AF386415

THE HUNT FOR HITLER

THE HUNT FOR HITLER

HOW I DISCOVERED THE TRUE STORY OF THE FÜHRER'S FATE

CYRIL JONES

FRONTLINE
BOOKS

THE HUNT FOR HITLER
How I Discovered the True Story of The Führer's Fate

First published in Great Britain in 2026
by Frontline Books
An imprint of
Pen & Sword Books Ltd
Yorkshire - Philadelphia

Copyright © Cyril Jones
ISBN 9781036195465

The rights of Cyril Jones to be identified as Author of this work
have been asserted by them in accordance with
the Copyright, Designs and Patents Act 1988.
A CIP catalogue record for this book is available from the British Library

Typeset by Lapiz Digital
Printed and bound in the UK by CPI Group (UK) Ltd,
Croydon, CR0 4YY.

Printed on paper from a sustainable source by
CPI Group (UK) Ltd, Croydon, CR0 4YY

The Publisher's authorised representative in the EU for product safety is
Authorised Rep Compliance Ltd., Ground Floor, 71 Lower Baggot Street,
Dublin D02 P593, Ireland.
www.arccompliance.com

For a complete list of Pen & Sword titles please contact
PEN & SWORD BOOKS LTD
47 Church Street, Barnsley, South Yorkshire, S70 2AS, England
E-mail: enquiries@pen-and-sword.co.uk
Website: www.pen-and-sword.co.uk
or
PEN & SWORD BOOKS
1950 Lawrence Rd, Havertown, PA 19083, USA
E-mail: uspen-and-sword@casematepublishers.com

CONTENTS

LIST OF PLATES

LIST OF RUSSIAN ABBREVIATIONS

CPSU	Communist Party of the Soviet Union
FSB	Federal'naya sluzhba bezopasnosti Rossiyskoy Federatsii, Russian Federation's main security agency, successor to the KGB.
GRU	Main Intelligence Directorate, Soviet/Russian military intelligence WW2
GSFG	Group of Soviet Forces in Germany WW2
KGB	Komitet Gosudarstvennoy Bezopasnosti. Committee for State Security. Soviet Union's main security agency (1954–91).
MGB	Ministerstvo Gosudarstvennoy Bezopasnosti. Ministry of State Security.
NKVD	Narodny Komissariat Vnutrennikh Del'. People's Commissariat for Internal Affairs predecessor of the KGB.
SMERSH	Smert Shpionam, 'Death to Spies'. Soviet Army Counter-Intelligence WW2
USSR	Union of Soviet Socialist Republics

LIST OF GERMAN WAFFEN-SS RANKS

SS	Schutzstaffel. Germany's WW2 paramilitary elite corps
SS-Oberst-Gruppenführer	Colonel General
SS-Obergruppenführer	General
SS-Gruppenführer	Lieutenant General
SS-Brigadeführer	Major General
SS-Standartenführer	Colonel
SS-Obersturmbannführer	Lieutenant Colonel
SS-Sturmbannführer	Major
SS-Hauptsturmführer	Captain
SS-Obersturmführer	First Lieutenant
SS-Untersturmführer	Second Lieutenant
SS-Sturmscharführer	Sergeant Major
SS-Hauptscharführer	Master Sergeant

For
Rose & Toby

After being told by General Krebs that Hitler was dead I thought 'So we have been fighting for five and a half years for someone who committed suicide? Having drawn us into this terrible disaster, he himself chose the easy way out and left us to fend for ourselves? We must now end this madness as soon as possible. I will order all fighting to cease immediately.'

General Helmut Weidling
Commander, Berlin Defence Area, 1945
Testimony to Red Army Interrogators,
4 January 1946

Chapter 1

BEGINNING OF THE END

**SPECIAL REPORT BY G. K. ZHUKOV AND
K. F. TELEGIN TO I. V. STALIN**

3 May, 1945
Top secret
To: Supreme Commander Marshal of the Soviet Union

Comrade Stalin

On 2 May, 1945 in the city of Berlin in the grounds of the Reich Chancellery of the Reichstag in the Wilhelmstrasse, where Hitler's headquarters were lately situated, burned bodies were discovered that were identified as those of Reichsminister of Propaganda Dr Goebbels and his wife.

On 3 May this year in the same area, at Goebbels' headquarters (a bunker about 80 metres deep) the six corpses of Goebbels' children were discovered and removed.

All indications on the children's corpses were that they had been killed by powerful poisons.

The Chief of SMERSH Counter-Espionage Department of the 1st Byelorussian Front Lieutenant General Comrade Vadis personally showed the corpses to the prisoners: Vice-Admiral Voss, Grand-Admiral Dönitz's representative at Hitler's headquarters, Schneider, in charge of the Reich Chancellery's garage, the cook Lange, and the chief technician of the Reich Chancellery Tziem [incorrectly named as Tzien in the original text].

They recognised the corpses as those of Goebbels, his wife and their children.

In the process of examining the corpses of Goebbels and his wife, gold NSDAP badges, two 'Browning No 1' pistols and a cigarette case bearing Hitler's monogram were discovered.

According to Voss, only one woman in Germany – Goebbels' wife – had such a gold badge which had been presented to her by Hitler three days before his suicide. Voss also identified Hitler's signature on the cigarette case.

Near the Reich Chancellery, in the courtyard of the Ministry of Propaganda, a corpse was discovered wearing a uniform of a general, who was identified by Voss as Lieutenant-General Krebs, the Chief of the General Staff of the German Army. Furthermore, in the lining of his uniform jacket near the left side pocket a strip of cloth was discovered bearing the name 'Krebs'.

On 1 May this year, Krebs visited the 8th Guard Army of our Front as an emissary to hold talks about capitulation. Examination of the body revealed a bullet hole in the right side of the chin with an exit wound in the back of the head, which proves his suicide.

3 May, 1945 Berlin

This telegram, sent to the dictator of the Soviet Union, Josef Stalin, by the two most senior commanders of the Red Army, now in control of the whole of Berlin, marked the beginning of the formal end of the Third Reich.

It was the first documented proof presented to Stalin that the leaders of Nazi Germany were either dead or incapacitated.

Except one. Where was Hitler?

This is the story of the final days of the Second World War and the events which immediately followed the discovery of bodies beneath the Reich Chancellery in Berlin on Wednesday 3 May 1945.

Much of it is told through the eyes of one remarkable person who took part in that operation and recounted her experiences years later after the death of Stalin, when she felt it was safe to do so.

***

As the car carrying Elena Rzhevskaya weaved its way through the ruins of Berlin she reflected on how it had come to this point – at this place.

In front of her was what remained of the Reich Chancellery, the heart of Nazi Germany, and she was about to enter the bunker beneath to interrogate the leaders of the Third Reich.

The date was Tuesday 1 May 1945. The Berlin garrison which had been defending the city from the Russian attacks had formally surrendered. Russian forces were now in complete control, and the Second World War was now at an end.

Elena Rzhevskaya knew the task in front of her. As a German speaker she had interrogated hundreds of German soldiers over several years and she knew the techniques. But this was going to be different. Perhaps she would find herself interrogating Hitler himself.

Only a few hours earlier Russian soldiers had sealed off the Reich Chancellery. They knew only that Hitler and his entourage had his headquarters there. It wasn't long before they found the bunker and made their way in.

Elena Rzhevskaya and the officers accompanying her steeled themselves and went inside.

***

Chapter 2

ELENA RZHEVSKAYA

To fully understand what happened in the bunker we must jump forward almost 50 years and look back at the events through the eyes of Elena Rzhevskaya herself.

In June 1991 she opened the door of her modest apartment in Lenigradsky Prospekt, Moscow, and invited me and a film crew into her living room.

She accepted a bouquet of flowers and told me I was the first journalist she had agreed to speak to on the record. Not only that, she agreed to be filmed. It was later pointed out to me that this was extremely courageous on her part as this was still the Soviet Union, albeit under Mikhail Gorbachev.

It seems she agreed because she was intrigued by what I had found inside the Russian film archives – a pristine can of 35mm film, previously unseen, shot in and around the Berlin bunker in May 1945. I had come across this film as part of my research into what happened to Hitler's body after the Russians took control of the bunker. The film, incorporating Elena Rzhevskaya's story was told in the documentary *Hitler. The Final Chapter*, broadcast worldwide in 1992.

I had been surprised that my request for an interview had been accepted. At the time she was 72 years old, but still retained vivid memories of the time she'd spent interrogating Germans inside the bunker.

'You know', she said 'it was our fault.' When I asked her what she meant she replied 'Our fault that the whole thing became a mystery. It was that tyrant [Stalin] who started all the confusion. We should have told the Allies the full story. After all, they had told us about Himmler's death, and shown us photographs of his corpse. We should have done the same thing; we created the mystery.'

4

In the final weeks of the Second World War, as Nazi Germany faced imminent defeat, Heinrich Himmler – head of the SS and one of the principal architects of the Holocaust – attempted to negotiate a separate peace with the Western Allies. In late April 1945, he asked Count Folke Bernadotte of the Swedish Red Cross to transmit an offer of surrender to General Dwight D. Eisenhower, Supreme Commander of the Allied Forces. When Adolf Hitler learned of Himmler's secret negotiations on 28–29 April, he was enraged, stripped Himmler of all his offices, expelled him from the Nazi Party, and ordered his arrest.

Himmler became a fugitive and tried to evade capture by disguising himself as a sergeant of the Secret Field Police, using forged identity papers under the name 'Heinrich Hitzinger' and shaving off his moustache. Himmler travelled with a small group of aides through northern Germany, hoping to avoid detection and possibly escape abroad.

On 21 May 1945, Himmler and two companions were stopped at a checkpoint in Bremervörde, northern Germany, set up by former Soviet prisoners of war. The group was detained due to suspicions raised by their appearance and the forged documents they carried, which bore a stamp recognised by British military intelligence as having been used by fleeing SS members. Over the next two days, Himmler was moved between several holding camps.

On 23 May 1945, Himmler was brought to the British 31st Civilian Interrogation Camp near Lüneburg. During a routine interrogation conducted by Captain Thomas Selvester, Himmler finally admitted his true identity. A medical examination was ordered, during which Himmler bit into a hidden potassium cyanide capsule concealed in his mouth. Despite efforts to save him, he died within 15 minutes. His body was subsequently buried in an unmarked grave near Lüneburg, the location of which remains unknown.

'When the Allies showed us the photo we already knew about Hitler, and that's when we should have told them', Rzhevskaya said.

'But we couldn't, as Stalin had given strict orders that we were to say nothing. Stalin told the Allies that Hitler was still alive. There was nothing we could do, we were very angry.'

'I was personally threatened. Stalin told my superiors to make sure I didn't say anything.'

This threat by Stalin and Soviet authorities hung over Elena Rzhevskaya's head for many years after the war. 'In October 1945, just before I was demobilised, Major Boris Bystrov, my immediate superior in the counter-intelligence unit, whom I had known for several years, reminded me to keep the secret, and told me that I was being watched.'

He said 'You know, you are the youngest of us, and you will outlive us. One day you can write about it.'

The main point Rzhevskaya wanted to make was that, yes, senior Soviet military officials did lie to the Allies in 1945, but that was because of an order from Stalin, 'and we had to obey that order, we dare not do otherwise. We didn't like it, and I've spent much of my life trying to put it right. Now I'm in a position to do that, because I was there and I know what happened.'

I should note that this conversation took place on 21 June 1991, only a few weeks before the attempted coup against the Soviet President Mikael Gorbachev. He had introduced a new era in Soviet society, called 'Glasnost and Perestroika'.

Glasnost encouraged a more open society by allowing for greater freedom of speech and access to information, as well as more open discussion of the problems within the Soviet system, including criticisms of the government and communist party. Perestroika involved restructuring the Soviet economy, aiming to address its inefficiencies and shortages, by introducing elements of a market economy and giving more autonomy to businesses and ministries, though it didn't necessarily end the centrally planned system. Gorbachev hoped that these reforms would improve relations with the West, particularly in the context of the Cold War. It was this new policy Rzhevskaya was taking advantage of, and she felt she could speak freely.

Three years prior to our interview Elena Rzhevskaya had published a book in Russian entitled *Berlin, May 1945*. This told the story of her wartime experiences and the events in the bunker but had not received much publicity. Few in the West were aware of it. She now had an opportunity to speak directly to a Western audience.

Before our filmed interview began Rzhevskaya looked at a video copy of the film I had procured from the Russian Archives. 'How did you get this?', she asked. I explained that it had been obtained legally by a Russian film company, and sold on to me on the understanding that it would be used in my documentary.

It was clear that the film fascinated her. 'I've never seen this before', she said.

But I was there when it was filmed. This happened soon after we entered the bunker. The bodies of the Goebbels family were among the first things we found. At that stage we hadn't found Hitler's corpse, although we knew he was dead, because Krebs had told us.

I don't think the cameraman filmed much else because it was very dark, as the power kept going on and off. I was there when they showed

[Vice Admiral] Voss the bodies. You can't see me there because I was slightly to one side.

I remember one time when we were searching for Hitler's body and we left the bunker to go to a suburb of Berlin. When we returned all the lights had gone out. Unfortunately for us responsibility for security at the bunker had been taken over by a different part of the military, and we had to draw our weapons to force them to comply.

Another problem was that our soldiers had found the bunker's supply of alcohol, so you can imagine the problems that caused.

After watching the video for about half an hour, Rzhevskaya said she was ready to begin filming.

'I think', she said, 'I should tell you the story from the beginning.'

Elena Rzhevskaya was born in October 1919, to a Jewish family in the Belorussian town of Gomel. The family name was Kagan, and they later moved to Moscow. At the time of the German attack on the Soviet Union she was 22 and joined the war effort. She was initially sent to work in a munitions factory, a re-purposed clock factory and later studied to be a nurse, but she was determined to find her way to the Front.

She had learned German as a child, a skill which was obviously useful so she was transferred to a school for interpreters. There she met Pavel Kogan, a budding young poet, and after a short time they married, although they didn't have time to register it. Soon after they had a young daughter, Olga.

After graduating and given commissions as Lieutenants (as were all war interpreters), they were posted to different military units. Young Olga was left behind to be cared for by Elena's parents.

Pavel was a very gifted poet and knew hundreds of poems by heart. Although his poems were never published in his lifetime, they became popular among Russian students in the immediate post-war period. Initially he was declared unfit for military service as he suffered from severe myopia and chronic bronchitis, but like almost all of his contemporaries he was determined to assist in the war effort.

From the front he wrote to his father:

What can I write about myself: I am alive and well, cheerful, fighting. I really want to believe that I will stay alive and that we will all meet here, on Pravda Street. Only here, at the front, did I understand what a dazzling, what a charming thing life is. Next to death, this is very well understood. And for the sake of life, for the sake of your wonderful grey head, I will die, if necessary, because a person with a normal head and heart cannot reconcile himself to fascism.

On 23 September 1942, Pavel headed a reconnaissance group on the Sugar Loaf Hill, near Novorossiysk, a key Soviet port on the Black Sea, which had just been captured by German troops. The group came under fire, and it was there that the poet died at the age of 24.

'Do you know what was one of most important documents we were given as part of this course?' Elena asked me. 'A book of German swear-words', she said, laughing.

Many years later she wrote:

> I was not prepared practically for the war at all, only emotionally, but we went to war believing it would be the most important thing we did in our lives. It would seem we were not mistaken. And something else: emotions have proved more durable than many practical things, certainly than my leaky boots.
>
> People shoot, kill, bury, rush into the attack, go out on reconnaissance, and that is war. But the starving women with their bags, without proper boots, wandering God knows where with their hungry children, the old people, the refugees, the people burned out of their homes – they are the real horror of war.

It wasn't long before she found herself in the midst of battle, and what became known as the 'Rzhev Meat Grinder', a series of battles in and around the city of Rzhev, about 250km west of Moscow. It was one of the two most momentous battles the Soviets ever fought, the other being the 'Battle of Stalingrad'.

The battle of Rzhev which took place over a 14-month period, produced staggering casualties. At least three million German and Soviet soldiers were killed or wounded. Rzhevskaya herself was lucky not to be killed. She showed me a Russian icon with a hole in the middle. 'That's a bullet hole', she said, 'and it was meant for me.' After the war, when she began writing as a profession, she gave herself the pen name 'Rzhevskaya', in memory of the battle.

Chapter 3

THE BATTLE FOR BERLIN

In February 1945, over a period of seven days, Prime Minister Winston Churchill, President Franklin Roosevelt and Josef Stalin, the leaders of the United Kingdom, the United States and the Soviet Union, met at Yalta in Crimea, to finalise strategies for ending the war and begin planning for a post-war recovery, as well as the division of Europe.

It had already been decided that Germany would be divided into a number of Occupied Zones administered by British, American, French and Russian forces. Berlin, though located deep in the Soviet zone, would also be divided into four sectors. This meant that even if Western Allied forces had taken Berlin first, they would have had to turn over much of it to the Soviets.

At that time the Red Army was much closer to Berlin than the Western Allies. By early April 1945, Soviet forces were around 50 miles from Berlin, while the Western Allies were about 300 miles away. The Commander in Chief of Allied Forces, General Dwight Eisenhower, saw no strategic benefit in capturing Berlin since it would have to be handed over to the Soviets anyway,

He also believed that attacking Berlin would result in enormous casualties for American and British troops. The Soviets were willing to bear the cost, and anyway Stalin was determined to take the city. Eisenhower prioritised capturing southern Germany, Czechoslovakia and Austria to prevent a possible Nazi last stand in the Alps, known to the Nazis as the National Redoubt.

With both Allied and Soviet forces advancing rapidly from different directions, moving beyond the Elbe risked confusion and possible friendly fire incidents. Coordination between the two armies was difficult, and Eisenhower did not want an accidental confrontation with the Soviets. Also, the Nazi leadership had heavily fortified Berlin. The Wehrmacht and SS were prepared to fight to the last man, and the fanatical defence would have been brutal for any attacking force. To the Allies it made sense for the Russians to take it.

Stalin saw Berlin as the ultimate prize, both as the Nazi capital and as a sign of Soviet military dominance. The Soviet Union had suffered enormous losses during the war, with tens of millions of soldiers and civilians killed. Allowing them to capture Berlin was seen by the Allies as a form of recognition for their sacrifices and contribution to the defeat of Nazi Germany. And since the Soviets had already committed vast resources and manpower to reach Berlin, it was strategically preferable for them to bear the burden of the battle. Roosevelt and Churchill also recognised Stalin's determination to secure Berlin as a symbol of Soviet military might and as leverage in post-war negotiations.

In consequence the Allies' decision to stop at the Elbe River was a combination of political agreements, military strategy and practical considerations. The Western Allies focused on eliminating remaining German resistance while the Soviets took Berlin, setting the stage for the division of Germany and the Cold War. The Allied leaders were already anticipating the geopolitical division of Europe and the onset of the Cold War. By allowing the Soviets to capture Berlin, they tacitly acknowledged their emerging sphere of influence in Eastern Europe. Whether they would have made the same decision in hindsight is moot, but it nonetheless reflected the delicate balancing act of wartime alliances and the realities of geopolitical strategy at the close of the war. While it resulted in the Soviet occupation of Berlin and the subsequent division of the city during the Cold War, it was viewed at the time as a pragmatic choice to secure the defeat of Nazi Germany and manage the post-war order.

The Battle of Berlin was led by the Red Army's 1st Belorussian Front, 1st Ukrainian Front, and 2nd Belorussian Front, with additional support from the 1st Polish Army. These three fronts were commanded by some of the USSR's most experienced generals.

The 1st Belorussian Front was led by Marshal Georgy Zhukov, probably Russia's greatest-ever general. His strategy was to assault Berlin from the east and north-east, crossing the Oder River near the Seelow Heights. He was located directly to the east of Berlin, between the Oder and Neisse Rivers with Approximately 768,000 troops and over 3,000 tanks. He was supported by significant artillery, including rocket launchers (Katyushas). His plan was to launch a frontal attack on Berlin via the heavily fortified Seelow Heights, acting as the main thrust of the assault. The 1st Polish Army was attached to the 1st Belorussian Front, tasked with supporting the offensive and participating in the assault on Berlin.

The 1st Ukrainian Front was led by Marshal Ivan Konev. His primary objective was to attack from the south, envelop Berlin, and potentially link up with Zhukov's forces to encircle the city. He was located south of Berlin, near the Neisse River with over 700,000 troops and 2,200 tanks. He also had strong air and artillery support. He would advance through the university city of Cottbus and push north toward Berlin, blocking any potential German reinforcements from the south.

Leading the 2nd Belorussian Front was Marshal Konstantin Rokossovsky who would secure the northern flank of the Soviet advance and prevent any German counter-attacks. He lay north of Berlin, near the Oder River, facing the remnants of Army Group Vistula. He had around 650,000 troops with significant tank and artillery support. He intended to cross the Oder River near Stettin (modern Szczecin) and advance westward to cut off German escape routes to the Baltic Sea.

The German defence of Berlin was led by Army Group Vistula, commanded by General Gotthard Heinrici. The German forces numbered roughly 300,000 soldiers, although many were poorly equipped and inexperienced. They were supported by a small number of tanks and aircraft. Positioned along the Seelow Heights and inside Berlin were additional Volkssturm (militia) units and Hitler Youth forming part of the city's defence.

In total the Red Army deployed over 2.5 million troops, 6,250 tanks, 7,500 aircraft and tens of thousands of artillery pieces for the Berlin operation. The Soviet forces had spent weeks preparing for the Berlin offensive, including stocking up massive stockpiles of ammunition, food, fuel, and medical supplies

Over 40,000 artillery pieces were concentrated along the Oder River. The Soviets planned a massive artillery barrage to weaken German defences before the assault. The Soviet Air Force dominated the skies, with thousands of aircraft providing close air support and bombing raids on German positions. And Soviet troops were deployed in echelon formations, ensuring that fresh reserves were always available to sustain the offensive.

They paid an enormously high price for the victory. During the Berlin Operation, Zhukov, commander of the 1st Belorussian Front, had continually repeated the order 'to break through to the city's suburbs at any price and immediately inform me [so that I can] report to Comrade Stalin and release an announcement to the press'. 'At any price' translated to 361,367 servicemen killed and wounded in Berlin from 16 April to 8 May 1945 – an average of 15,712 men a day. This was a colossal price when compared to the Battle of Stalingrad (1942–3): 6,392 men a day.

The Soviet attack began on 16 April 1945 with a massive artillery barrage (the largest of the war), followed by an assault on the Seelow Heights by Zhukov's 1st Belorussian Front. Two days later Soviet forces breached the Seelow Heights after fierce fighting and advanced toward Berlin. By 21 April they had reached the outskirts of Berlin, and on 25 April the city was fully encircled by Soviet forces from the north, east, and south, with German forces trapped inside.

At 3:50 am on Tuesday, 1 May under a white flag, General Hans Krebs, Chief of the General Staff of the German Armed Forces, was brought into the Command Post of the Soviet Union's 8th Guards Army. Waiting for him was its commander, General (later Marshal) Vasily Chuikov. Krebs told Chuikov that he was authorised to negotiate the surrender of German Armed Forces. He also told him that Hitler was dead.

Immediately on hearing this news Chuikov rang the Commander in Chief of Soviet Forces, General, and later Marshal Zhukov, and within minutes Zhukov was on the phone to the Soviet leader, Josef Stalin.

He was at his summer cottage. The call was answered by a duty general who said: 'Comrade Stalin has just gone to bed.'

'Please, wake him up. The matter is urgent and can't wait till morning.'

In a little while Stalin was on the line. Zhukov reported to him about Hitler's suicide and a letter from Goebbels proposing armistice. Stalin answered: 'Now he's done it, the bastard. Too bad he could not have been taken alive. Where is Hitler's body?'

Zhukov said 'According to General Krebs Hitler's body was burned.'

'Tell Sokolovsky that there can be no talks – either with Krebs or any other Hitlerites, only unconditional surrender', said the Supreme Commander. 'If nothing special happens, don't call me till morning. I want to have a little rest before tomorrow's May Day Parade.'

The end came on 2 May 1945, when Berlin capitulated to the Red Army. Once the order was given to surrender, weapons began piling up by Berlin's Town Hall – machine guns, assault rifles and ordinary rifles. Abandoned German artillery pieces had their barrels pointing at the ground. Marshal Zhukov described the final hours in his autobiography. He wrote:

On 1 May the 248th Rifle Division under General N. Z. Galai and the 230th Rifle Division under Colonel D. K. Shishkov of the 5th Assault Army under General Berzarin stormed and seized the State Post Office and attacked the building of the Finance Ministry situated opposite the

Reich Chancellery. On 1 May the 301st Division (commander Colonel V. S. Antonov of Berzarin's Army) in cooperation with the 248th Rifle Division stormed and captured the Gestapo building and the Aviation Ministry.

Under infantry cover a self-propelled artillery battalion rushed forward. A. L. Denisyuk, commander of a self-propelled gun, installed it in the aperture of the fence and saw the grey building of the Reich Chancellery about a hundred metres away, showing through the foggy mist. A huge eagle with a swastika adorned its facade. Denisyuk gave the command, 'Fire on the Nazi marauder!' The Nazi coat-of-arms was knocked off.

The final battle for the Reich Chancellery, in which the 301st and 248th Rifle Divisions were engaged, was strenuous. The fighting at the approaches to and inside the building was especially fierce. Striking was the courage of Major Anna Nikulina, instructor of the political department of the 9th Rifle Corps. Together with the assault group of F. K. Shapovalov's battalion, she made her way through the break in the roof, approached the metal spire and tied to it the Red flag she had carried under her jacket with a piece of telegraph wire. The Soviet Flag unfurled over the Reich Chancellery.

By 15:00 on 2 May the enemy was crushed. The remnants of the Berlin garrison, over 134,000 men, surrendered. Many of those who had fought arms in hand apparently deserted in the last few days and went into hiding.

2 May 1945, was a day of great jubilation for the Soviet people, the Soviet Armed Forces, our Allies, and the peoples of the whole world.

The Order of the Supreme Commander read:

'The troops of the First Byelorussian Front supported by the troops of the First Ukrainian Front after stubborn street fighting have completed the routing of the Berlin group of German forces and today on 1 May, have gained full control of Berlin, the capital of Germany – the centre of German imperialism and the hotbed of German aggression'.

Later that day a small Soviet military unit weaved its way through the rubble of Berlin. Leading the group was Colonel Vasily Gorbushin, who was charged with taking over the bunker beneath the Reich Chancellery which had been identified as the headquarters of Adolf Hitler.

Shortly before the group's arrival the bunker had been sealed by Soviet troops of the 1st Byelorussian Front, and the occupants held prisoner. They were detained until they could be interrogated by Russian investigators.

The interrogation squad comprised members of a Russan counter-intelligence group called SMERSH, a Russian acronym that stands for 'Смерть шпионам' (*Smert Shpionam*), which translates in English to 'Death to Spies'. It was created in 1943 by order of Stalin. Its primary mission was to combat espionage and treason within the Soviet military and territories under Soviet control

It operated under the auspices of the Red Army and was tasked with identifying, capturing, and neutralising spies, saboteurs, and other perceived enemies of the Soviet state. One of its tasks was the vetting of captured prisoners of war to identify spies or collaborators. SMERSH was known for its brutal tactics, including torture and summary executions, to extract confessions and eliminate threats. It was dissolved in 1946 and its functions were absorbed into the broader Soviet state security apparatus, including the MGB (Ministry of State Security), which later became the KGB.

The head of the SMERSH interrogation unit who questioned those captured in the bunker was Colonel Ivan Klimenko, of the 79th Rifle Corps, 3rd Assault Army, 1st Belorussian Front, (who, coincidentally, was one of the men who found Hitler's corpse). He led a small group of investigators whose translator was Elena Rzhevskaya. The two later became friends and corresponded with each other over many years. Rzhevskaya insisted, however, that she was never a member of SMERSH.

Zhukov himself inspected the Reich Chancellery along with Colonel-General Berzarin, Lieutenant-General Bokov, member of the Military Council of the Army, and some other officers who had taken part in the assault 'in order to make certain of the suicide of Hitler, Goebbels and other Nazi leaders'. Zhukov later said that on arrival they found themselves in an embarrassing situation. They were told that the bodies of the suicides had allegedly been buried by the Germans, but no one knew who exactly did it or where. Different hypotheses were put forth.

'The POWs, mostly wounded, knew nothing about Hitler and his entourage', Zhukov said.

In the Reich Chancellery only a few dozen people were found. Apparently, at the last moment the high-ranking officers and the SS men had left the building by secret tunnels and gone into hiding in the city.

We looked for the place where the bodies of Hitler and Goebbels were burned, but could not find it. Admittedly, we saw the ashes of some fires but they were obviously too small. Most likely German soldiers had used them to boil water.

When we had almost finished inspecting the Reich Chancellery, it was reported to us that the bodies of Goebbels's six children had been found in an underground room. Shortly afterwards the bodies of Goebbels and his wife were found close to the bunker. Dr. Fritsche, who was brought to identify the bodies, testified that they were those of Goebbels and his wife.

Zhukov said that at first circumstances made him doubt the truthfulness of the account of Hitler's suicide, all the more so because they could not find Hitler's private secretary Bormann either. At the time he thought that Hitler might have escaped at the last moment when there was no hope of any help for Berlin from without. 'I stated that surmise at a Berlin press conference for Soviet and foreign correspondents', he said.

> Sometime later, after an inquiry and the questioning of Hitler's personal medical staff, etc. we started to receive additional, more concrete evidence confirming Hitler's suicide. I became convinced that there were no grounds for doubting Hitler's suicide. Most of the Nazi ringleaders, among them Göring, Himmler, Keitel and Jodi, fled from Berlin in different directions in good time.
>
> Like reckless gamblers, they, together with Hitler, hoped till the last moment to draw a lucky card which would save Nazi Germany and themselves. On 30 April, and even on 1 May, the Hitlerite ringleaders still tried to deter final defeat by starting negotiations to summon to Berlin the newly-brought-to-light Dönitz government allegedly to make decision on Germany's surrender.
>
> General Krebs, an experienced military diplomat, did his utmost to involve us in long-drawn-out negotiations, but his ruse failed. General Sokolovsky, who was empowered to carry on negotiations, told Krebs categorically that the cessation of hostilities was only possible after complete and unconditional surrender of the Nazi troops to the Allies. That was the end of their talk. And since the Germans at that time refused to agree to unconditional surrender, our troops were ordered to finish the enemy off immediately.

For the specialist search team, the most immediate task was to find the leaders of the Third Reich. Because of the inadvertent admission by Krebs that there was a bunker under the Reich Chancellery, they went looking for it.

The Reich Chancellery from which Adolf Hitler prosecuted the war had been specially designed for him by his favourite architect, Albert Speer, who he later appointed Minister of Armaments and War Production. It stood only 500m from the Reichstag.

It replaced the old Reich Chancellery, originally the Palais Radziwiłł on Wilhelmstraße, which was acquired by the Prussian state in 1869 and became the official chancellery after German unification in 1871. The building was expanded and modernised over the years, serving as the administrative heart of the German Empire, the Weimar Republic, and, briefly, the early Nazi regime. Notably, it was here that President Paul von Hindenburg appointed Hitler as chancellor on 30 January 1933. The Reich Chancellery was the central seat of government for Germany's chancellors from the late nineteenth century, but it became especially infamous as the headquarters of Hitler and the Nazi regime. The complex included both the Old Reich Chancellery and the New Reich Chancellery, each with distinct histories and architectural significance.

By the mid-1930s, Hitler considered the Old Chancellery inadequate for his vision of a world power's headquarters. The building underwent further renovations, including the addition of a large reception hall and a conservatory, and the construction of the Vorbunker (an air-raid shelter), which would later be connected to the more famous Führerbunker.

Construction on the new Chancellery began in early 1938 and was completed in less than a year, a remarkable feat given the building's scale and complexity. The building's architecture was grandiose and neoclassical, featuring a monumental façade, vast halls, and high ceilings. The interior was lavishly decorated with red marble, exotic woods, and massive sculptures. The most famous space was the Marble Gallery, a 146m-long corridor designed to awe visitors and project an image of overwhelming authority.

It had more than fifty rooms (most of them no bigger than a boxroom). It also housed a powerful communications centre, and had food supplies and a kitchen. An underground garage was connected to it. There were two ways into the underground complex: from the internal garden of the Reich Chancellery, and from the Chancellery's vestibule, from which a fairly broad and gentle staircase led downwards.

The two-storey Führerbunker was much deeper down than the bomb shelter under the Reich Chancellery and its reinforced concrete ceiling much thicker. It was described by Hitler's bodyguard, Hans Rattenhuber, as the most solid of any built in Germany. The reinforced concrete ceiling of the bunker was eight metres thick.

The Reich Chancellery was not just an office complex; it was the epicentre of Hitler's dictatorship. Here, he received dignitaries, planned military campaigns, and staged the rituals of Nazi power. The building's design was integral to the regime's propaganda, serving as a stage for the performance of Hitler's rule and the myth of the Führer as the embodiment of the German state.

The Vorbunker was the original shelter, completed in 1936, located just beneath the Old Reich Chancellery. It was intended as a temporary air-raid shelter and included basic facilities such as dormitories, a generator room, washrooms, and hermetically sealable gas doors for protection against chemical attacks. These bunkers were not only meant for physical protection but also to allow Hitler and his inner circle to continue directing the war effort and government operations even under siege. The complex had its own power supply, air filtration, and communication systems, making it possible to function independently for extended periods.

Chapter 4

INTO THE BUNKER

Russian assault detachments eventually broke through the final defensive ring and burst into the Reich Chancellery on the morning of 2 May 1945. But although the Russians now knew that the bunker lay beneath the Reich Chancellery, it took them several hours to find it. Russian engineers with mine detectors were called in and a systematic search was begun.

Soviet Intelligence officers arrived a short time later, with orders to start the search immediately. The action was directed by Lieutenant Colonel Ivan Isayevich Klimenko, Commander of the Counter Intelligence Section, 79th Rifle Corps, also known as SMERSH. Klimenko, a professional soldier since 1936, had started on his way to Berlin in 1941 at Yelnya, where he had his first encounter with the Germans. Five times he was caught in encircling battles, and in extricating himself he had marched on foot approximately 1,100km.

He arrived at the Chancellery, however, in an Army truck. With him in the truck were three other officers, and in a truck following them there were five soldiers. They owed their mission to the fortuitous accident that the Chancellery had become part of the fighting sector of their Corps. This 79th Rifle Corps under the command of Major General Pepevertkin had advanced in the battle from the north toward the Reichstag Building and the Chancellery. The 150th Division under Brigadier General Zhatilov had hoisted the red banner on the German Parliament, a building which Zhukov had pointed out to his armies as a widely visible goal.

Simultaneously, the 301st Division under General Antonov, which belonged to the 5th Assault Army of General Berzarin and was advancing from the south, had occupied the Gestapo building in Prinz Albrecht Strasse and the adjacent Air Ministry. At dawn on 1

May the gunners of the 301st Division posted their guns in front of the Chancellery.

Rzhevskaya recalls a firefight in the vestibule of the Chancellery with the remnants of the guard, most of whom, however, had fled. Next came the descent. Military and civilian staff began coming out of the corridors, the boxrooms and the rest of the complex with their hands up. The wounded were sitting or lying on the floor.

'There was groaning. In the underground complex and in the storeys of the Reich Chancellery shooting broke out repeatedly.'

She remembers the route to Hitler's bunker being rather long and complicated. An entrance from the enclosed garden led directly to the Führerbunker.

Descending the stairs, you immediately came to a long corridor with numerous doors opening off it.

We needed to get our bearings immediately, to locate all the exits and block them, get the lie of the land and start searching. In the very mixed collection of people occupying the complex it was no simple matter to identify those who could be helpful, people who would know more than others about Hitler's fate and could guide us through the labyrinthine complex. We conducted a first sketchy enquiry.

Down there we found a portly 40-year-old, Karl Schneider, one of the Chancellery's garage mechanics. He testified that on 28 or 29 April, he could not remember which exactly, the telephone operator on duty in Hitler's secretariat gave him an order to deliver all the petrol he had to the Führer's bunker. Schneider sent eight cans, each containing twenty litres of petrol. Later the same day, he received a further order from the operator to send firelighters. He had eight and sent them all.

Schneider had not himself seen Hitler and did not know whether he was in Berlin, but on 1 May he was told by the head of the garage and by Hitler's chauffeur, Erich Kempka, that the Führer was dead. Rumours were circulating among the security soldiers that he had committed suicide and that his body had been burnt. Putting these rumours together with the orders he had received, Schneider concluded that the petrol he had sent had been used to burn the Führer's body.

Then, on the evening of 1 May, he had another call from the duty telephonist, again demanding that all available petrol should be sent to the Führer's bunker. Schneider siphoned petrol from the fuel tanks of the cars and sent another four cans.

'What had that call been about? Who had the petrol been meant for this time?' Together with Karl Schneider and Wilhelm Lange (a cook), Major Bystrov, Lieutenant Colonel Klimenko and Major Khazin went out into the garden. The ground had been churned up by shells, the trees mutilated, and their charred branches were strewn underfoot. The lawns were blackened by fire and soot, and there was broken glass and piles of bricks everywhere.

'How were they to determine where the bodies had been burned?'

The four men began an inspection of the garden and, three metres from the garden exit of the Führerbunker, found the half-burnt bodies of Goebbels and his wife. So that was what the second supply of petrol had been for.

Twenty years later, in a letter to Rzhevskaya, Lieutenant Colonel Ivan Klimenko, her immediate superior, said 'the German found them first' referring to Schneider. 'If it had been any later, the torrent of Red Army soldiers pouring into the Reich Chancellery would have trampled the bodies to pieces without even noticing what was under their feet.'

The first bodies found in the bunker itself were those of Generals Wilhelm Burgdorf and Hans Krebs. The two officers were in the corridor lounge, sitting before a long table littered with glasses and bottles. Both men had shot themselves, but they were identified by papers found in their uniforms.

Krebs, of course, had only a few hours before unsuccessfully tried to negotiate a surrender with the Russians on the orders of Goebbels. Burgdorf, a fanatical hard-line Nazi, was one of Hitler's key adjutants.

Burgdorf had played a key role in the forced suicide of Field Marshal Erwin Rommel, who was implicated in the 20 July 1944 plot to assassinate Hitler. On 14 October 1944, acting on Hitler's orders and accompanied by General Ernst Maisel, Burgdorf confronted Rommel at his Rattenhuber home and presented him with the choice of suicide (with the promise of a state funeral and protection for his family) or facing a trial for treason. Rommel chose suicide and died by cyanide poisoning, with Burgdorf present as a witness.

The charred bodies of Josef and Magda Goebbels were carried back down into the bunker and placed next to the bodies of the children. Lieutenant Colonel Boris Polevoy, who had earlier been among the first to report on the atrocities at Auschwitz after its liberation, said 'only Joseph Goebbels' face was recognisable'.

'To see the children was horrid', he said. 'The only one who seemed disturbed was the eldest, Helga. She was bruised. All were dead, but the rest were lying there peacefully.'

Soviet doctors immediately examined the youngsters. There were burn marks around their mouths, leading the doctors to believe that the children had been given a sleeping potion and had then been poisoned while they slept by cyanide tablets which had been crushed between their teeth. From Helga's bruises, the doctors speculated that she had awakened during the poisoning, had struggled and had had to be held down.

Looking on was Elena Rzhevskaya and her colleagues, as well as the head of the search team, Major (later Major-General) Alexandr Bystrov, chief of the Political Section (essentially the top political officer) of the Soviet 21st Army.

The bodies were carried up to the Reich Chancellery Court of Honor to be photographed and tagged for identification purposes. Rzhevskaya described the scene:

> Few Berliners could get in to see anything. There were small groups of officers and soldiers. There was filming for the newsreels, and Goebbels was surrounded by a few commanders keen to be in the picture.
>
> I was standing to one side, and saw Bystrov, standing stock-still, his dark, haggard face almost unrecognisable. Leaning forward, he was staring, transfixed, at the body of Goebbels.
>
> The whole scene, with the blackened body on its platform, in the ragged remnants of its Nazi uniform, with the yellow, noose-like tie which had somehow survived round the bare, black neck, its ends gnawed by fire and now stirring in the wind, seemed like an exhibit from history's chamber of horrors.
>
> When I later read that passage in Goebbels' diary where he gleefully records the Führer's approval of his notion of introducing a yellow star to identify Jews, I wondered if there had not been something symbolic about that yellow noose round the neck of its inventor.
>
> Before killing himself, Goebbels slaughtered his own children, closing the circle of murder with poison and fire, the means put to so much use in the concentration camps.

Reflecting years later, Rzhevskaya said she shuddered but was not frightened by the scene, 'and not only because we had seen so many terrible things in four years of war, but rather because those charred remains did not seem human: they seemed satanic. The dead children, that was frightening. Six children: five girls and one boy, exterminated by their parents.'

One of the senior captured German officers who was brought to the site was Vice Admiral Hans-Eric Voss, a close confidant of Joseph and Magda Goebbels and one of the last people to see both Hitler and Goebbels alive before their suicides.

Voss was present when Hitler announced his intention to commit suicide and thanked his staff for their service. After Hitler's death,

Voss attempted to escape from Berlin but was captured by Soviet forces on 2 May. He had been entrusted with the mission of reaching Admiral Dönitz in order to hand him the supreme authority Hitler had bequeathed him, and the order to continue the war at all costs. There was to be no question of capitulation!

After his capture Major Bystrov drove Voss through the streets of defeated Berlin. Bystrov said Voss stared stonily through the car window the whole time looking at the smoking ruins. A crowd of Berliners stood at a camp kitchen where a Russian cook was ladling out hot soup; overturned barricades, over which the car drove before crawling on through narrow alleys carved through streets blocked by fallen masonry, rubble and rubbish.

'Do you know these children?' Bystrov asked. Voss nodded in the affirmative and, asking permission, sank wearily into a chair. 'I saw them only yesterday. This one is Heidi', he said, pointing to the youngest girl. A few minutes earlier Voss had identified Goebbels and his wife. He told the assembled Russians that Goebbels and his wife Magda had resolved many weeks earlier that they would rather take their own lives than be captured.

Werner Naumann, Goebbels' aide, said later he had tried for weeks to dissuade Magda Goebbels, but she remained firm. At about 8:30 on 1 May Naumann said he had been talking with Goebbels and his wife when suddenly Magda 'got up and went into the children's rooms. After a short while she returned, white and shaken.'

'Almost immediately, Goebbels began making his good-byes. He said a few personal words to me – nothing political or about the future, just good-bye', Naumann said.

As Goebbels left the bunker he asked his adjutant, Guenther Schwagermann, to burn his and his family's bodies after death. Then, as Naumann watched, Joseph and Magda Goebbels went slowly up the stairs and into the garden. Goebbels was wearing his cap and gloves. Magda was 'shaking so badly she could hardly walk up the stairs'. No one ever saw them alive again.

The children were dead, too, and at the hand of a most improbable killer. 'Only one person', said Naumann, 'went into the children's rooms in the last moments before Joseph and Magda took their own lives, and that was Magda herself.'

SS Colonel Helmut Kunz was a dentist who found himself in the bunker by accident. On 4 May Rzhveskaya interrogated him. He had been called there to assist Magda Goebbels with a dental problem. After treating her he had found himself complicit in the murder of the children. 'He was feverishly agitated', Rzhveskaya said. 'He could not get over what he had experienced. Magda Goebbels had asked him to assist her with injecting the children.'

Admiral Voss said

> Goebbels came back to his study, and, together with his wife, I went to their apartment [in the bunker], where Goebbels' wife took a syringe filled with morphine from a cupboard in the front room and handed it to me, after which we went to the children's bedroom. At this time the children were already in bed, but not sleeping. Goebbels' wife announced to the children, 'Children, do not be frightened. The doctor is going to give you a vaccination which is being given now to children and soldiers.' With these words, she left the room, and I was left alone in the room and proceeded to give the morphine injections. After that I again went into the front room and told Frau Goebbels that we should wait about ten minutes for the children to fall asleep and at that time I looked at the clock. It was 20:40.
>
> Kunz told her that he doubted he had the mental strength to help administer poison to the sleeping children, so Magda Goebbels asked him to find Hitler's personal physician, Ludwig Stumpfegger, and send him to her.
>
> When I returned with Stumpfegger to that room next to the children's bedroom where I had left Goebbels' wife she was not there, and Stumpfegger went straight to the bedroom. I stayed waiting in the next room. Four or five minutes later Stumpfegger came out of the children's bedroom with Goebbels' wife and, without saying a word to me, left immediately.
>
> Goebbels' wife also said nothing to me, only cried. I went with her down to the lower floor of the bunker to Goebbels' study, where I found the latter in a highly nervous state, pacing up and down the office. Entering the office, his wife stated 'Everything is finished with the children, now we need to think about ourselves', to which Goebbels replied, 'Quickly. We have little time.'

Rzhevskaya said Magda Goebbels told Kunz she had been given the morphine and the syringe by Stumpfegger. He did not know where she had obtained the ampoules of poison. She might have been given them by Hitler who, as we later learned, had been issuing them at the end of April.

'Kunz returned to the hospital in a very depressed state', we were told by Werner Haase, the head of the hospital whom we interrogated after him. He came into my room, sat on the bed and clutched his head in his hands.'

Haase asked him 'Are Goebbels and his family dead?' He replied, 'Yes'. To my question as to whether he had been alone, Kunz replied,

'I was helped by Dr Stumpfegger'. 'I was not able to get anything more out of him', Haase said

Vice Admiral Voss, Dr Kunz, Lange the cook, Schneider the garage mechanic, Wilhelm Eckold the head bodyguard of Goebbels, Wilhelm Ziehm, technical administrator of the building of the Reich Chancellery, and many others formally identified Goebbels.

'Although the body was charred, it was readily recognisable by anyone who had met Goebbels or seen him from a distance', Rzhevskaya said. 'He could have been recognised even from the caricatures of him in our Soviet press. He had a very distinctive appearance, his head disproportionately large for his puny body and noticeably squashed at the sides. He had a slanting forehead and his face narrowed markedly to his chin.'

Even Zhukov, the Red Army's highest-ranking officer, was revolted by the deaths of the six children. He and the Army High Command in Berlin were inspecting the Reich Chancellery at the time the children's bodies were found. He later wrote in his autobiography: 'I must admit I had not the heart to go down and look at the children killed by their own mother and father.'

Rzhevskaya said she had to shake off her feelings of revulsion to continue with her task, as she was the only German-speaking Russian in the bunker. She said it was dark in the underground complex, and with the ventilation not working it was stuffy, dank and gloomy.

I had to sort through a vast number of papers and documents by the light of humble oil lamps. There were on-the spot accounts of street fighting in Bormann's files, reports from the Berlin Nazi Party leadership about the hopelessness of the situation, their lack of ammunition, the demoralised state of the soldiers. There was Bormann's correspondence, and Hitler's personal papers.

My priority in searching through these papers was to find anything that would shed some light at least on what had been happening there in the last few days, that would add a brush stroke or give a clue as to how everything had ended.

Here was Bormann sending telegram after telegram to his adjutant, Hummel, in Obersalzberg, all bearing the red stamp 'Geheim', Secret! From the nature of his instructions it was clear they were preparing to move Hitler's headquarters to Berchtesgaden. They had been planning to get out of Berlin.

Here was a folder containing information from their enemy's sources, radio intercepts from the last days of April: Reuters news agency reports from Allied headquarters, broadcasts from Moscow about combat operations on the fronts, telegrams about events in the rest of the world, from London, Rome, San Francisco, Washington and Zurich. These sources were used at Hitler's headquarters to gain a sense of what was happening on other sectors of the front, and in Berlin itself, in the last days of April. By this time, direct contact with the troops had been finally lost.

She said all the papers in the folder were typewritten in huge letters, and she had never before come across such a strange font: 'It was as if you were reading through a magnifying glass. What was that for? Later I learned that Hitler's secretary, Gertraud Junge, retyped all the papers on a special typewriter. For reasons of image, Hitler did not want to wear spectacles.'

Among the documents was a report from a foreign radio station about the execution of Mussolini and his mistress, Clara Petacci. With a blue pencil, Hitler had underlined the words 'Mussolini' and 'hung upside down'. This discovery seemed to Rzhevskaya to be significant: the news of Mussolini's fate made it clear to Hitler that he needed to avoid discovery of his body after his death. 'We searched for documents and, having familiarised myself with them, I annotated them. They were then forwarded, as already mentioned, to front headquarters, as were our own papers, interrogation reports and all other documentation.'

Chapter 5

GOEBBELS' DIARY

One of Rzhevskaya's major finds at the time was Goebbels' diary. It was found in one of two suitcases of documents. There were ten or so thick notebooks from different years, covered in closely written, heavy handwriting in straight lines. The letters had a barely noticeable slant to the left and were tightly squeezed together. The first books of the diary dated from 1932, before the Nazis came to power, and the last ended on 8 July 1941.

'We discovered later that this was only the date on which the handwritten diary ends. From the following day, 9 July 1941, and almost to the end, he dictated his entries each day to two shorthand typists', Rzhevskaya said:

> I greatly regretted not being able to sit down and study this diary, which it was not easy to decipher. It would have needed many days of diligent work, and we were having to count the minutes. Our immediate task was to establish what had happened to Hitler and where we could find him. I had no option but to forward the diaries to front headquarters. With the war at an end, such documents were of purely historical interest and considered to be of no value.

Rzhevskaya mused that in the years that followed, when she recalled Goebbels' diary she feared the notebooks had been lost along with a host of other documents, but a time came when she had the opportunity to read very carefully a part of this diary, to whose discovery she had contributed and which had been preserved in the Russian archive.

> It was the last handwritten notebook dating from May, June and early July 1941. Realising that this diary was a tremendously valuable historical document, I quoted abundantly from it in my book (translated, naturally,

into Russian). I thus presided over the first publication from this body of handwritten diaries, revealing their whereabouts to the world.

Nobody, of course, had any intention of making the original of the diary available for a foreign edition, and accordingly this chapter is all but missing in the [East] German edition of my book that was edited in the USSR.

However, the mere mention of the existence of this notebook and the exact date on which it ended, 8 July 1941, proved to be enough. [West] German historians already had Goebbels' typewritten diaries at their disposal, which began from the following day, 9 July 1941, and now they knew that the manuscript diary was extant and preserved in an archive in Moscow. They began seeking access to it, and in 1969 microfilm copies were conveyed to the Germans. In 1987 all the surviving pages of the manuscript diary were published, and became an international best-seller.

The last notebook of that diary is uniquely interesting historical testimony, reflecting as it does the facts and atmosphere of preparations for the attack on the USSR. It discloses the nature of the provocations and the methods of disinformation undertaken at the time by Nazi Germany.

The first mention of the attack on the USSR appears in the diary on 24 May, 1941. Goebbels sent his representative to Alfred Rosenberg, who was to become minister for the occupied eastern territories, to coordinate their activities in the impending operation.

'Russia must be broken down into component parts', Goebbels said, '. . . the existence of such a colossal state in the east cannot be tolerated'. He was also busy with active disinformation, spreading false rumours about a supposedly imminent invasion of Britain in order to mask Germany's true intentions. 'The rumours we have sown about the invasion are working. There is a climate of exceptional nervousness in England', he said.

The entry for 31 May reads: 'Operation Barbarossa is developing. We are beginning the first big deception. The entire state and military machinery is being mobilised. Only a few individuals are informed about the true course of events. I am obliged to send the whole ministry off on a false trail, risking, in the event of failure, the loss of my prestige . . .

'Little by little we are elaborating the theme of the invasion. I ordered a song to be composed about it, a new theme, increasing the use of broadcasts in English, training a propaganda company for England, etc. Two weeks allowed for everything . . . If nobody blabs and, given the small circle of initiates, one can count on that, the deception will succeed. Forward march.

'A busy time is beginning. We will prove that our propaganda is unrivalled. The civilian ministries suspect nothing. They are working in the direction set for them. It will be interesting when the balloon goes up.'

Fascinating as they may have been, Rzhevskaya knew she had to tear herself away from the diaries and continue the search for Hitler, or what remained of him.

As she continued her search Goebbels' body was carried out of the bunker on the leaf of a door, on to the Wilhemstrasse in front of the Chancellery. Berliners, Red Army soldiers and others gathered round to witness one of the most potent examples of the downfall of a bizarre dream. Many gathered around to have themselves photographed beside the body, a sort of post-war 'Selfie'.

Down in the bunker Rzhevskaya continued talking to captives who had remained in the bunker.

'Which one of you was the last to see Hitler? Who saw him here at all, alive in the underground complex? What is known about what has happened to him?'

She returned to Karl Schneider, the garage mechanic who had previously told her about sending petrol to Hitler's bunker. Whether Hitler was in Berlin at all until 1 May he had no idea. Personally, he said he did not see him. On 1 May, however, in the Chancellery garage he said he had heard from Hitler's chauffeur, Erich Kempka, and from the person in charge of the garage that Hitler had committed suicide. 'The news went round by word of mouth', he said 'Everyone was repeating it but no one really knew for sure.'

A 50-year-old man introduced himself to the searchers as Wilhelm Lange, chef of the Führer's domestic commissariat in the Reich Chancellery and a specialist pastry cook. He said 'I last saw Hitler at the beginning of April 1945 in the garden of the Reich Chancellery, where he was taking a walk with his German sheepdog which answered to the name of Blondi.'

'What do you know about the fate of Hitler?'

'Nothing for sure. In the evening of 30 April, Hitler's dog handler, Sergeant Major Tornow, came to me in the kitchen for food for the puppies. He was upset about something and told me, "The Führer is dead and nothing remains of his body". There were rumours among the Reich Chancellery staff, he said, that Hitler had poisoned or shot himself and that his body had been burnt. He did not know whether or not that was true.'

He continued: 'The technical administrator of the Reich Chancellery, Wilhelm Ziehm then said "The last time I saw Hitler was at 12 noon on 29 April. I was summoned to the Führer's bunker to fix a malfunctioning ventilator. While doing the job I saw Hitler through the open door of his office."'

'By the morning of 4 May that's all we had discovered', Rzhevskaya said. 'Nothing for sure, as Lange the chef had said, and even this information had to be extricated from an accumulation of other contradictory, sensational misinformation.'

The searchers were given fantastic stories, including that Hitler had been flown out on a plane piloted by Hanna Reitsch three days before Berlin fell; that his 'death' had been staged, and the broadcast announcement about it was a ruse; that Hitler had been spirited away from Berlin through underground passages and was hiding in his 'impregnable' stronghold in South Tyrol.

Rzhevskaya said people who were in possession of more modest, but crucial information were so traumatised by everything they had experienced that they muddled dates and facts, even though what they were recollecting had happened only two or three days previously.

> First here, then there, alternative stories bubbled up and burst, each more sensational than the last. Rumours circulated that Hitler had had doubles.
>
> To exclude these speculations definitively, one after another, took time. The search was being conducted at a furious pace: it was easy to race off on the wrong track and come to false conclusions. Complications, sometimes ridiculous, hampered the search.

In the meantime, Stalin had become displeased that the discovery of Goebbels' remains was publicised. 'The search for Hitler', he decreed, 'would proceed in strict secrecy.' Elena Rzhevskaya's counterintelligence unit was downsized to three: Colonel Vasily Gorbushin (in charge of the search), Major Bystrov, and herself. They were prohibited all contact with the press and photographers. And it was at this point that Stalin specifically instructed that Rzhevskaya keep her mouth shut.

'Under very difficult conditions', Rzhevskaya said, 'it was essential to coordinate the efforts of the intelligence agents and sort through everything methodically and swiftly, to block off all the false trails and target the search.'

> Again and again, metre by metre, we painstakingly examined the empty underground complex beneath the Reich Chancellery. There were overturned tables, broken typewriters, glass and paper underfoot; box-rooms and more substantial rooms, long corridors and crossings.
>
> There was damage to the concrete walls and, here and there in the corridors, pools of water. Damp, dank air. The ventilators had not

worked well even when Hitler was there and now were not working at all. It was difficult to breathe and it was murky. Round every corner something seemed to be rustling or moving, or there was a silence you felt might at any moment be broken by gunfire from some desperate Nazi officer.

The crunching of boots on broken glass, echoing gasps from soldiers who had stormed the Reich Chancellery and now, prowling through the last residence of the German government, were coming upon crates of expensive liqueurs.

They were calling out to each other as if finding their way through a forest, their torches lighting up the theatrical setting of the last hours of the Third Reich. Sometimes we heard the click of safety catches and a menacing 'Khende khokh', 'Hände hoch!' in a heavy Russian accent, directed into the darkness where the sound of our footsteps was coming from.

It was a difficult, unpredictable situation. Above us, on the surface of Berlin, the war was over, but down here, underground, the search continued in the chaos. Our searching was tireless; we were completely focused, conscious of a tremendous responsibility, the culmination of four years of warfare. We had to find our bearings in what was, at first, the thoroughly confusing topography of the underground complex, to discover hiding places and check them. The hunt was on to find Hitler.

General Krebs had already been found, lying in the courtyard in a grey-green tunic with the epaulettes torn off. He had poisoned himself too.

But as to the whereabouts of Hitler, we still had 'nothing for sure'. If we proceeded from the testimony of Vice Admiral Voss, who had been told about Hitler's death by Goebbels (to whom Hitler had bequeathed the authority of Reich Chancellor); if we accepted the hypothesis of Schneider, the garage mechanic, as to what his petrol had been needed for; the missing link in the chain was someone who had actually taken part in burning the bodies, or had seen how and where it happened, or had at least heard about it in detail.

The garden of the Reich Chancellery, which subsequently was found to have been the setting for this drama, was so churned up that it was hardly going to be possible to determine where the cremation had taken place.

Meanwhile, rumours abounded. Somebody had been told by somebody else that Hitler had been reduced to ashes and that Axmann, the Reichsführer of the Hitler Youth, who had participated in a group attempt to break out, had made off with the ashes. Axmann, at that time, had given us the slip.

If Hitler had been totally incinerated, that would confirm what dog handler Tornow had told Lange the chef: 'The Führer is dead and nothing remains of his body.' If that was so, if there were no remains or they were never going to be found, we would never be able to show the world irrefutable evidence he was dead. Hitler's disappearance would remain a mystery and provide fertile soil for all manner of myths, something in which only his adherents could have an interest.

The information we had was now collated. We were looking for people who could clarify what had happened. Meanwhile, more and more people came trampling through the Chancellery, soldiers and commanders, staff officers and people who had flown in from Moscow, and journalists we needed to steer well clear of.

They wandered through the apartments in the Reich Chancellery, came down into the underground complex looking for Hitler's rooms. As a token of their encounter with history, they carried off with them this and that as a souvenir. Everybody wanted to be here, everybody had a right to be here. Really, though, this was no time for tourists.

We searched the complex, the garden, inside the building above ground, and in nearby stretches of the street. On the morning of 4 May, I had a quiet, domesticated and completely civilian man sitting in front of me, a little stoker nobody in the Reich Chancellery had noticed. As a technician, he had been sent to the Führer's bunker to mend the malfunctioning ventilator.

He had already told us that, while he was in the corridor, he had seen the bodies of the Führer and Eva Braun being taken out of Hitler's rooms, wrapped in grey blankets. She was wearing a black dress. He was not trying to persuade us of anything, just telling what he had seen.

In a chorus of louder, more assertive voices the ring of truth was somehow missing. The stoker himself was so unassuming, so humble, that it was difficult to believe he could have any role to play in events of this magnitude. Vice Admiral Voss seemed far better suited to the role, only he had no direct evidence to give.

The stoker was the first German from whom I heard about Hitler's wedding. At the time, in a Berlin where the fighting and the fires had barely died down, it struck me as ridiculous beyond belief. I looked again at the humble, ordinary man who was matter-of-factly thinking through the bizarre scenes he had witnessed in the last three or four days, as if they were something from an infinitely remote past. The truth was that we had moved not just from one day to the next, but out of one epoch and into another.

I have forgotten the stoker's name. He juts out of the tome of history, an anonymous bookmark pointing us to the right page. Incredulous, inattentive, we had not taken the time to read it carefully. [His name was actually Johannes Hentschel, specifically responsible for the machine room providing power and water. He was an electro-mechanic who worked in the Reich Chancellery and later the Führerbunker. Hentschel stayed behind even after most others had left or died, ensuring the bunker's essential services continued for the wounded in the Reich Chancellery above.]

Elena Rzhevskaya said the search team's biggest problem was the mass of conflicting statements being made by survivors and witness.

But there was one almost casual remark [SS Colonel] Kunz made that we could not ignore. He said that Goebbels' wife, telling him about Hitler's suicide, did not add anything definite about how he had done it but,

'There were rumours', Dr Kunz told us, 'that his body was to be cremated in the garden of the Reich Chancellery.'

'Who exactly did you hear that from?' Colonel Gorbushin asked. 'I heard it from Rattenhuber, the SS Obergruppenführer responsible for security at the Führer's headquarters,' he said, 'The Führer has left us alone, and now we have to drag his body upstairs.'

In Goebbels' rooms we find in two suitcases, besides his diaries, several screenplays sent to him by their authors; and a huge album, an anniversary gift from Nazi Party comrades for his fortieth birthday. It contains sheets of photographs, reproducing page after page of Goebbels' manuscript *The Little ABC of the National Socialist*.

It was difficult to work in the underground complex itself, where the electricity supply failed periodically, and I spent many hours analysing documents in one of the halls of the Reich Chancellery. It was the reception hall where people waited for Hitler to appear, I think, or some other. I am not sure exactly. (I had trouble working out the layout of the Reich Chancellery.) Everything seemed to have been overturned.

Perhaps this was where the SS security guards had made their last stand; also, the army had passed this way, and had no reason to respect the furnishings in the grand rooms of the headquarters of Nazism.

Tables had been knocked over, glass lampshades smashed, chairs had been overturned and their seats ripped open. Everywhere were shards of glass from the windows. I still remember the special floor of this room, entirely covered by a velvety grey velour, now trampled and torn by Red Army boots. The reconnaissance squads were bringing in sacks full of documents and dumping them on that special flooring.

In Goebbels' rooms we also found several files in a suitcase that contained Magda Goebbels' personal papers. What did she bring with her when she moved to the underground complex on 22 April from her house on Göringstrasse? There were inventories of the furnishings in the country house in Lanke, and in the castle in Schwanenwerder, which had been built by the time of the war with the Soviet Union. Everything was listed: fittings, cabinets with silver, dinner services and figurines.

Nothing was overlooked: every ashtray, every cushion in the innumerable rooms, every last handkerchief of Dr Goebbels and its place in the linen cupboard, every toilet paper holder. And so, from one room to the next, in the main building and the outbuildings: bedrooms, offices, children's and adjutants' bedrooms, guest rooms, halls, vestibules, stairs, corridors, terraces, servants' rooms, and cinemas. An inventory of Goebbels' wardrobe. Eighty-seven bottles of assorted wines.

There were bills detailing the cost of furnishing the castle, about which Goebbels writes enthusiastically in his diary, and sundry department store bills going back as far as 1939 and addressed to Magda Goebbels.

Inventories of the children's clothing, individually for each one of them. All their dresses, coats, hats, shoes, ski suits and underwear are listed. Items that are new, and items handed down from the eldest daughter to the second in seniority, from the second to the third, and so on. And items that, for the present, were being held in reserve. A certificate awarded to her as a participant in the Olympic Games, signed by the Führer.

There was also a paper, sent to Magda Goebbels, stamped with the seal of the National Socialist German Workers' Party and signed by one of the Party leaders of the Berlin district. It contained the forecasts of a fortune-teller. He predicted in April 1942 there would be a parachute landing of Allied forces on the coast of France in early June 1942 and that fierce battles would follow. These would be at their fiercest in August 1944. In mid-June of that year, the prophecy continued, the Germans would use a new aerial weapon which would cause untold destruction, especially in England. This would lead to domestic political difficulties in Britain that would hamper the further advance of the Allies.

Also, according to the fortune-teller fierce fighting against the invading troops would last from August until November 1944, but in early November the Allies would suffer their greatest defeat in the entire war. In April 1945, Germany would be ready to redirect all its strike force to the Eastern Front, and after fifteen months Russia would finally be conquered by Germany. Communism would be eradicated, the Jews driven out, and Russia would break down into smaller states. In summer 1946, German submarines would be equipped with a new and terrifying weapon with the aid of which, in the course of August 1946, the remnants of the British and American fleets would be destroyed.

But none of this provided direct clues as to what had happened to Hitler. A folder belonging to Martin Borman, Hitler's private secretary, contained an important document, a radio-telegram Bormann had sent from the Reich Chancellery shelter to his adjutant twelve days earlier, on 22 April 45.

To Hummel. Obersalzberg.
Proposed relocation overseas and south agreed.
Reichsleiter Bormann

What did that mean? Bormann was evidently preparing a hideaway for himself far beyond the borders of Germany. And here is how matters stood beyond the borders of his diary, which I also found was in the archive. If I had had Martin Bormann's notebook-cum-diary in front of me then, I would have read the following in the last entries:

> Sunday 29 April.
> A second day begins with a hurricane of gunfire. During the night of 28 April the foreign press reported Himmler's offer of surrender. Marriage of Adolf Hitler and Eva Braun. The Führer dictates his political and personal will. The traitors Jodl, Himmler and the generals have abandoned us to the Bolsheviks. Again a hurricane of gunfire. According to an enemy report, the Americans have burst into Munich!
> 30 April 45.
> Adolf Hitler a
> Eva H.

Next to their names Bormann had drawn an inverted runic cross, an emblem of death.

If we'd been able to read that document earlier, we would have had important confirmation that Hitler had died on 30 April, but we did not have sight of the diary. It was found in the street by reconnaissance agents of our neighbouring army and we did not get to see it.

Admittedly, the peculiar circumstances in which the diary was found would probably not have allowed us then, at the preliminary stage of inspecting it, to trust it uncritically: it could have been a forgery, planted for us to find.

Today [1991] however, we can say with complete confidence that this is the genuine diary of Martin Bormann, which he dropped while trying to break through the ring of Soviet troops as a member of Mohnke's group, probably when he was fatally injured!

The diary, although recording events at quite a different level, is absurdly like the diaries of the very stupidest German front-line soldiers, which in turn are closely similar to each other. The similarity is no sign of democratic ways but of the monstrous uniformity of thinking that Hitler counted on and Nazism cultivated.

Although the Reich Chancellery was only 550m or so from the Reichstag, it was in the zone allocated to Rzhevskaya's neighbouring 5th Assault Army, which captured it. They were not allowed to cross that dividing line, but the fighting was over and she said everything was a muddle.

'Absolutely anybody who got the chance came rushing into our army's zone, which contained the Reichstag, in order to be able to say, "I was here", to sightsee, to write their name on the Reichstag, to go inside.' With a smile she said, 'I was one of them. I left my name on the Reichstag only three days later.'

Rzhevskaya said that 3 May 1945 gave her a great feeling of exhilaration.

The discovery of the bodies of Goebbels and his family was made very public, which seemed only natural. On that day nobody in charge thought differently. Journalists, photographers and newsreel reporters were allowed to record everything. In the first days of victory, people experienced what they believed was a dawning of freedom. They acted rationally and normal.

But they soon discovered they had been deluding themselves, because Stalin was outraged that people had taken the initiative to make this event so public and somebody evidently got a flea in his ear. From the following day a screen of strict secrecy went up round the search for Hitler. There was to be no contact with the press or photographers, and all reports were to go directly to Stalin, bypassing the Army command.

So there was nothing we could do. We couldn't talk to the journalists, or any civilians, not even military officers outside of our immediate circle, which included SMERSH, who then took complete control of the search.

We had two problems. The first was trying to understand from the conflicting information of the Germans what had happened, and then trying to keep everyone on our side in the dark.

And there were apparently some bizarre moments. Rzhevskaya described how on 3 May a group of generals from the 1st Byelorussian Front headquarters were passing through the Chancellery garden. One or other of them decided one of the bodies looked like Hitler. It was immediately pulled out of the pond and Germans were called to identify it. Their unanimous verdict was, 'Not the Führer'.

The situation was further complicated when German Vice Admiral Voss identified the corpse as Hitler's. Rzhveskaya believes he was being deliberately deceptive, as he must have been able to accurately identify Hitler. But the searchers needed further proof, so they waited until a former member of staff of the Soviet embassy in Berlin, who had seen Hitler before the war several times, flew in from Moscow.

Accordingly, a gentleman with a little moustache and his hair falling to one side of his face and wearing a pair of darned socks duly reposed for a considerable time in the vestibule of the Reich Chancellery, then in the hall, until the diplomat finally arrived and confirmed: 'Not Hitler'.

Newsreel and photojournalists had meanwhile been having a field day photographing and filming the body and, proudly labelling it 'Hitler', later depositing their handiwork in the archive and the historical film library. No member of the press was allowed anywhere near the actual remains and they were not photographed.

Maybe the connoisseurs of some sensations will be disappointed, but I must say there were no doubles whatsoever. We were involuntarily creating them ourselves. The fact was that General Berzarin, the commander of the 3rd/6th Army, said that the person who found Hitler would get the title of Hero of the Soviet Union. So when they really saw someone, found some bodies and a moustache, so they would bring this person to the commandant, and our journalists, even famous ones, were writing later on 'I saw eight doubles' in this place

Unsurprisingly, the false Hitler was later blithely spliced into a Soviet documentary film but, under pressure from an agitated foreign press, he was disavowed and the film withdrawn. The posthumous adventures of this unknown man did not end there, however. He spawned a whole constellation of doubles whereas, in reality, Hitler never had any. Neither was the screen life of the false Hitler over.

Only a few years ago [mid-1980s] after the ill-fated film he was again resurrected from the archive by journalists and the photo was shown on television, masquerading as the body of Hitler.

No doubt there will be a next time, because this piece of film is still making the rounds. I hope that I can kill this nonsense by talking to you on film. It was quite crazy.

Chapter 6

DISCOVERY OF THE BODIES

And then, suddenly, the search for Hitler's body took a surprising turn, and chance took a hand.

Rzhevskaya explained that on Saturday, 5 May, a unit of her army, 79th Corps, was leaving Berlin for a new deployment and the SMERSH group which had already been involved in the search went with their commander, Lieutenant Colonel Klimenko, purely out of curiosity, to take a last look at the Chancellery garden and the place where Goebbels had been found.

As Klimenko later explained, in a letter to Rzhevskaya, that was near the emergency exit from Hitler's bunker. He said that on 4 May one of the group, Private Ivan Churakov, noticed a bomb crater 3m or so to the left of the door. The soil in it was loose and seemed to have been thrown in recently. He jumped down into the crater and, from the ground which had settled under his weight, something became visible. They dug down and found the black, charred bodies of a man and a woman. They pulled them out of the crater and took a good look at them. They did not recognise the man as Hitler, and indeed he was completely unrecognisable. The analogy with the charred body of Goebbels did not occur to them, and they did not look more closely at their find. The main thing that threw them off the scent was that Klimenko had heard Hitler's body had already been found and was lying in the Reich Chancellery. That dead German in the darned socks hoodwinked them. The men filled in the crater again and left.

So the bodies of Hitler and Eva Braun were in fact discovered on 4 May, but it was not realised what they were. In a 1965 letter to Elena Rzhevskaya Klimenko said he did not report finding these bodies to anyone.

'That could have turned out to be a fatal mistake', Rzhevskaya said but fortunately the search team came to hear of it. They already had enough facts to understand whom the soldiers had dug up. Colonel Gorbushin insisted that those who had made the discovery be brought back.

'In that same letter, Klimenko tells me that when he returned to his SMERSH unit, he himself began to wonder whether those bodies we had reburied were the bodies of Hitler and Eva Braun.' This seemed all the more likely because, before leaving the Reich Chancellery, he had gone to look at the other Hitler and learned he had been identified as 'not the Führer'.

Klimenko sent the soldiers back to the Reich Chancellery under the command of his deputy, Captain Deryabin. The names of those who found the bodies are immortalised in a document drawn up the following day.

Berlin. Army on active service.
Declaration
This fifth day of the month of May 1945.
I, Senior Guards Lieutenant Alexey Alexandrovich Panasov, and Privates Ivan Dmitrievich Churakov, Yevgeny Stepanovich Oleynik and Ilia Yefremovich Seroukh in Berlin, in the area of Hitler's Reich Chancellery, near the place where the bodies of Goebbels and his wife were discovered, next to Hitler's personal bomb shelter, found and recovered two bodies, one female, the other male.
The bodies are badly burned, and it is not possible to identify them without further information.
The bodies were situated in a bomb crater three metres from the entrance to Hitler's shelter and covered with a layer of earth
Senior Guards Lieutenant (Panasov)
Private Churakov Private Oleynik
Private Seroukh
The ground in the crater was dug over and two dead dogs found, a sheepdog and a puppy.
A further declaration was drawn up:
We have found and recovered two slaughtered dogs.

Characteristics:

1. German sheepdog (female) with dark grey fur, of large stature, having round its neck a collar in the form of a fine chain. No injuries or blood found on the body.
2. Of small stature (male), with black fur, without a collar, no injuries, bone of the upper half of the mouth punctured, blood in that area.

The bodies of the dogs were in a bomb crater 1.5 m apart under a light covering of earth.

There are grounds to believe that the killing of the dogs occurred 5-6 days ago, since there is no bad smell from the bodies and the fur is not becoming detached.

For the purpose of discovering items that might serve to confirm to whom these dogs belonged and the causes of their death, we carefully dug over and examined the soil at the place from where the bodies of the dogs were recovered. Here there were discovered:

1. Two dark-coloured glass tubes for medicine.
2. Sundry burnt sheets from typographically printed books and small scraps of paper with original handwriting.
3. A metal medallion of elliptical shape on a fine chain of beads 18-20 cm long, on the reverse side of which is an engraved inscription: May I be always by your side.
4. German currency amounting to 600 marks in notes of 100 marks.
5. A metal tag of elliptical form [with the number] 31907.

The bodies of the dogs and the items discovered at the place of discovery and recovery have been photographed and are stored at the SMERSH counterintelligence department of the corps, as witness the present Declaration.

Captain Deryabin
Senior Guards Lieutenant Panasov
Sergeant Tsibochkin
Privates Alabudin, Kirillov, Korshak, Gulyaev.

The dogs were readily identified. The sheepdog was Hitler's personal dog, as was written in another declaration. It was 'tall, with long ears'!

At this moment, Rzhveskaya told me, she realised that she was witnessing history, and recalled it in detail.

In the garden it was light and windy. The soldiers stood in a circle: Churakov, Oleynik, Seroukh, Senior Lieutenant Panasov. The wind was tugging at bits of burnt tin, wire, broken branches strewn around on the lawn.

On a grey blanket, contorted by fire, lay black, hideous human remains caked with lumps of mud.

I was there to witness that.

The charred bodies, and those of the two dogs, were placed in Red Army ammunition boxes measuring 163cm in length, by 55cm wide, and 53cm in height.

What followed was another bizarre scene in what had already been a bizarre period. She looked at me with a smile on her face and said 'This is really weird'.

As dawn broke on 6 May, two bodies were heaved over the fence of the Reich Chancellery garden into a waiting truck and driven off.

Rzhveskaya explained.

The problem was that the 5th Assault Army, whose commander, General Berzarin, was the commandant of Berlin, was restoring order and clearing the Reich Chancellery and underground complex of all the people who had been flooding in. Sentries were posted at the entrance with orders to admit no one.

For us there was an added complication. For the intelligence services of the 5th Assault Army it remains to this day a source of enduring intolerable irritation that such a notable success was achieved on their patch not by them but by gatecrashers from our 3rd Assault Army.

We were not about to leave our spoils in the hands of anybody else, abandoning the project before we had seen it through to a conclusion ourselves.

So that was the ploy we resorted to: kidnapping the bodies of Hitler and Eva Braun, wrapped in sheets and, behind the backs of the sentries, spiriting them over the fence to where a truck with two large crates was waiting.

So began the posthumous adventures of Hitler's body. The search team had sifted through all the details of his last days to establish everything that had happened, and had confirmation and the evidence that Hitler and Eva Braun had been hastily concealed in a bomb crater.

OFFICIAL REPORT ON THE BURIAL OF THE CORPSES OF HITLER, GOEBBELS AND OTHER PERSONS

Top Secret
4 June, 1945 the 3rd Assault Army

On 4 June, 1945, the commission including Chairman of the Commission – Chief of 'SMERSH' Counter-Espionage Section of the 3rd Assault Army Colonel Miroshnichenko and the members of the Commission, Deputy Chief of the 'SMERSH' Counter-Espionage Section of the 3rd Assault Army Colonel Gorbushin, Chief of the 4th Sub-Section of the 'SMERSH' Counter-Espionage Section of the 3rd Assault Army Major Bystrov, Commander of the 5th detached company Senior Lieutenant Gorokhov, Commander of a platoon of the 5th detached company Senior Lieutenant Byelobragin, Sergeant-Major Bakalov and Privates Hyretdinov and Teriaev, of the 5th detached company, compiled the following report:

On 2 May, 1945, a group of officers of the 'SMERSH Counter-Espionage Section of the 3rd Assault Army in the city of Berlin, discovered in the grounds of Reich Chancellery several metres from the emergency exit of Hitler-Goebbels' bunker, the corpses of German Reichminister of Propaganda of Dr. Josef Goebbels and his wife Magda Goebbels, and in the course of the examination of the interior of the bunker, the corpses of Goebbels' children were found in a bedroom: daughter Hilde, son Helmut, daughter Helga, daughter Hedda, daughter Heide and daughter Holde,

At the same time, the body of the Chief of the German General Staff General Krebs was found in the courtyard of the Ministry of Propaganda.

All these corpses were delivered to the 'SMERSH' Counter Espionage Section of the 3rd Assault Army in the city of Buh [Buch, a Berlin suburb].

In a further search on 5 May, 1945, several metres from the place where the corpses of Goebbels and his wife had been discovered, two badly-burnt bodies were discovered in a bomb-crater. These were the corpse of the Reichschancellor of Germany Adolf Hitler and the corpse of his wife Braun. These two corpses were also taken to the 'SMERSH' Counter-Espionage Section of the 3rd Assault Army – the city of Buh [Berlin]. All the bodies brought to the 'SMERSH Counter-Espionage Section of the 3rd Assault Army were subjected to the following procedures: forensic medical examination and identification by persons who knew them when alive.

After the forensic medical examination and all operations to identify them were completed, all the corpses were buried near the city of Buh.

Because of the relocation of the 'SMERSH Counter-Espionage Section of the Army, the corpses were exhumed and moved first to the region of the city of Finow, and later, on 3 June, 1945, to the region of the city of Rachenau, where they were finally buried.

The corpses were in wooden coffins in a 1.7 metre deep grave, laid out in the following order: From east to west: Hitler, Eva Braun, Goebbels, Magda Goebbels, Krebs and Goebbels children.

At the western end of the grave there is also a basket containing the bodies of two dogs, one of which belonged to Hitler personally and the other to Braun, Eva.

The location of the burnt bodies: Germany, province of Brandenburg, the vicinity of the city of Rathenau, forest to the east of the city of Rathenau, along the road from Rathenau to Schrechow, before reaching the village of Neu Friedrichsdorf, 325 metres from a railway bridge, along a forest road, from a milestone numbered 111 north-east-wards 4-side marker bearing the same number 1, a distance 5 metres. From this 3rd pole due east it is a distance of 62 metres. The grave was filled in and smoothed over and small pine trees planted on it forming the number 111.

Chairman of the Commission Colonel Miroshnichenko
The members of the Commission: Colonel Gorbushin, Major Bystrov, Senior Lieutenant Gorokhov Senior Lieutenant Byelobragin, Sergeant-Major Bakalov Red Army Private Hyretdinov, Red Army Private Teriaev.

Chapter 7

THE AUTOPSY

In a small park 20km north-east of the centre of Berlin stood a small building with medical facilities and equipment. In May 1945, despite all the destruction around it, it had not been damaged. On 8 May a medical team specially chosen for the task began an autopsy on the two charred bodies, as well as the dogs. Colonel Gorbushin's search team had dwindled down to three people, including Rzhevskaya as interpreter. They too were present. Gorbushin had ordered all the bodies, including the Goebbels family, as well as the bodies of Generals Hans Krebs and Wilhelm Burgdorf to be delivered to this building. Elena Rzhevskaya, who had fond memories of Gorbushin, said he was determined 'for the sake of history' to establish the truth.

The medical team led by the Chief Forensic Pathologist of the First Belorussian Front, Doctor Faust Shkaravsky, was also determined to conduct as scientific an examination as possible, so that there could be no doubt. Shkaravsky was an experienced pathologist. He had graduated from the Medical Institute of Kiev, Ukraine, in 1925, and was later on the faculty of forensic medicine at the Kiev Medical Institute and the Institute for Advanced Medical Studies. Shortly before the war broke out he was sent to the Leningrad Academy of Military Medicine. He participated in the battles of Stalingrad and Kursk, and advanced to be Chief Expert of Forensic Medicine for two Red Army divisions. He had performed approximately 1,000 autopsies, and was familiar with the methods and procedures, having instructed students in anatomy.

Although they were aware that they were probably conducting an autopsy on Hitler himself, this had not yet been firmly established, so the examination proceeded on what were, simply, two charred corpses.

The autopsy itself was carried out by the Acting Chief Anatomical Pathologist of the 1st Byelorussian Front Major Anna Marants, who dissected the corpse of Hitler under Dr. Shkaravsky's supervision. Their report reads:

DOCUMENT NO. 12
Concerning the forensic examination of a male corpse disfigured by fire (Hitler's body)
Berlin-Buch, 8.V., 1945
Mortuary CAFS No. 496 (Abbreviation for Mobile Army Surgical Hospital)

The Commission consisted of Chief Expert, Forensic Medicine, 1st Byelorussian Front, Medical Service, Lieutenant Colonel F. I. Shkaravsky; Chief Anatomist, Red Army, Medical Service, Lieutenant Colonel N. A. Krayevski; Acting Chief Anatomical Pathologist, 1st Byelorussian Front, Medical Service, Major A. Y. Marants; Army Expert, Forensic Medicine, 3rd Assault Army, Medical Service, Major Y. I. Boguslavski; and Army Anatomical Pathologist, 3rd Assault Army, Medical Service, Major Y. V. Gulkevich, on orders of the member of the Military Council 1st Byelorussian Front, Lieutenant General Telegin. They performed the forensic-medical examination of a male corpse (presumably the corpse of Hitler).

Results of the examination:

A. EXTERNAL EXAMINATION
The remains of a male corpse disfigured by fire were delivered in a wooden box
(Length 163 centimetres, width 55 centimetres height 53 centimetres. On the body was found a piece of yellow jersey, 25 x 8 cm., charred around the edges, resembling a knitted undervest.

In view of the fact that the corpse is greatly damaged, it is difficult to gauge the age of the deceased. Presumably it lies between 50 and 60 years. The dead man's height is 165 cm.
(the measurements are approximate since the tissue charred), the right shinbone measures 39 cm.

The corpse is severely charred and smells of burned flesh. Part of the cranium is missing.

Parts of the occipital bone, the left temporal bone, the lower cheekbones, the nasal bones, and the upper and lower jaws are preserved.

The burns are more pronounced on the right side of the cranium than on the left. In the brain cavity parts of the fire-damaged brain and of the dura mater are visible. On face and body the skin is completely missing; only remnants of charred muscles are preserved. There are many small cracks in the nasal bone and the upper jawbones. The tongue is charred; its tip is firmly locked between the teeth of the upper and lower jaws.

In the upper jaw there are nine teeth connected by a bridge of yellow metal (gold). The bridge is anchored by pins on the second left and the second right incisor. This bridge consists of 4 upper incisors 2 canine teeth, the first left bicuspid and the first and second right bicuspids as indicated in the sketch. The first left incisor consists of a white platelet, with cracks and a black spot in the porcelain (enamel) at the bottom. This platelet is inset into the visible side of the metal (gold) tooth. The second incisor, the canine tooth, and the left bicuspid, as well as the first and second incisors and the first bicuspid on the right, are the usual porcelain (enamel) dental plates, their posterior parts fastened to the bridge. The right canine tooth is fully capped by yellow metal (gold). The maxillary bridge is vertically sawed of behind the second left bicuspid.

The lower jawbone lies loose in the singed oral cavity. The alveolar processes are broken in the back and have ragged edges. The front surface and the lower edge of the mandibula are scorched. On the front surface the charred prongs of dental roots are recognisable. The lower jaw consists of fifteen teeth, ten of which are artificial. The incisors and the first right bicuspid are natural, exhibiting considerable wear on the masticating surface and considerably exposed necks. The dental enamel has a bluish shimmer and a dirty yellow colouration around the necks.

The teeth to the left (and right) are artificial, of yellow metal (gold), and consist of a bridge of gold crowns. The bridge is fastened to the third, the fifth (in the bridge, the sixth tooth), and the eighth tooth (in the bridge, the ninth tooth). The second bicuspid to the right is topped by a crown of yellow metal (gold) which is linked to the right canine tooth by an arching plate. Part of the masticating surface and the posterior surface of the right canine tooth is capped by a yellow metal (gold) plate as part of the bridge.

The first right molar is artificial, white, and secured by a gold clip connected with the bridge of the second bicuspid and the right incisor.

Splinters of glass, parts of the wall and bottom of a thin-walled ampule, were found in the mouth. The neck muscles are charred, the ribs on the right side are missing, they are burned. The right side of the thorax and the abdomen are completely burned, creating a hole through which the right lung, the liver, and the intestines are open to view.

The genital member is scorched. In the scrotum, which is singed but preserved, only the right testicle was found. The left testicle could not be found in the inguinal canal.

The right arm is severely burned, the ends of the bone of the upper arm and the bones of the lower arm are broken and charred. The dry muscles are black and partially brown; they disintegrate into separate fibres when touched. The remnants of the burned part (about two thirds) of the left upper arm are preserved. The exposed end of the bone of the upper arm is charred and protrudes from the dry tissue. Both legs, too, are charred. The soft tissue has in many places disappeared; it is burned and has fallen off.

The bones are partially burned and have crumbled. A fracture in the right thighbone and the right shinbone were noted. The left foot is missing.

INTERNAL EXAMINATION

The position of the internal organs is normal. The lungs are black on the surface, dark red on the cut surface, and of fairly firm consistence. The mucous membrane of the upper respiratory tracts is dark red. The cardiac ventricles are filled with coagulated reddish-brown blood. The heart muscle is tough and looks like boiled meat. The liver is black on the surface and shows burns; it is of fairly firm consistence and yellowish-brown on the cut surface. The kidneys are somewhat shrunken and measure 9 x 5 x 3.5 cm.

Their capsule is easily detachable; the surface of the kidneys is smooth, the pattern effaced, they appear as if boiled. The bladder contains 5c. yellowish urine, its mucous membrane is grey. Spleen, stomach, and intestines show severe burns and are nearly black in parts.

NOTE:
1. The following objects taken from the corpse were handed over to the SMERSH Section of the 3rd Assault Army on 8 May 1945:
2. a maxillary bridge of yellow metal, consisting of 9 teeth;
3. a singed lower jaw, consisting of 15 teeth.
4. According to the record of the interrogation of Frau Käthe Heusermann it may be presumed that the teeth as well as the bridge described in the document are those of Chancellor Hitler.

NOTE: In her talk with Chief Expert of Forensic Medicine, Lieutenant Colonel Shkaravsky, which took place on 11 May 1945, in the offices of CAFS. No. 496, Frau Käthe Heusermann described the state of Hitler's teeth in every detail. Her description tallies with the anatomical data pertaining to the oral cavity of the unknown man whose burned corpse we dissected. [Käthe Heusermann's role in identifying Hitler's teeth is explored in the following chapter.]

signed (Shkaravsky) Chief Expert, Forensic Medicine, 1st Byelorussian Front, Medical Service, Lieutenant Colonel

signed (Krayevski) Chief Anatomical Pathologist, Medical Service, Red Army, Lieutenant Colonel

signed (Marants) Acting Chief Anatomical Pathologist, 1st Byelorussian Front, Medical Service, Major

signed (Boguslavski) Army Expert, Forensic Medicine, 3rd Assault Army, Medical Service, Major

signed (Gulkevich) Army Anatomical Pathologist, 3rd Assault Army, Medical Service, Major

CONCLUSION

Based on the forensic-medical examination of the partially burned corpse of an unknown man and the examination of other corpses from the same group (Documents Nos. 1–11),

the Commission reaches the following conclusions:

1 Anatomical characteristics of the body:

Since the body parts are heavily charred, it is impossible to describe the features of the dead man. But the following could be established:

a) Stature: about 165 cm. (one hundred sixty-five)

b) Age (based on general development, size of organs, state of lower incisors and of the right bicuspid), somewhere between 50 and 60 years (fifty to sixty).

c) The left testicle could not be found either in the scrotum or on the spermatic cord inside the inguinal canal, nor in the small pelvis,

d) The most important anatomical finding for identification of the person are the teeth, with much bridgework, artificial teeth, crowns, and fillings (see documents).

2. Cause of death:

On the body, considerably damaged by fire, no visible signs of severe lethal injuries or illnesses could be detected.

The presence in the oral cavity of the remnants of a crushed glass ampule and of similar ampules in the oral cavity of other bodies (see Documents Nos. 1, 2, 3, 5, 6, 8, 9, 10, 11, and 13), the marked smell of bitter almonds emanating from the bodies (Documents Nos. 1, 2, 3, 5, 8, 9, 10, 11), and the forensic-chemical test of internal organs which established the presence of cyanide compounds (Documents Nos. 1, 2, 3, 4, 5, 6, 7, 8, 9, 10, 11) permit the Commission to arrive at the conclusion that death in this instance was caused by poisoning with cyanide compounds.

signed (Shkaravsky) Chief Expert, Forensic Medicine, 1st Byelorussian Front, Medical Service, Lieutenant Colonel
signed (Krayevski) Chief Anatomical Pathologist, Medical Service, Red Army, Lieutenant Colonel
signed (Marants Acting Chief Anatomical Pathologist, 1st Byelorussian Front, Medical Service, Major
signed (Boguslavski) Army Expert, Forensic Medicine, 3rd Assault Army, Medical Service,
Major
signed (Gulkevich) Army Anatomical Pathologist, 3rd Assault Army, Medical Service, Major

Next came the autopsy on the second badly charred corpse, assumed to be that of Eva Braun, who referred to herself in the brief hours after the marriage as Frau Hitler.

Again, the official report reads:

1 Anatomical characteristics of the body:
In view of the fact that the body parts are extensively charred, it is impossible to describe the features of the dead woman.
The following, however, could be established:
a) The age of the dead woman lies between 30 and 40 years, evidence of which is also the only slightly worn masticating surface of the teeth.
b) Stature: about 150 cm.
c) The most important anatomical finding for identification of the person are the gold bridge of the lower jaw and its four front teeth.
2. Cause of death:
On the extensively charred corpse there were found traces of a splinter injury to the thorax with hemothorax, injuries to one lung and to the pericardium, as well as six small metal fragments.
Further, remnants of a crushed glass ampule were found in the oral cavity. In view of the fact that similar ampules were present in other corpses, (Docs. Nos 1-11), that a smell of bitter almonds developed upon dissection, (Docs. Nos 1-11), and based on the forensic-chemical tests of the internal organs of these bodies in which the presence of cyanide compounds was established (Docs. Nos 1-11), the Commission reaches the conclusion that notwithstanding the severe injuries to the thorax the immediate cause of death was poisoning by cyanide compounds.

In both cases the experts were faced with the most seriously disfigured of all thirteen corpses. Because of this obstacle to the examination two sentences need to be particularly stressed:

'Splinters of glass, parts of the wall and bottom of a thin-walled ampule, were found in the mouth and 'In the oral cavity yellowish glass splinters of a thin-walled ampule were found'

These findings permitted the Commission to conclude that death was caused by poisoning with cyanide compounds.

This conclusion is in no way contradicted by the splinter injuries in Eva Braun's body. These could not possibly have been inflicted on her in the bunker. Most probably they occurred during the burning in the garden, which was under artillery fire. Only shell splinters could have caused the injuries and the haemorrhage in the pleura.

It was clear from the autopsy, therefore, that both Hitler and Eva Braun died of cyanide poisoning. This was a decisive finding, as it contradicted some of the statements made by witnesses in the bunker when interrogated by Red Army officers.

In a letter Shkaravsky later wrote to Elena Rzhevskaya, he set out a precise account of how the commission came into existence, and is worth quoting in full.

A few words about the situation in which this examination of the '13' was carried out. In the first days of May 1945 (on the 2nd or 3rd, I don't remember exactly), the headquarters of the 1st Belorussian Front was located in a small town about 30 kilometres from Berlin. One afternoon I was called by the head of the Military Sanitary Directorate of the Front, Major General of the Medical Service Barabashov {59.1} and received an order to urgently go on a business trip to the Berlin suburb of Buch to conduct a 'particularly important' examination on the instructions of the Political Directorate of the Front (General Telegin).

I immediately left and in Buch I contacted SMERSH of the 3rd Assault Army. Unfortunately, the head of SMERSH and his deputy were very unfriendly. Despite my high official position, they did not want to talk to me, much less allow me to conduct any kind of examination. I was told that we did not invite you and do not need your help. They simply did not want to 'share the laurels of victory', because they found the corpses of Hitler and Goebbels.

My position was unenviable. For the first time in my life, in my forensic medical practice, I, a forensic medical expert, was not allowed to carry out an examination, especially an examination on the instructions of the Front Political Directorate. But it was so, it was war, and war has its own special laws.

I intuitively felt that the examination was going to be unusual and interesting. After all, 'SMERSH' on the first day did not want to tell me what there was: whether there were corpses, whose, where, etc., they were simply silent. I decided not to retreat, but to wait and, conversely, to advance. The owners of the corpses, i.e. 'SMERSH', I declared that history would condemn them for such a peculiar attitude (in fact, a criminally barbaric attitude towards examination). As a result, with great difficulty I managed to convince them that I did not need their 'laurels', that I, as a forensic expert, must, by law, establish the truth and help them.

In addition, I persistently told them that with their tactics of endless waiting, corpses (I, of course, primarily thought about human corpses) from the stage of valuable objects and material evidence, due to the law of rotting, would turn into the stage of a rotten, stinking mass, of no use to anyone, especially in the case of poisoning.

Everything would be lost for the investigation. This had an effect on them, and they finally showed their cards and declared that there really were corpses and that they were waiting for instructions from Moscow, but for now they would not do anything.

However, I insisted, and, very reluctantly, they showed me the objects of examination. Of course, I was not presented or informed of any documentary information about the corpses (who, what, when, where, etc.). A shame! But that's how it was. I, the chief forensic expert of the front, was strictly forbidden to photograph corpses! I agreed to everything, just to perform an autopsy . . .

On the same day, Deputy beginning [*sic*] 'SMERSH' of the 3rd Assault Army (Colonel, I don't remember his last name) in the Berlin suburb of Buch led me to a small German cottage located in the garden. [The colonel in question was most likely Colonel Gorbushin.] The house was guarded by sentries, its windows and doors were closed. Entering the house, I saw 9 corpses on the floor on the first floor. The room was completely empty of furniture. The corpses lay in some order. These were the corpses of Goebbels, his wife, 6 children of Goebbels and the corpse of General Krebs.

The room thermometer showed +16°C. The first thing I did was personally open the windows in order to at least slightly lower the temperature in the room and help preserve the corpses.

Then I gave instructions (according to an old professional habit, I am the master of the corpses during the examination!) to 'SMERSH' so that ice would be immediately delivered to preserve the corpses. And I must tell the truth, this instruction of mine was carried out with military precision. By evening there was about a ton of ice in the room, and this was the case all the time until 9 May i.e. until the day of the autopsy of the last corpse. This event actually saved the corpses for us, and we opened them without being rotten.

And this was extremely important in this particular case, when there was poisoning with hydrocyanic acid (cyanide compound), i.e. a very unstable substance and quickly deteriorates in a corpse. (Remember the attempted poisoning of Rasputin with cyanide). If the corpses had rotted, during a forensic chemical study of blood and organs we would not have found cyanide compounds and the question about the cause of death of this entire group of 'heroes', and in particular Goebbels and Hitler, would have remained open. History would have lost a lot.

And now everything is clear! During a quick examination of the corpses, I immediately noticed the colour of the corpse spots; they were a bright crimson colour, which happens in cases of death from poisoning with cyanide compounds. My assumptions were also confirmed by the presence of a pleasant smell of bitter almonds, which was especially clearly felt when the chest of children's corpses was pressed. I immediately conveyed my thoughts on this matter to the deputy chief, 'SMERSH'. This placed him somewhat in my favour.

And then, on 4, 5, 6 May I regularly visited SMERSH 2-3 times a day, waiting for a response from Moscow, i.e. I waited by the sea for weather, but there was no weather. Moscow was silent! Waiting with me were the members of the commission who had arrived to participate in the examination; these were the main specialists of the 1st Belorussian Front and the 3rd Assault Army (5 doctors in total).

Everyone is tired of such aimless waiting, and even the owners themselves, i.e. 'SMERSH', and on 7 May, having replaced anger with mercy, the head of 'SMERSH' of the 3rd Assault Army allowed me (the commission) to perform an autopsy on the corpses of 2 dogs and 2 of Goebbels' smallest children.

I repeat, I was strictly forbidden to photograph corpses! But I managed, and when the sentry left the room where the autopsy was being carried out, I managed to photograph the corpse of Goebbels and his 2 daughters. I have these pictures!

Now briefly about the corpses, about their autopsies. The autopsy was carried out in the sectional surgical field mobile hospital No. 496, located on the outskirts of Berlin – Buch. I note that the autopsy was carried out by a commission consisting of 5 specialists from the front and the 3rd Army, and I headed the commission.

Acts No. 1, 2, 8, 9, 10 and 11 are acts on the autopsies of Goebbels' children; children age 6-15 years. The clothes on the corpses were simple, but clean {59.2} There was no damage to the corpses; There were small fragments of a glass ampoule in each mouth. From private conversations with SMERSH employees, it turned out that the doctor of the Goebbels family administered morphine to the children before the poisoning and, already in a state of morphine sleep, inserted an ampoule with hydrocyanic acid, crushing it; death followed immediately.[96]

A forensic medical examination of blood and organs from corpses, which was carried out on my instructions in front-line sanitary and epidemiological laboratory No. 291, revealed the presence of cyanide compounds, i.e. the death of all children was caused by poisoning with cyanide compounds (hydrocyanic acid).

Acts No. 5 and 6. refer to the corpses of Goebbels and his wife. The picture in the section is similar to the picture of autopsies of corpses of the first group, i.e. there was poisoning from cyanide compounds. But both corpses were significantly charred. From conversations it became clear that these corpses were burned in a fire at the Reich Chancellery, in the courtyard of which they were discovered.

Act No. 7 – autopsy of the corpse of Major General {59.3} of the German army Krebs. On the corpse is the clothing of a German army general, without shoulder straps; cadaveric spots are bright crimson in colour, the smell of bitter almonds upon autopsy. The cause of death is the same – poisoning with hydrocyanic acid.

On 5-7 May 2 dog corpses and 2 charred corpses were delivered – Hitler and Eva Braun. No documentation. All these corpses were also opened by us without any objections from SMERSH. (Acts No. 12, 13, 3, 4.)

Everywhere the picture is the same, there are glass fragments (ampoules) in the mouth, the bright crimson colour of the blood, the smell of bitter almonds and the presence of cyanide compounds during forensic chemical examination of the organs. Death from hydrocyanic acid poisoning.

It is necessary to dwell in more detail on the autopsies of 3 corpses. The corpse of a small shepherd (dog); he had a penetrating bullet wound to the head with brain damage and a penetrating bullet wound to the chest. These two perforating wounds were quite possibly caused by one shot.

In our act, we indicated that the method of killing this dog could be as follows: an ampoule of hydrocyanic acid was introduced into the dog's mouth, possibly with food, she crushed it with her teeth and immediately threw it out, but a certain amount of poison got into the respiratory tract, convulsions occurred, but death did not occur immediately, then the dog was shot.

The corpse of Eva Braun, significantly burnt. There is multiple penetrating intravital shrapnel wound of the chest with injury to the heart sac, lung, with large haemorrhage into the pleural cavity, as well as small metal fragments in the lungs. There are fragments of the ampoule in the mouth again!

We believe that Eva Braun's body was hit by fragments of a mine or artillery shell.

And finally, 3. The corpse of our main 'hero' – Adolf Hitler. The commission did not see any documents where it was said, even in a presumptive form, that this was Hitler's corpse. Just talk! Therefore, two questions immediately arose before us: a) to establish the cause of death of the deceased and b) to identify the corpse, i.e. to establish whether this is really Hitler's corpse, because there was a lot of talk about doubles, about dummies. Everyone was talking, and, of course, they were saying different things.

On the first question, everything immediately became clear by analogy: fragments of a glass ampoule in the mouth, the smell of bitter almonds felt during the autopsy of the corpse, and the positive results of a forensic chemical examination of the corpse for cyanide compounds {59.4}. The result is hydrocyanic acid poisoning.

I emphasise that no fatal injuries or signs of significant diseases were found during the autopsy.

The second question is more complex – identification of the corpse.

We approached this very seriously and established the following: the upper jaw of the corpse was a single massive golden bridge with 9 teeth, some of them were gold. The lower jaw is also a very massive golden bridge of a special design, with a large amount of gold, 15 teeth, of which 10 are gold. It is characteristic that this bridge had an external massive golden arc! Silicate teeth were strengthened on special thin steel pins.

It is clear that the presence of such valuable individual features in the corpse raised the urgent question of the need to study Hitler's dental medical history and interrogate dentists'.

Interviewed later, Professor Krayevski, a member of the autopsy commission, was asked which detail of the autopsy he remembered most clearly. 'Probably the smell of bitter almonds, which we all noticed. For an anatomical pathologist or a forensic physician this smell says unmistakably: Poisoning by cyanide compounds.'

Professor Krayevski also commented on one particular detail which had been established at the dissection of Hitler's internal organs: the missing second testicle. In medical parlance this defect is known as monorchism. Krayevski remarked that monorchism is a fairly frequent phenomenon and as a rule is congenital: such a defect did not exclude a normal sexual life. The autopsy commission then turned to the examination of the remaining bodies. In all cases they found that death was by cyanide poisoning.

In the 80 years since Hitler's death, Western medical opinion has cast doubt on Scharavsky's autopsy, specifically the conclusion that

Hitler died of cyanide poisoning, saying there were no toxicological reports to verify that conclusion.

All experts agree, however, on the dental evidence that confirmed the identity of the charred corpse as that of Hitler.

The doubts caused by the absence of a toxicology report remain even though the official reports states:

On the *forensic-chemical tests of the internal organs* of these bodies in which the presence of cyanide compounds was established the Commission reaches the conclusion that notwithstanding the severe injuries to the thorax the immediate cause of death was poisoning by cyanide compounds.

Clearly the autopsy commission had access to a forensic laboratory, even though they were standing in the ruins of Berlin. There is no record of where these tests were carried out but most likely at the nearby Charite hospital, which had continued to function throughout the battle of Berlin.

We can, however, be certain that one of four things happened in the bunker.

1. Hitler swallowed a cyanide capsule and died.
2. Hitler swallowed a cyanide capsule then shot himself.
3. Linge shot the corpse after Hitler's death.
4. Hitler shot himself and the cyanide capsule was inserted into his mouth post-mortem.

This last assertion can probably be discounted because the autopsy says it found cyanide in the internal organs. Contrary to popular opinion biting into a cyanide capsule will not cause instantaneous death. Cyanide capsules were randomly distributed among the Nazi hierarchy at the end of the war, and many committed suicide by this means. Himmler, for instance, bit into a capsule concealed in his mouth after he was arrested. The fatal dose of potassium cyanide for an adult is typically 200–300 mg (about 1.5–3 mg/kg body weight. Military and espionage 'suicide pills' (like those used by Nazi leaders) were specifically designed to contain at least this much.

Death after biting into a cyanide pill occurs extremely rapidly – typically within minutes, but not instantly, and is not considered painless; the experience can involve significant distress and discomfort before rapid loss of consciousness and death.

After ingesting a lethal dose of cyanide symptoms like headache, confusion, seizures, and loss of consciousness begin, within seconds to a few minutes. Death usually follows within several minutes to less than 30 minutes after ingestion of a lethal dose, depending on the amount and individual factors. Animal studies show loss of consciousness in about 6.5 minutes and cessation of breathing in around 18 minutes after ingestion. Cyanide interrupts the body's ability to use oxygen, causing rapid shutdown of the central nervous and cardiovascular systems, leading to cardiac arrest. It would have been possible, therefore, for Hitler to bite into a cyanide capsule and then shoot himself.

Witnesses, however, specifically General Weidling, the last German Commander of Berlin, says Hitler was in poor state of health, describing him to Red Army interrogators as a 'mental and physical wreck'. Film of Weidling's testimony to Red Army interrogators shows him demonstrating how Hitler's arms shook violently

Toxicology tests for cyanide were possible in 1945 using chemical colour tests (like the Prussian blue test) on biological samples. These tests could confirm cyanide poisoning if performed soon after death, but their reliability was limited by the technology, rapid cyanide metabolism, and sample conditions at the time. However, in the case of Hitler, both body decomposition and fire damage could have significantly hindered or even prevented the detection of cyanide.

Cyanide is highly volatile and rapidly metabolised after death, making it difficult to detect as time passes. Studies show postmortem blood samples can lose up to 79 per cent of cyanide concentration within 24 hours, and detection becomes increasingly unreliable as decomposition advances. (Hitler's autopsy occurred eight days after his suicide.)

Although rare, there are documented cases where cyanide was detected in decomposed bodies years after death, usually when decomposition fluids were well-preserved and sampled. However, this is exceptional and depends on preservation conditions. In 1945, chemical tests for cyanide (like the Prussian blue test) were less sensitive and required relatively fresh biological samples. Delays in autopsy or sampling would have made detection much less likely.

High heat and burning can destroy or dissipate cyanide in tissues, making detection extremely challenging or impossible. In fire victims, cyanide can sometimes be detected if the person inhaled smoke containing hydrogen cyanide, but the intense heat often degrades biological markers and can even produce cyanide artifacts during decomposition or burning, which complicates interpretation.

In the context of Hitler's death, where the bodies were partially burned and left for hours before recovery, the likelihood of successfully detecting cyanide with 1945 technology was very low. Advanced decomposition and fire damage would have drastically reduced the chances of a positive cyanide test.

Even today, detection in such conditions is rare and requires specialised circumstances or preservation. In 1945, therefore, significant decomposition or fire damage would have made cyanide detection by toxicology tests extremely unlikely, and a negative result would not rule out poisoning under those circumstances.

One notable feature of the body presumed to be Hitler was that part of the cranium was missing, and this became a problem, because there had been inconsistencies in the testimonies of witnesses who had been in the bunker at the time of Hitler's death. One witness who had been arrested in the bunker, suggested that Hitler had a gun and that Hitler may have shot himself.

In January 1946, Lieutenant-General A. Z. Kobulow, Chief of the General Department of Prisoners-of-War and Internees (GDPWI) NKVD USSR, signed an analytical report concerning a version of Hitler's suicide based on these contradictions. He posed the following questions:

> Why had none of the sources stated what had happened to Hitler's remains after they were burned; why was there no information that a doctor had been called to certify death: why were there contradictions in statements about carrying the bodies out into the Reich Chancellery's garden and about who participated (i.e. who actually carried the bodies and who merely accompanied them); why were there discrepancies in witness statements concerning the external appearance of the bodies; about whether the corpses of the Nazi leaders were burned completely; why the remains were discovered by soldiers of a SMERSH platoon before the location had been indicated by the guard Mengershausen and so on.

On this basis it was decided to consolidate all available material from several departments for detailed and rigorous verification of the whole body of the facts.

A commission, known as 'Operation Myth' was set up to conduct further excavations at the site at which Hitler and Eva Braun's corpses had been found, and a fragment of skull was discovered. Their report said:

The left incipital portion of a skull with an exiting bullet hole was found. It should be noted that in the report of 8 May 1945 (the Autopsy Commission report) upon examination of the burned corpses, it was stressed that the top of the skull is partially absent. During this further examination, traces of blood were discovered on the upholstery of the sofa in the bunker in which, according to (Heinz) Linge (Hitler's chief valet and a senior SS officer), the Führer had committed suicide.

Due to the relocation of the SMERSH Counter-Espionage Department of the 3rd Assault Army, the corpses that had been examined in May, 1945 were re-buried in a forest near the city of Rathenow, Brandenburg, at the beginning of June.

On the orders of Lieutenant-General P. V. Zelenin, the Chief of SMERSH for the Soviet Occupational Force in Germany, on 21 February, 1946 the remains were re-buried in the grounds of a military base in Magdeburg where the SMERSH Counter-Espionage Section of the 3rd Assault Army was based.

Commenting on the autopsy report, Elena Rzhevskaya said that:

To us the manner in which Hitler committed suicide was immaterial, and neither were we versed in the traditions of the German Army: they were of no interest to us. The fact remains that Dr Faust Scharavsky and his competent colleagues carried out at that time a thorough medical examination and concluded that Hitler had taken poison.

Hitler's personal adjutant, Otto Günsche, standing outside the door, did not hear a shot but did notice a strong smell of bitter almonds when the door was slightly open.

Some people, Hitler's secretary Gertraud Junge, for example, did hear a shot. She said, 'When I left Hitler's office and went up the stairs to the shelter landing, I heard two shots. I imagine the shots were fired in Hitler's office'. Be that as it may, people decided that Hitler shot himself. Thus, Hitler's orderly, Bauer, who shortly after met the SS guard Mengershausen, told him that. Other close associates of the Führer said the same.

Was there really a shot in Hitler's room, or did those awaiting the end outside the doors imagine it? And if there was, who fired it? The testimony of the head of Hitler's bodyguard, Hans Rattenhuber, sheds light on this.

At about three or four in the afternoon, when I went into the anteroom I noticed a strong smell of bitter almonds. Högl, my deputy, told me with distress that the Führer had just committed suicide.

At that moment Linge came to me. He confirmed the news of Hitler's death, adding that he had just had to carry out the most difficult order the Führer had given him in his life.

I looked at Linge in surprise. He explained to me that just before he died, Hitler ordered him to leave the room for ten minutes, then re-enter, wait another ten minutes, and carry out the order. At this, Linge quickly went into Hitler's room and returned with a Walther pistol which he put on my desk in front of me. From its special exterior finish I recognised it as the Führer's personal pistol. It was now clear to me what Hitler's order had been.

Hitler, evidently uncertain that the poison would prove effective because of the many injections he had been having every day for a long time, ordered Linge to shoot him after he took it.

Reichsjugendführer Axmann, who was present during this conversation, took Hitler's pistol and said he would hide it until better times.

Rattenhuber evidently did not know another circumstance that prompted Hitler to give that order to Linge. The problem was that, when the poison was tested on a second dog, the poisoned puppy struggled against dying for a long time and was then shot.

This was established at the autopsy of the dead dogs found in the crater, although at first it was overlooked and is not mentioned in the report detailing how they were found.

The conclusion reached by the doctors was that the manner in which the dog was killed appears to have been as follows: it was first poisoned, possibly using a small dose of cyanide compounds, and then, when it had been poisoned and was in its agony, it was shot. This may have heightened Hitler's fear, as he watched the poisoned dogs, that the poison might not work. In his testimony, Rattenhuber wrote: 'Linge shot Hitler'.

Rzhevskaya imagined that Linge's hand might have been shaking when he shot at the dead Führer and the bullet missed him. So if a shot really did ring out in Hitler's room, was it Linge who pulled the trigger? But there was no sign of a shot.

Rzhevskaya claims that the decision to conduct 'Operation Myth' came not from Stalin, but was born of the rivalry between two government departments: the Ministry of Internal Affairs and the SMERSH Counter-intelligence Department. Witnesses who had earlier been taken to Moscow were returned to Berlin: Hitler's adjutant (Günsche), his valet (Linge), and other staff who served him who were in Russian captivity. However, no matter how much pressure was applied to get them to admit that Hitler was alive, they answered as one: He is dead and we cannot make him alive.

The apparently created a dilemma for the commission, since the original autopsy commission headed by Dr. Shkaravsky had established that Hitler was poisoned, so an assertion appeared in print that he had simultaneously taken poison and shot himself.

Many experts doubt the feasibility of performing these two actions simultaneously. The account given in the testimony of the head of Hitler's bodyguard, Rattenhuber, said Hitler, fearing the poison would be insufficiently effective, ordered his valet to shoot him after he had been poisoned, and the order had been carried out. And perhaps the 'bullet exit wound' is the missing evidence of Linge's shot.

Faust Shkaravsky confided in a letter to Rzhevskaya that he still had a feeling of ongoing unfairness: 'the Commission was strictly forbidden to photograph Hitler's body, whereas the Commission was photographed in full force next to Goebbels' body strapped to the dissection table. There are also plenty of photographs taken during the investigation. But with Hitler, oh, no!' he said.

The 1945 autopsy report was lodged in the Russian Archives and kept secret, but it surfaced 20 years later in a book by one of Elena Rzhevskaya's wartime interpreter colleagues, journalist Lev Bezymenski. Bezymenski's book *The Death of Adolf Hitler. Unknown Documents from Soviet Archives* did not disclose how he came to possess the report. Elena Rzhevskaya believes they came from the Soviet Archives, but there is doubt about this. She and Bezymenski had been fellow students at the interpreters' school in Moscow, and corresponded for a number of years.

The report remained a secret until 2025 when exactly 80 years after the events, the Russian Federal Security Service (FSB) declassified archival documents concerning Hitler's death, the examination of his and Eva Braun's bodies, and the circumstances in the Führerbunker at the end of the Second World War.

These documents included the original Soviet forensic report from 8 May 1945, describing the examination of a male corpse, presumed to be Hitler, found near the bunker, and testimonies and interrogation records from Hitler's close aides, such as Heinz Linge and Otto Günsche, who described the suicide, the burning of the bodies, and the identification process. They confirmed everything that had been included in Bezymenski's book nearly 60 years earlier.

Born in 1920 in Kazan, Lev Bezymenski studied philosophy in Moscow and entered the Soviet Armed Forces in 1941, first as a private and later as an officer in Stalingrad, Kursk and Berlin. An excellent scholar of German, he served as interpreter at the hearings of Field Marshal Paulus, the German commander who surrendered to the Russians after the Battle of Stalingrad. As a member of Marshal Zhukov's staff, he participated in the Battle of Berlin, but did not participate in the search for Hitler.

His book was first published in the USSR under the title *The End of a Legend*. It was translated into German and published there under its new title, mentioning *Soviet Archives*. This could have been done for marketing purposes to lend credence to its contents. It was also published in the UK in 1968, but it was heavily criticised by the historian Hugh Trevor-Roper, who suggested it was Soviet propaganda for historical purposes. This, remember, was at the height of the Cold War.

Recollecting my conversation with Rzhevskaya in 1991, she mentioned that Faust Scharavsky, had a personal copy of the autopsy reports. Scharavsky, who after the war served as chief forensic expert of the Kiev Military District, and head of its forensic laboratory, died in 1975. Shkaravsky remained in contact with Rzhevskaya and wrote to her about the commission's work. But it appears that she herself did not see the original documents during her time at the Soviet Archives researching her own books. They do not appear in any of her writings, lending credence to the notion that Bezymenski came by them via the Commission's members. At least one member of the Commission discussed its findings with Bezymenski.

Elena Rzhevskaya herself believed that, at some point in an unclear future the conspiracy of silence would come to an end, so the facts needed to be established immediately that could not be challenged.

> Already some of our superiors, detecting currents that were coming down from 'above', were looking askance at our zeal, keeping us at a distance because of their instinct of self-preservation.
>
> As the secretiveness increased, almost all the people who had worked with us were taken out of the loop so that eventually we were down to three people, me, Colonel Gorbushin and Major Bystrov.

Scharavsky's admission that he took photographs in secret is further evidence that there was collusion between members of the Autopsy Commission and Lev Bezymenski. Some of the photographs (perhaps all) appear in Bezymenski's book, including one of the full complement of doctors. These photographs have not been published in any other book or form since the book was first published in 1968. I included them in my documentary *Hitler. The Final Chapter*, and they are repeated here in this book.

Collaborating with Bezymenski was a risky thing to do. Why would they have done it?

We'll probably never know, but the most likely answer is timing.

All members of the Autopsy Commission were sworn to secrecy, as were all members of the SMERSH squad, and those who took part in the search for Hitler. It is clear this irked Scharavsky, who believed the knowledge about Hitler's fate should be made public. But in 1945 it was too dangerous. Stalin continued to deceive the West and insist that Hitler was still alive, possibly in South America. No one dared challenge him.

Then, in March 1953, Stalin died. His death, at the age of 74, of a cerebral haemorrhage, was a shock to the people of the Soviet Union, but a relief to many. He was a tyrant who had been responsible for the death of millions of people during the 'Great Purges' of the 1930s. He was feared and idolised at the same time.

Soviet society took a while to readjust to the new era. Nikita Khrushchev became the leader of the Soviet Union six months later, in September 1953, when he was elected First Secretary of the Communist Party of the Soviet Union, following a power struggle. This position made him the most powerful figure in the USSR, as the Communist Party was the central authority in Soviet governance.

Khrushchev further consolidated his leadership in March 1958, when he also became Chairman of the Council of Ministers (Premier), combining the top party and government roles. This dual role gave him formal control over both the party and the state until his removal in October 1964.

Three years after Stalin's death Khrushchev gave a 'secret' speech at a closed session of the 20th Congress of the Communist Party of the Soviet Union. This event marked a pivotal moment in Soviet and global communist history, initiating a process known as de-Stalinisation. The speech fundamentally shattered the myth of Stalin's infallibility and transformed how Stalin was perceived within the Soviet Union. Before the speech, Stalin had been venerated as a near-deified leader, and Soviet citizens were raised on constant praise of his 'genius'. Khrushchev's denunciation, delivered in a closed session but quickly circulated among party members, caused widespread shock, confusion, and disillusionment among both the Communist Party elite and the wider public

Khrushchev condemned Stalin for his use of mass terror, particularly during the Great Purge when countless innocent party members were falsely accused, tortured, and executed. He highlighted Stalin's role in the unwarranted arrest and execution of loyal communists, the purges of the Red Army's leadership, and the deportation of entire ethnic groups during and after World War 2.

Khrushchev criticised Stalin for fostering a 'cult of personality', arguing that Stalin had elevated himself above the party and the people, distorting Marxist-Leninist principles and ruling as a dictator rather than a collective leader.

The speech accused Stalin of serious blunders, such as failing to prepare the Soviet Union for the Nazi invasion in 1941 and mishandling wartime leadership. Khrushchev also condemned Stalin's foreign policy mistakes, notably the break with Yugoslavia.

Khrushchev referenced Lenin's Testament, in which Lenin had warned about Stalin's potential for abusing power, and cited personal correspondence illustrating Stalin's problematic behaviour even during Lenin's life.

Khrushchev's denunciation focused on Stalin's actions against the Communist Party and its members, largely omitting the broader terror campaigns against ordinary Soviet citizens and avoiding criticism of earlier policies such as forced collectivisation and the repression of intellectuals. He did not implicate other party leaders (including himself) who had been complicit in Stalin's crimes

The speech had immediate consequences. It launched a period of relative liberalisation, known as the 'Khrushchev Thaw'. Censorship was relaxed, thousands of political prisoners were released or rehabilitated, and a limited cultural renaissance occurred. It permanently damaged Stalin's reputation and altered the trajectory of Soviet policy. It also set the stage for later reforms and contributed to the eventual weakening of Soviet control over Eastern Europe.

Bezymenski's book first appeared in 1957, not long after Khrushchev's denunciation. Although he was not a member of the Hitler search squad, he had contacts amongst many of those who had taken part, including Elena Rzhevskaya.

As a journalist he would have been aware of the work of the Autopsy Commission, and their names. The new liberalised era would have allowed him to explore the possibility of a book on Hitler's death, and, probably knowing about the Commission's feelings about secrecy, approached them.

While this is speculation, his efforts seem to have borne fruit, hence the book, and publication of the photographs taken clandestinely inside the morgue.

Chapter 8

PROOF OF IDENTITY

With the Commission's work completed, attention now focused on proving the identity of the corpse believed to be Hitler. And once again Elena Rzhevskaya was in the thick of the action alongside Major Bystrov and Colonel Vasili Gorbushin, under the command of Andrei Mirozhnichenko, Chief of Counter Intelligence in the 3rd Assault Army.

During the autopsy it was found that Hitler's dentures and teeth had come through surprisingly intact. The autopsy report includes two large non-standard sheets of paper documenting Hitler's teeth in meticulous detail. The experts removed the dentures (and lower jaw). Now the crucial task was, at all costs, to find Hitler's dentists. And this is where Rzhevskaya found herself at the centre of history.

In Berlin-Buch on 8 May, the very day when the document of surrender of Germany was ratified in Karlshorst, although I did not yet know that, Colonel Gorbushin called me in and handed me a box, saying it contained Hitler's teeth and that I was answerable with my head for its safe-keeping.

It was a second-hand, burgundy red box with a soft lining and covered with satin, the kind of thing made to hold a bottle of perfume or cheap jewellery. I had no idea how Gorbushin had come by it.

Now, however, what it held was the irrefutable proof that Hitler was dead. In forensic medicine this is held to be the fundamental anatomical item that clinches any argument about a person's identity. Moreover, this evidence could be preserved for many years to come.

The box was entrusted to me because the safe was still back with the second echelon and there was nowhere secure to put it. Why me? For the simple reason that everything connected with Hitler was being kept top secret and must not be allowed to leak out from Gorbushin's group which, as already mentioned, had dwindled by now down to just three people.

All that day, so pregnant with the sense of imminent victory, it was decidedly tiresome to be carrying a box about, and to turn cold whenever I thought of the possibility of accidentally leaving it somewhere. It burdened and oppressed me.

The situation in which I found myself was odd, unreal, especially when I look back at it now, out of the context of the war. War is itself pathological, and everything that happened during the war, everything we went through, simply cannot be translated into the concepts of peacetime and does not fit into the familiar psychological categories.

Already by this time, the sense of history surrounding the fall of the Third Reich was fading. We had experienced too much. The death of its leaders and everything connected with that seemed nothing out of the ordinary.

I was not the only one feeling that way. When I was called to front headquarters to translate Goebbels' diaries, I met up with Raya, our telegraphist, and saw her trying on a white evening dress that had belonged to Eva Braun and which had been brought to her from the underground complex of the Reich Chancellery by Senior Lieutenant Kurashov (who was in love with her).

It was a long dress, reaching almost to the floor, with a plunging neckline, and Raya did not care for it. As a historic memento it was of no interest to her. Shoes from a box labelled 'Für Fr. Eva Braun' were just right and she appreciated them far more.

Towards midnight on 8 May, I was about to go to bed in the downstairs room I had been allotted in a two-storey house when I suddenly heard someone calling my name from the first floor. I hastily ran up the very steep wooden staircase. The door to the room was wide open, and Major Bystrov and Major Pichko were standing beside the radio craning their necks.

It was strange really, because we were expecting this, but when the newsreader finally came on air to announce solemnly, '*The signing of the instrument of unconditional surrender of the German armed forces*', we just stood there, overwhelmed.

The task of locating Hitler's dentists in the chaos of devastated Berlin, would have daunted anyone, but on 9 May, this first morning when the war was over, we sallied forth on our quest.

From the intact outskirts we drove back into the ruins of Berlin. In places smoke was still rising, the city's air still filled with the fumes of battle. The barricades, crushed by tank tracks, had yet to be dismantled. In places ruins not yet cool still smoked. There was rubble everywhere. The city was full of refugees from the eastern lands, but everyone who could had fled Berlin before the assault, getting away from the bombing and the impending siege. Who could we approach?

Somehow, though, the gods were with us. How else was it possible that in this tortured, vanquished city of three million souls, we found the assistant of Professor Hugo Blaschke, Hitler's dentist?

At the Charite Hospital the team found a student from the dentistry department who knew Blaschke, and he volunteered to take them to him.

They headed toward the Kurfurstendamm, one of Berlin's most fashionable streets. Rzhevskaya said it was in the same state as all the others but No. 213, at least the wing of it which housed Blaschke's surgery, was still intact. At the entrance they were met by a man with a red ribbon in the buttonhole of his dark jacket, a signal of welcome and solidarity with the Russians. He introduced himself as Dr. Bruck. On inquiring about Blaschke's whereabouts Dr. Bruck told them that he had flown from Berlin to Berchtesgaden together with Hitler's adjutant.

Gorbushin asked him if he knew any of Blaschke's employees. 'Of course I do', he said, 'You mean Kathchen? Käthe Heusermann? She is at home in her apartment right on our doorstep.' The young student volunteered to go and find her, and while the group waited they were seated in soft armchairs in which the Nazi leaders had sat before them, as patients of Dr Blaschke. Since 1932 Blaschke had been Hitler's personal dentist, and, as it turned out, he had a dark past.

Hugo Johannes Blaschke, born 1881, was Hitler's personal dentist from 1933 until April 1945. Born in Neustadt, Poland), Blaschke studied dentistry in Berlin and at the University of Pennsylvania, later training as a dental surgeon in London. He opened his own dental practice in Berlin in 1911 and served as a military dentist during the First World War. After the war, he returned to private practice in Berlin.

Blaschke's association with the Nazi elite began in 1930 when Hermann Göring became his patient. Göring recommended him to Hitler in 1933, and after successfully treating his toothache, Blaschke was appointed as Hitler's personal dentist.

He also provided dental care for other high-ranking Nazis, including Eva Braun, Joseph Goebbels and Heinrich Himmler. Blaschke joined the Nazi Party in 1931 and the SS in 1935, rising to the rank of SS-Brigadeführer (equivalent to Major General) by 1944. He was also the chief dentist for the SS and played a significant role in the dental care system for the Nazi leadership.

In the final days of the Third Reich, Blaschke accompanied Hitler to the Führerbunker in Berlin but was ordered to leave the city as the Red Army approached. After the war, he was detained and interrogated by the Allies. He was classified as a 'fellow traveller' during the denazification process and continued to practice dentistry in Nuremberg until his death in 1959.

His role extended beyond dental care for Nazi leaders, however; he was directly implicated in the collection and use of gold teeth extracted from concentration camp victims. The Nazis systematically removed gold teeth and fillings from murdered Jews and other prisoners in the camps. These were collected under orders from the SS leadership, notably Heinrich Himmler, and the gold was used for various purposes, including dental work for senior Nazis and SS officers, and the gold teeth he was wearing on his death likely came from concentration camp survivors.

Blaschke had about 5kg of dental gold from concentration camps at his disposal for treating senior Nazis. Historian Henrik Eberle stated that Blaschke placed ten gold fillings in Hitler's mouth in 1944, and the most likely source of this gold was the supply from concentration camps, primarily taken from Jewish victims. Gold from other sources was scarce in wartime Germany, making the use of concentration camp gold highly probable.

A 1941 letter from one of Blaschke's subordinates to the office of SS commander Heinrich Himmler confirmed that Blaschke had a stockpile of 50kg of dental gold – enough to last for years. Blaschke was also involved in organising dental stations in concentration camps and was questioned after the war about the extraction of gold from deceased Jewish prisoners.

When asked by a US prosecutor if his dentists had pulled teeth from dead Jews, he reportedly replied, 'That's why we are here, or not'.

While some sources suggest there is no direct documentary proof that gold from Holocaust victims was used in Hitler's own dental work, the evidence strongly indicates that such gold was used for the dental prostheses of SS officers and likely for other senior Nazis.

The evidence linking Blaschke to the extraction of gold teeth from concentration camp victims is based on several documented facts and testimonies. His involvement extended to establishing dental stations in concentration camps, where teeth were extracted from victims without anaesthesia, as per SS directives.

Blaschke was sentenced to 10 years in prison for war crimes and crimes against humanity, with his involvement in the organisation and use of dental gold from camp victims cited as part of the evidence against him.

In Dr. Blashke's surgery on the Kurfurstendamm Dr. Bruch explained to the Russians that Käthe Heusermann, Dr Blaschke's assistant, had been his student and later his own assistant before the Nazis seized power. Later she and her sister helped Bruck to disappear, because he was a Jew and needed to live under a false name.

Rzhevskaya described her first impressions of Heusermann as she entered the surgery.

A slim, tall, attractive woman in a dark blue flared coat came in. She had on a headscarf over luxuriant blonde hair. 'Käthchen', Bruck said familiarly, 'these people are Russians. They seem to need you for something.'

Even before he had finished she burst into tears. She had already suffered from encountering Russian soldiers. 'Käthchen!' Dr Bruck said in embarrassment, 'Käthchen, these people are our friends.' Bruck was considerably shorter than Käthe, but he took her hand as if she were a small child and stroked the sleeve of her coat.

They had found themselves at opposite ends of the Nazi regime. She, as a member of the staff serving Hitler, was in a privileged position, while he, persecuted and living outside the law, was given support by her family, for which she might have paid a terrible price.

Looking around, Käthe saw me sitting on the sidelines. She came straight over and sat down next to me. Without a moment's hesitation we began talking to each other. Käthe Heusermann was thirty-five. She told me her fiancé was a teacher and now, as a non-commissioned officer, was somewhere in Norway and she had heard nothing from him for a long time.

Dr Blaschke had invited her to be evacuated with him to Berchtesgaden, but she refused. She had been working for Blaschke since 1937, and last saw Hitler in mid-April in the Reich Chancellery when she was receiving a ration of cigarettes. With the permission of Magda Goebbels she had left the Reich Chancellery, but continued to go there for rations, which she shared with Dr Bruck.

It was from her I heard that Magda Goebbels had not been happily married; she complained about her husband's infidelities and had wanted to leave him, only the Führer insisted on her keeping together their exemplary German family. She quite liked Magda, or at least sympathised with her.

Colonel Gorbushin began the interrogation.

'Where is the medical history on Adolf Hitler's teeth?' he asked Käthe Heusermann. 'Here, in the files', she answered. Frau Heusermann quickly searched in the file box and pulled out a card which proved to be the medical history of Adolf Hitler. The entries gave evidence that the Führer had had very poor teeth in need of frequent repair.

The Russian team also needed the X-ray pictures of Hitler's teeth, but they were not at the clinic. When Gorbushin asked where they might be, Käthe Heusermann answered that they ought to have been kept in Professor Blaschke's office in the Chancellery.

Wasting no more time in the clinic, they drove to the Chancellery, taking Käthe Heusermann along. Here they went down to the basement, found Professor Blaschke's dental office, and with Käthe Heusermann's assistance soon discovered X-ray photographs of the Führer's teeth and a few gold crowns that had been prepared, but time to put them to use had run out on dentist and patient. Käthe Heusermann informed them that crowns and bridges for Hitler and Eva Braun had been prepared by a dental technician named Fritz Echtmann, whose address she knew.

'We found Echtmann at home', Gorbushin said. 'I explained the purpose of our visit and asked him to come with us. He was readily willing. Frau Heusermann and Echtmann were interrogated by Kagan [Rzhevskaya's maiden name] assisted by Major Bystrov, who spoke German.'

In answer to their questions Käthe Heusermann and Fritz Echtmann described Hitler's teeth from memory in minute detail. Their information about bridges, crowns and fillings corresponded precisely with the entries in the medical history and with the X-ray pictures that we had found. Next they asked them to identify the jawbones which had been taken from the male corpse. Frau Heusermann and Echtmann recognised them unequivocally as those of Adolf Hitler.

> In a similar procedure they next asked the dentists to describe Eva Braun's teeth. After they had both answered the questions exhaustively, Bystrov placed before them the gold bridge which had been taken from the mouth of the female corpse during the autopsy. Käthe Heusermann and Fritz Echtmann declared without hesitancy that this prosthesis belonged to Eva Braun. Fritz Echtmann added that the special construction of the bridge prepared for Eva Braun was his own invention and that so far no dental prosthetist had used a similar method of attachment.

Next, the medical experts met again. After examination of the medical history, X-ray pictures, and the jawbone with the teeth of the charred male corpse which had been found on 4 May in the garden of the Chancellery, the experts came to the definitive conclusion that these were Adolf Hitler's teeth.

That trip back into the Führerbunker had its own drama. Rzhevskaya mentioned once again that their entry into the bunker was blocked.

> The sentry grounded his rifle, but barred our way; he had been ordered not to let anyone pass without a special permit from the commandant of

Berlin. Gorbushin whipped out his pistol and pushed the sentry aside. The man was taken aback. He would have had every right to shoot, but we needed to get in.

We opened the heavy oak door. To the right was the assembly hall: the door had been torn off its hinges, chandeliers had fallen to the floor. To the left was the gentle descent to the bomb shelter. Hitler had worked here until 21 April, when our artillery fired a volley of shells into the centre of Berlin and he moved to the Führerbunker.

We passed through the vaulted vestibule and down two flights of stairs, with one dim torch between the three of us. It was dark, deserted and spooky. In the radio studio from which Goebbels broadcast, a Red Army soldier was sleeping with his helmet slipped down over his ear. Only Käthe could find her way around in this Tomb of the Pharaohs. She led us to a boxy little room which, until recently, had been at the disposal of her boss, Dr Blaschke.

We searched through a box with a card index, looked in the desk and a locker. With Heusermann's help we found the X-rays of Hitler's teeth and his dental records. We were lucky, incredibly lucky. We found gold, crowns which, according to Käthe, had been made for Hitler although, as she admitted in her memoirs written many years later, here she was slightly overdoing it: the crowns were in fact for one of the secretaries. She was understandably anxious to stay on the right side of us. Fortunately those crowns did not figure again in the investigation.

We left, taking with us our incredibly important finds, the most miraculous, the most wonderful of which was Käthe Heusermann herself.

Rzhevskaya had taken a shine to Käthe Heusermann, and so began an unusually friendly relationship between two people who only a few days earlier had been enemies.

On 11 May Dr. Faust Scharavasky met with Käthe Heusermann. He had with him Hitler's medical history. He noted that she had helped to prosthetise Hitler's teeth in her capacity as a specialist in stomatology. 'I remember very clearly how frightened she was during the interrogation', he said in a later interview with Lev Bezymenski.

However, the interrogation proceeded very smoothly, really like an ordinary conversation between doctors. I, a Soviet physician, was speaking with a German doctor. In the course of our conversation, which lasted between two and three hours, Frau Heusermann gladly ate some of our candy.

Her fear soon evaporated. She described minutely the specific features of Hitler's dental prostheses and drew them with her own hand. I even started to argue with her, because I had overlooked one detail when examining the teeth and had miscounted the steel pins. She turned out to be right.

Having finished with the theoretical part of our conversation, we proceeded to the practical part, that is, I wanted to check the correctness of her statements against the prostheses themselves, which were in my desk. I took them out and placed them before Frau Heusermann. She repeated everything again in detail and declared categorically that the prosthesis I had shown her was in fact Hitler's dental prosthesis. The picture was clear beyond doubt, for Frau Heusermann as well as for me as forensic expert.

The charred body found in the bunker was without doubt that of Adolf Hitler, together with his wife of a few hours, Eva Braun.

By 11 May 1945, with the investigation nearing its end SMERSH agent Lieutenant Colonel Klimenko detained a member of Hitler's SS bodyguard, Harry Mengershausen. Rzhevskaya described him as a handsome, broad-shouldered fellow, now wearing civilian clothes.

Mengershausen said he could indicate the place where the bodies were hidden, covered with earth and rubble. When he was taken back to the garden he pointed out the crater, not knowing that the bodies had already been removed from it.

The Russians accepted his evidence and wrote a report, which concluded the work of the SMERSH team. After that everything to do with the bunker was undertaken by the Army and Front Headquarters.

At this time almost all the witnesses who had remained in the bunker had been interviewed. It was now possible to determine, more or less, depending on whether they were to be believed, what had happened in the bunker, and make sense of the supposed gunshot in Hitler's study.

Major Bystrov interrogated Mengershausen and I translated. We were sitting on logs in the courtyard of our Front's headquarters.

Mengershausen told us that on 30 April he was guarding the Reich Chancellery, patrolling the corridor where the kitchen and green dining room were situated. Additionally, he was monitoring the garden because at a distance of 80 metres from the green dining room was the Führer's bomb shelter.

Mengershausen said 'Patrolling the corridor and approaching the kitchen, I met someone I knew to be the Führer's orderly, Bauer, who was going to the kitchen. He told me that Hitler had shot himself in his bunker. I enquired as to the whereabouts of the Führer's wife, and Bauer told me she too was lying dead in the bunker, but he did not know whether she had poisoned or shot herself. I talked to Bauer for only a few minutes: he was hurrying to the kitchen. In the kitchen food was being cooked for Hitler's entourage. He returned shortly afterwards to the bunker.

'I did not believe Bauer's report of the death of Hitler and his wife and continued to patrol my area. Not more than one hour after meeting Bauer, as I came out to a terrace situated 60–80 metres from the bunker, I suddenly saw the personal adjutant, Sturmbannführer Günsche, and Hitler's valet, Sturmbannführer Linge, carrying the body of Hitler from the emergency exit of the bunker and placing it 2 metres from the exit. They went back and a few minutes later brought out Eva Braun, who was dead, and whom they put in the same place.

'Some way from the bodies there were two twenty-kilogram cans of petrol, Günsche and Linge began to pour petrol over the bodies and set fire to them.'

Bystrov asked him whether any of the other guards had seen the bodies of Hitler and Braun being burned. Mengershausen did not know for sure. 'Of all the security guards I was the closest to Hitler's bunker at that time', he said. He bent down and began to outline a map of the garden on the ground with a piece of wood.

Rzhevskaya said:

So, we had found our missing link – somebody involved in or who had witnessed the actual cremation. who would have been so helpful in the first phase of our mission, when we were hunting Hitler.

From his post Mengershausen said he had been able to see only Günsche and Linge but, shielded by the bunker, hiding from the shellfire, Goebbels, Bormann and the others were observing the burning of the bodies. Nearby, a battle was raging; the Reich Chancellery was under intense bombardment.

Asked how he could identify Hitler, Mengershausen said 'The bodies that were carried from the bunker were definitely those of Hitler and his wife, Eva Braun. I knew Hitler by his face and his clothes. He had black trousers worn over high boots and grey-green uniform jacket. Under the uniform jacket, I could see a white shirt-front and a necktie. None of the Nazi Party leaders except for Hitler wore such a uniform, and I had seen him in this uniform several times. [that's why] I remembered it exceptionally well.'

'When Hitler was being carried out I clearly saw his face in profile – his nose; hair and moustache. So, I confirm that it was definitely Hitler', he said.

'Hitler's wife Braun, when she was being carried out of the bunker, was dressed in a black dress, with several pink flowers made of cloth on the breast. I saw her several times wearing this dress in the bunker.

Besides, I saw her face – it was oval, thin, with a straight, narrow nose and fair hair. Thus, knowing Hitler's wife Braun very well, I state that it was definitely her body that was carried out of the bunker.'

He described the wailing of shells, the crash of explosions throwing up columns of soil, the smashing and whistling of flying window glass, how the buffeting wind disturbed the clothing on the bodies. 'The fire flared up and then died down as the petrol burned off. More petrol was poured over them and again ignited', Mengershausen said.

Then what did Mengershausen do? He escaped, acting on his own initiative and without waiting for new orders. 'That same day, 30 April, I changed into civilian clothing and hid in a cellar.' He was wearing a raincoat that was too short for him and obviously belonged to somebody else. His long arms protruded from the sleeves.

Major Bystrov handed him a photograph of the Reich Chancellery garden. Rzhevskaya translated, 'Tell me what you see in this photo'. 'This is a photo of the emergency exit from Hitler's bomb shelter', he said. 'I know this place well and can show you where the bodies of Hitler and his wife Braun were burned, and also the place where they were buried.'

'With one cross I am indicating on the photo where the bodies of Hitler and Braun were burned, with two crosses the place where they were buried, and with three crosses the emergency exit from Hitler's bunker.'

Rzhevskaya said the next time she saw that photo with Mengershausen's crosses on it was in the Council of Ministers Archive.

Mengershausen, however, had not told them the whole truth. In his written testimony sometime later, he acknowledged that he not only watched the bodies burn he was also involved himself.

The head of Hitler's bodyguard, SS Gruppenführer Hans Rattenhuber, testified that the bodies of Hitler and Eva Braun did not burn well, and he went downstairs to arrange for more fuel to be sent. 'When I came back up, the bodies had already been sprinkled with a little soil. The sentry Mengershausen told me it was impossible to stand at his post because of the intolerable smell and that he, together with another SS soldier, had, on the instructions of Günsche, pushed them into a pit where Hitler's poisoned dog lay', he said.

Going on to describe the behaviour of those in the shelter, who set about preparing to escape the moment they became aware of the Führer's death, Rattenhuber once more mentioned Mengershausen: 'I was startled by the cold calculation of SS guard Mengershausen, who made his way into Hitler's office and removed a gold badge from the Führer's tunic, which was draped over a chair, hoping that "They'll pay a good price for this relic in America".'

Mengershausen's testimony was the missing link the search team had needed in order to produce an evidence-based reconstruction of the last hours of Hitler's life and the exact nature of his death.

It was time to summarise. Reports that Hitler had been positively identified went first to front headquarters, and from there to the top. Rzhevskaya said those involved in these initial investigations had a sense of great personal responsibility to obtain irrefutable evidence, recognising only too well that a lack of clarity about Hitler's death would be harmful. It could only facilitate his intention of disappearing without a trace, turning into a myth, and thereby fuelling the fanaticism and galvanising the Führer's adherents. Nazism was very centred on Hitler personally, and the peoples of the USSR, who had put everything they had into winning the victory over Nazism, had an inalienable right to know that the last full stop had been written in this history.

> Having obtained incontrovertible evidence, I really believed that all the nonsensical rumours would be swept away and truth would prevail. I wrote a brief letter to my family, which they have preserved, to say that I had taken part in an important mission, that we would shortly be returning to Moscow, and I would see them soon.
>
> I was sure we would be sent to Moscow with all the data and principal witnesses to the identification. I was sure that Käthe Heusermann, for her services to history, would be appreciated and rewarded. Nothing stirred. Everything stayed just as it was. Now what was going to happen?

While many were captured or killed, a number of prominent Germans managed to break out, at least temporarily, from the bunker in the chaotic final hours.

They left in several groups using underground tunnels and the U-Bahn (subway) system to reach the Friedrichstrasse station, aiming to cross the Spree River via the Weidendammer Bridge. One of them, Heinz Linge, who was captured by the Russians, later testified that he teamed up with SS-Obersturmbannführer Erich Kempka.

> In full uniform we climbed through a window of the New Reich Chancellery cellar. Under a hail of shell and mortar fire we crossed Friedrich-Strasse to the railway station where a couple of our panzers were standing and still offering the Russians battle. Towards midnight on the Weidendamm bridge we came upon Stumpfegger, Baur and Bormann who had lost their bearings, arrived by a roundabout route and were now separated from the Russians by an anti-tank barrier.
>
> As three of our panzers and three armoured vehicles rolled up, Bormann decided to break through the Russian lines using a panzer.

Kempka jumped up, stopped the vehicles and told the leading panzer commander what was required. Under the protection of this panzer heading for the tank barrier, Bormann, Naumann and Stumpfegger doubled forward while I watched. The panzer was hit by a projectile from a Panzerfaust. The people alongside it were tossed into the air like dolls by the explosion. I could no longer see Stumpfegger nor Bormann. I presumed they were dead, as I told the Russians repeatedly in numerous interrogations later.

Kempka escaped Berlin by traveling through the city with a small group of remaining bunker survivors. Initially, he disguised himself in civilian clothes with the help of a Yugoslav woman who claimed to Soviet soldiers that Kempka was her husband, allowing him to evade immediate capture by the Soviets. Kempka eventually made his way to Wittenberg and then Munich, where he obtained false identification papers from a German woman who worked for the Allies as an interpreter.

From Munich, Kempka continued south to Berchtesgaden, Hitler's mountain retreat in Bavaria. There, on 20 June 1945, he was captured by US Army troops. Kempka was held by the American authorities until October 1947. He became the first direct witness in Allied hands able to confirm the details of Hitler's death in the bunker.

Martin Bormann, Hitler's private secretary and head of the Nazi Party Chancellery, and Ludwig Stumpfegger, Hitler's personal physician together with Artur Axmann, Leader of the Hitler Youth escaped across the Spree River. In December 1972, construction workers in West Berlin uncovered two skeletons near Lehrter station, close to where eyewitnesses had last seen Bormann and Stumpfegger. A retired postal worker, Albert Krumnow, had reported that he and colleagues buried two bodies in the area in May 1945, one of whom was identified by an SS doctor's paybook as Stumpfegger. In 1998, DNA testing definitively confirmed the identification of Bormann by matching the remains to a living relative. After confirmation, Bormann's remains were cremated and his ashes were secretly scattered at sea in 1999 to prevent the site from becoming a neo-Nazi shrine. The skeleton believed to be Stumpfegger matched his height and physical characteristics. Composite photographs and facial reconstruction further supported the identification. Fragments of glass found in the jawbones of both skeletons suggested they had bitten cyanide capsules to commit suicide. While Bormann's identity was later confirmed by DNA testing, Stumpfegger's identification rests on forensic and circumstantial evidence, which is considered highly reliable. The remains of Stumpfegger were ultimately buried in Munich's Nordfriedhof cemetery

Others to escape were Hans Baur, Hitler's personal pilot, who was wounded and captured by Russian soldiers. Heinz Linge and Otto Günsche, Hitler's SS adjutant, also escaped but were quickly captured and were to prove crucial to the story of Hitler's final moments.

Traudl Junge, Gerda Christian, Else Krüge, Hitler's secretaries escaped in a group led by SS Brigadeführer Wilhelm Mohnke (bunker defence commander), but were later captured by Soviet troops. Among others who escaped was Constanze Manziarly, Hitler's diet cook, who escaped with the secretaries; her ultimate fate remains unknown but she disappeared after capture. Rochus Misch, bunker telephone operator, escaped and was later captured by the Soviets.

Diplomat Johannes Hewel escaped but committed suicide when capture was imminent. Erich Kempka (Hitler's chauffeur), escaped, but was later captured by US forces. Franz Schädle (commander of Hitler's bodyguard), attempted to escape but committed suicide after being severely wounded.

Axmann and Kempka managed to evade immediate capture but were arrested weeks or months later by Allied forces. Artur Axmann was Reich Youth Leader of the Nazi Party, who deployed 16 and 17-year-olds to defend Berlin in 1945. After his escape he tried to organise a Nazi underground movement, but was captured by the US Army in December 1945. In 1958, a Nuremberg de-Nazification court sentenced him to 39 months' imprisonment but he was released immediately as he had served this period while on remand before his trial. He subsequently became a businessman in the Canary Islands, and died in Germany on 24 October 1996.

The transcripts of the interrogations of those who were in the bunker at the time, released decades later, enables us follow the sequence of events from the moment Hitler and his staff set up their headquarters there in mid-April 1945.

Several of these interrogations were conducted by Elena Rzhevskaya, as interpreter. 'In the beginning all we wanted to hear from these people was what happened to Hitler. It wasn't as if we were looking for criminal suspects,' she said. But after his charred corpse was discovered and identified, they were formalised. 'Once we had concluded our interrogations we moved on to other areas. I myself left the army in October 1945, so I was not a party to anything that happened after that.'

The death of Stalin in 1953 and the elevation of Nikita Khrushchev as leader of the USSR should have meant that the pretence about the fate of Hitler would no longer be necessary. Slowly, however, attitudes began shifting. In the mid-1950s and onwards Western writers and historians began serious studies of the Second World War and new books began to appear giving graphic eyewitness accounts of various battles and historic events. They were immensely popular and sold in the millions

Irish-American journalist and writer Cornelius Ryan's book *The Longest Day*, a detailed description of the preparations for and execution of the D-Day landings at Normandy in June 1944, was an instant best-seller. He later began researching the Battle of Berlin in April 1945, and approached Soviet officials for assistance, which was granted. Several Russians military officers gave first-hand accounts of the battle, and, as Ryan himself noted, he became the first Westerner to be informed by any Russian official that Hitler was dead. But it appears he was not given any further access to the details of his death.

At the same time Elena Rzhevskaya, by now an established writer living in Moscow, herself began prising open the locked doors of the Soviet archives in order to write an account of her own involvement.

> I was afraid of forgetting things about those events in Berlin, of letting them slip if I put everything off, so I began to write shortly after returning to Moscow, drawing on some entries in the notebook from that time.
>
> After Stalin's death, in 1954, I took the manuscript to *Znamya*, which specialises in prose about the army. Because of the subject matter, the manuscript was sent for permission to publish to the Foreign Ministry. It was returned with their resolution: 'At your discretion'. That is, they were not banning it. The editor, Vadim Kozhevnikov, was, however, highly circumspect in matters of discretion. He said to the editorial staff who were rooting for the manuscript, 'This has never been written about before. Why should we be the first? And anyway, who is she?' I was just someone off the street.
>
> The manuscript was, nevertheless, published in *Znamya* (No. 2, 1955). It contained all the details of the suicides of Hitler and Goebbels, the discovery of Goebbels' charred remains and those of his six children, murdered by their parents. They also kept in the testimony about the documents found in Hitler's bunker and the main find: the diaries of Goebbels. There was the story of the removal and burning of Hitler's body, and his burial there and then in the Reich Chancellery garden in a crater. In fact, everything except that we had found Hitler in that crater and identified him.

'So, in other words', I said, 'they left it hanging in the air whether this was fact or speculation. How did you manage to get round that ban?'

That happened in 1961, in my book *Spring in a Greatcoat*, and in a fairly roundabout manner. After the war, I was drawn to impressions of life in peacetime. I wrote novellas that were far removed from my own biography, about life without the war, although interlayered with it.

The 'Soviet Writer' publishing house was intending to publish a book consisting of two of my novellas, which I had already largely been paid for. It didn't come off. Of course, I was very upset, but it was not the first or last time that a setback, providing it was not fatal, turned out to be all for the good.

The publishing house had not forgotten the fee already paid and, two years later, suggested I should update the book. The writers Isaak Kramov and Boris Slutsky suggested I should slip in the Rzhev stories. So it was that in 1961 a book was published, titled *Spring in a Greatcoat* and containing stories about the war which had been lying around for 15 years. They were warmly received, and that encouraged me to return to writing prose about the war. In addition, however, the book included my uncensored documentary account of how we found Hitler's body. I put back in everything that had been taken out by *Znamya*, that is, everything about finding and identifying Hitler.

Happily, the censors paid no attention to the additions, because basically the text had already been published. And that is how, for the first time, the fact was made known that the Red Army had found Hitler's body, although I had no documents to back that up, except for the one copy Ivan Klimenko had sent me.

Having that publication behind me was very helpful when I was trying to get permission to work in the Council of Ministers Archive. The Writers' Union supported my application. I appealed to publishing houses and the Communist Party Central Committee, referring to the fact that I had been a participant in these events, that I was a writer who had already written about them, and that I now needed documentation for more in-depth and reliable work.

For a long time it all seemed hopeless. The answer was always the same: 'There is no access to these materials and no exceptions are likely to be made'. But on the crest of the wave of national pride as the twentieth anniversary of victory approached, a miracle occurred and the doors of the secret archive opened before me. It was September 1964, and I got to work in the archive for 20 days.

For me, the encounter with these documents was overwhelming. The intention had clearly been to leave them to moulder, silently covering up the mystery, and now it was my job to bring them out into the light, come hell or high water.

Rzhevskaya's books were warmly received in Russia and she became a minor celebrity. The Soviet Government even allowed her to tell part of her story in an episode of the massively popular British television documentary *The World at War*. The episode, entitled 'Women in War' briefly mentioned Elena Rzhevskaya, but did not relate her involvement in the discovery of Hitler's body and her adventures with Hitler's jaw fragments. I asked her about this and she gave a mischievous smile 'Because they never asked me', she said. 'Maybe they didn't know, I'm not sure, but I didn't volunteer it.' The implication was that it might have got her into trouble.

After the publication of her book, *Berlin, May 1945*, the Soviet authorities gradually relaxed their previous hardline attitude to access to wartime archives, but it wasn't until the turn of the twenty-first century, after the fall of the Soviet Union, that full access finally became available, and the true story emerged.

Russian historians and researchers were allowed access to archives that had been tightly controlled by the KGB (now the FSB). Among them were files related to the Soviet investigation into Hitler's death, including verbatim records of interrogations with Hitler's closest aides, internal reports to Stalin, and other classified documents.

With access to these files we can now put the events of the period leading up to and including the death of Hitler into context.

Chapter 9

HITLER'S FINAL COMMANDS

Hitler conceded for the first time that the war was lost in a meeting involving Jodl, Borman and Keitel at 5:30 pm on Sunday, 21 April 1945. 'We cannot win', he said to them. 'This is the end of Germany. I do not believe in the strength of the Army, the Air Force and the SS forces any longer.'

He then ordered Keitel, Jodl and Bormann to leave Berlin immediately. He repeated the order several times but Bormann and Keitel refused to obey. Only Jodl said he could not stay any longer and left at once. Admiral Dönitz called him on the telephone. Hitler listened to him and said 'Thanks', without saying anything else. Then von Ribbentrop telephoned, saying a split between the Western Powers and the East was expected 'soon'. Hitler thanked him and ended the call.

Soon after Goebbels arrived with his children. He said to Hitler 'Maybe we should turn our backs on the West and go on fighting the Russians.'

'There is no need for it', Hitler answered. 'We are lost.'

Just over a week later, in the first few days of May, SMERSH operatives captured about 800 high-ranking prisoners in the vicinity of the Reichstag and Hitler's Chancellery. All were questioned and became prisoners of war. Only one, however, had an intimate knowledge of what had occurred inside the bunker while the Russians fought their way into the city.

At the age of 54, German General Helmuth Weidling, noted for his artillery expertise and tactical skill, assumed command of the LVI Panzer Corps on 10 April 1945, as it became involved in the defence of Berlin. Thirteen days later, after resolving a misunderstanding that nearly led to his execution for an alleged unauthorised retreat, Weidling was personally appointed by Adolf Hitler as Commander of the Berlin Defence Area.

He led approximately 45,000 soldiers, including remnants of Wehrmacht and Waffen-SS units, police and Hitler Youth, as well as 40,000 poorly-armed militia and civilians. He organised the city into eight defensive sectors, and attempted to prevent unnecessary sacrifice especially of the Hitler Youth, and repeatedly requested permission to break out or surrender – initially denied by Hitler.

Since most of the senior German officers in the bunker were now either dead or missing, his is the only reliable eyewitness account we have by a senior German military figure of what happened. Written on 4 January 1946 in Moscow, it was made public for the first time in 2000 – 55 years after the event, and 45 years after his death.

We can follow the events of the final days through his own words. What follows is an extract of his testimony with minor edits.

The Russian Spring Offensive of 1945 on the Oder began on 14 April. The 56th Panzer Corps which I then commanded was in the Seelow-Wolkow area, to the west of Kustrin – directly in front of the Russian offensive. Soon after it started, as result of heavy fighting, there were deep penetrations of the left and right flanks of the sector I was defending, as well as at the rear of the Corps. Communications with the two neighbouring Corps and with the Army were cut, but my Corps managed to fight a defensive battle and retreat to the west, to the outer perimeter of Berlin's defensive area.

On 12 April, I sent Lieutenant-General Voigtsberger, a former commander of the 'Berlin' Division, to establish communications with 9th Army. Two days later, Voigtsberger returned from Army headquarters and excitedly reported that information had been received by them that I and my headquarters were supposedly moving to Döberitz, to the west of Berlin. For this reason, Hitler had ordered that I be arrested and executed.

Voigtsberger said he had insisted at 9th Army that such a movement would be impossible. The orders he brought with him from the 9th Army stated that the 56th Panzer Corps was to establish communication with the left flank of its neighbour to the right.

At first, I was unsure and unclear as to what to do, but the orders I received made our hearts beat faster because the idea of fighting in a city that had been destroyed was demoralising.

Together with my Chief-of-Staff Colonel Dürfing, I immediately started to prepare orders for the Corps to re-group on the night of 23/24 April. Colonel Refior then informed me by telephone of General Krebs' order to send a staff officer from the 56th Panzer Corps with a map of troop deployments to the Reich Chancellery.

For two reasons I decided to go to the Reich Chancellery myself. First, I wanted to know the reason for the order for my arrest and execution, and second I wanted, if possible, to ensure that my Corps avoided fighting in the ruined city.

At 6 pm, accompanied by the head of department 1-a, I arrived at the Reich headquarters of Major Knappe's Corps chancellery. From the sidewalk of Vossstrasse, a staircase led to an 'underground city' that was built between Wilhelmstrasse and Goeringstrasse. You can get an idea of the size of this shelter if you take into account that during the intensified raids on Berlin, 4–5 thousand of the city's children were fed and stayed there every night as Hitler's 'guests'.

We were immediately escorted into a small bunker. I was received by the Chief of the General Staff General Krebs and Hitler's personal aide-de-camp General Burgdorf. The meeting was somewhat cold, despite the fact that I knew Krebs well from the days of the Reichswehr, and later when he was Chief-of-Staff of the 9th Army and the Centre Army Group.

During the conversation that followed, I was easily able to convince both generals that I had no intention of, and nor was there any sense in, relocating to Döberitz, considering the military situation. They had to admit that they had taken for fact some insignificant rumour and now, after my explanation, they regretted their gullibility. Nevertheless, it turned out that I was to be removed after all, but they did not tell me this. Krebs told me they were very concerned about deep Russian penetration into eastern Berlin. They wanted to know what counter-action could be taken by the 56th Panzer Corps. When I informed them of the order my Corps had received from the 9th Army, Krebs shouted: 'Impossible, it's absolutely impossible! I'll immediately report to the Führer about it.' With these words, Krebs left me alone, and Burgdorf followed him like a shadow.

I instructed Major Knappe, who had accompanied me to notify the Chief of Staff by telephone that the Corps might still be needed in eastern Berlin that night. During the telephone conversation, the Chief-of-Staff said that he had received a telegram from the Department of Personnel of the Army signed by Burgdorf, saying that: 'General Weidling is transferred to the reserve of command personnel of the General Command of the Wehrmacht. Lieutenant-General Burmeister, commander of 25th Panzer Division, is appointed as commander of 56th Panzer Corps.'

I was extremely indignant. After all, it was only by chance that I had been able to rehabilitate myself here. But how many generals had suffered in recent times only because they had had no chance to disprove rumours about themselves?

While Krebs and Burgdorf were away, one of Krebs' officers gave me a brief report on the situation in Berlin. Hitler was staying in Berlin with some of his staff to personally direct the defence of the Capital. The flight of State officials from Berlin had begun on 15 April. The road to Munich was being called the 'Reich refugee road'.

Two Operational Headquarters were formed: the first *North Staff* under Field-Marshal Keitel and the second *South Staff* under Field-Marshal Kesselring. General Jodl was attached as Chief-of-Staff. One can judge how quickly and thoughtlessly this reorganisation was by the fact that the two Staffs took all the radio sets in Berlin with them. General Command in Berlin had to be content with a single remaining SS radio unit, connected to Himmler's headquarters.

I was also told briefly of a bombshell which had occurred on 23 April when Göring had sent a telegram from Berchtesgaden demanding a transfer of executive power from Hitler to him due to the fact that Hitler was not able to fulfil his duties in Berlin.

Then Krebs and Burgdorf returned from their report to Hitler. Krebs said to me 'You must report to the Führer immediately about the situation in your Corps. The order from the 9th Army is cancelled. Tonight the Corps will be used to the east of Berlin.' Then I gave vent to my indignation and declared that the Corp's situation should be reported by its new commander, General Burmeister. Together, the two generals barely managed to calm me down and they said that Hitler had decided to leave me in command of the Corps. Despite the fact that I was accompanied to the Führer's bunker by two generals, my papers were most carefully checked three times.

Finally, an SS Sturmbannführer took away my waist-belt and pistol. From the so-called Kolenhof, we went deeper into a labyrinth of shelters. Through a small kitchen we went into a kind of officers' mess where a lot of officers were dining. Then we went down another floor and found ourselves in the reception room outside the Führer's study.

It contained many people in grey or brown uniforms. Walking around the reception room I recognised only the Foreign Minister, Ribbentrop. Then a door opened and I found myself before Adolf Hitler. He sat in a rather small room in an armchair near a big table. When I entered. Adolf Hitler rose with obvious difficulty, leaning on the table with both hands. His left leg was trembling continuously. From his swollen face, two feverishly burning eyes stared at me. His smile changed into a frozen mask. He extended his right hand to me, with both his hands shaking like his left leg.

'Do I know you?' he asked. I replied that two years ago I had received a decoration from him – the Knight's Cross with Oak Leaves. Hitler said that he easily remembered surnames, but not faces. After that greeting, Hitler sank back into the armchair again. I reported on the situation of the Corps and said it had already begun to relocate south-east to regroup. If it were now ordered to about-face 180 degrees, there would be terrible confusion in the morning.

After a brief conversation with Krebs, Hitler again confirmed to me the order to send the Corps to the eastern sector of Berlin.

The ruined garden of the Reich Chancellery, above the bunker where the bodies of Adolf Hitler, Eva Braun and Magda and Josef Goebbels were burned.

Red Army soldiers Corporal Ivan Churakov (on the left) and Lieutenant Colonel Ivan Klimenko point to the spot where they found the bodies of Adolf Hitler and Eva Braun.

Winston Churchill and a group of British and Russian personnel inspect the petrol cans which were used to douse the bodies of Adolf Hitler and Eva Braun prior to lighting.

The entrance to Hitler's bunker near the spot where the bodies were found, as indicated by the single 'x' bottom right.

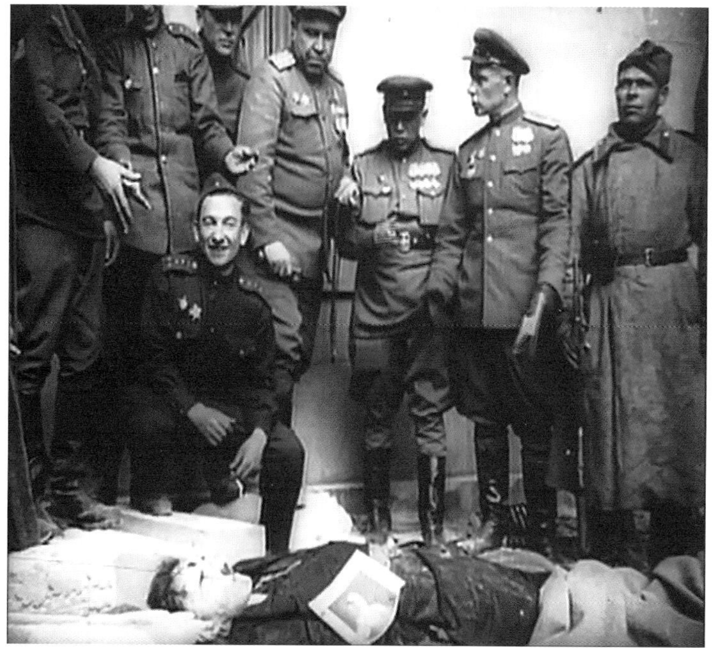

Russians inspecting a body that was initially, and incorrectly, believed to be that of Hitler.

Hitler's corpse photographed in a wooden box. The body was positioned on its left side. The right leg is protruding (on the left).

Victor Abakumov, the Head of SMERSH.

Lev Bezymenski, a SMERSH interpreter in 1945.

General Helmuth Weidling, the final commander of the Berlin Defence Area in April–May 1945, describing how he recalled the last time he saw Hitler.

The Autopsy Commission, including Dr Scharavsky, centre right, and Major Anna Marants, in the centre. The body is that of General Hans Krebs, Chief of the Army General Staff, who unsuccessfully tried to negotiate a ceasefire in Berlin.

The Morgue at Berlin-Buch.

Eric Kempka, Hitler's chauffeur.

Otto Günsche with Hitler.

Heinz Linge, Hitler's valet.

Traudl Junge, Hitler's Secretary, in 1942.

A portrait of Artur Axmann, leader of the Hitler Youth from 1940 to 1945.

Hugo Blaschke, Hitler's dentist.

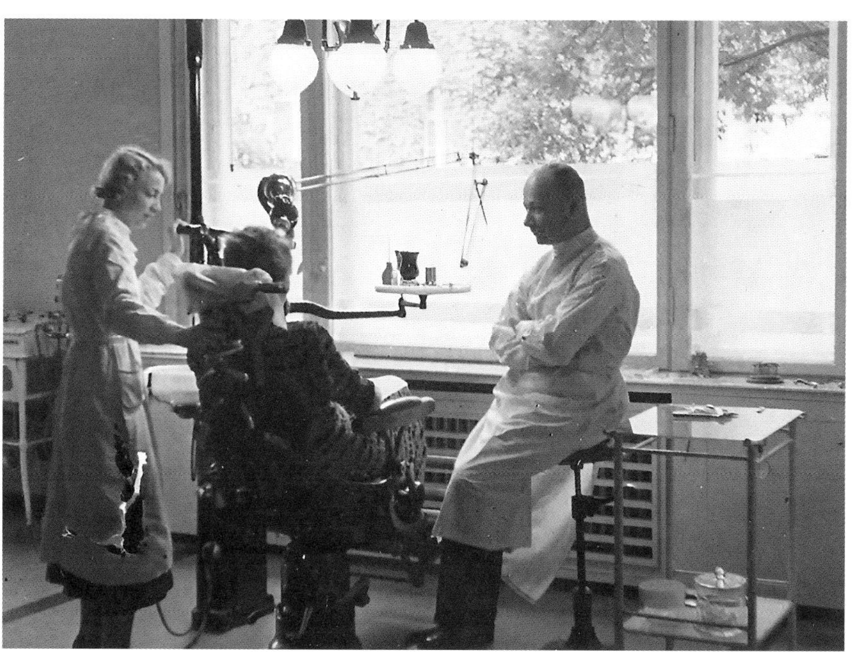

Käthe Heusermann as a young nurse with Dr. Fedor Bruck.

Elena Rzhevskaya in her study in Moscow,
June 1991.

Former Russian military interpreter Elena Rzhevskaya, on the right, and author Cyril Jones
pictured as they study film footage of Hitler's bunker, 1991.

At the end, Hitler expounded on his plan of operations for the relief of Berlin which I would describe as criminally amateurish. He spoke in a low voice, with long pauses, often repeating himself before suddenly turning to insignificant matters, that were strangely discussed at length.

Under Hitler's plan the 12th Assault Army under the command of Lieutenant-General Wenck would come from the south of Brandenburg and attack through Potsdam to the south-west sector of Berlin. Simultaneously, the 9th Army would receive an order to disengage from the enemy along the line of the Oder and launch an offensive in the south-east sector of Berlin.

As a result of the joint action of the two armies, the Russian forces to the south of Berlin would be destroyed. To ensure freedom of manoeuvre of the 12th Assault Army and the 9th Army, the following German forces would be sent against the Russians to the north of Berlin: from the Nauen region: the 7th Panzer Division and the 'Steiner' SS Assault Group from south of Fürstenberg. Later, that is when the Russian forces to the south of Berlin had been destroyed, the Russians north of the city would also be destroyed by the joint action of all four attacking groups.

When Hitler finished, it seemed to me as if I had heard it all in a dream. For several days and nights I had been involved in heavy fighting and knew that unless a miracle occurred the final catastrophe would come within days. There were only limited quantities of ammunition, almost no fuel and, above all, the troops were fighting without the will to resist because they no longer believed in victory.

Was a miracle possible? Was Wenck's Assault Army, about which Goebbels had talked so much in the last few weeks, what Germany was holding in reserve? Or was it only the fantasy of a fanatic who had lost touch with reality?

Struck by the sight of this human ruin who headed the German state, and badly depressed by the amateurishness that reigned within the ruling circles, I left Hitler's study. As I was leaving, Hitler rose, with obvious difficulty, and extended his hand to me. Nothing was said about my arrest, execution or dismissal.

In the adjutants' bunker Krebs explained my Corps orders to me on the map of Berlin. I was to take over four of the eastern and southern sectors of Berlin's defence area, out of the total of nine that still existed. Five sectors remained in the hands of the commander of the defence area. My Corps was under Hitler's direct command.

I said to General Krebs 'So Hitler is in fact the commander of the Berlin defence area?'

And I added some questions for him: 'Do you believe that Hitler's plan of operations includes raising the siege of Berlin? For example, he has simultaneously given the 9th Army defensive and offensive combat missions. Do you have any idea about the current state of the army? The left flank of my Corps is completely destroyed, and the pitiful remains of it is with the "Weichsel" Army Group. As for the neighbouring Corps to the right, all I know is that, it too, has been in heavy combat and is now in the same state as we are, probably worse. The rest of the 9th Army cannot be that strong. And yet despite this, under constant Russian pressure, the troops are to be removed from the Oder in order to fight in the eastern part of Berlin. You know, Krebs, I cannot follow Hitler's orders.'

General Weidling's doubts about Wenck's army were correct – it never arrived. Under the command of General Theodor Busse, it was effectively destroyed during the Battle of Berlin, specifically during the Battle of Halbe, which lasted from 24 April to 1 May 1945. Initially, the 9th Army was encircled by Soviet forces in the Spree Forest region south-east of Berlin. The surrounded army attempted a breakout to the west through intense Soviet resistance, aiming to link up with Wenck's own 12th Army in the hope that this would provide a route to surrender to the Western Allies instead of the Soviets.

This breakout attempt, known as the Battle of Halbe, was brutally costly. Of the roughly 80,000 soldiers originally encircled, about 30,000 managed to reach the safety of the 12th Army's lines; the rest were either killed, captured, or went missing. Civilian losses were also devastating, with about 10,000 civilians killed in the chaos. The survivors, including a mix of soldiers and many civilian refugees, then continued their retreat further west, eventually surrendering to US forces on the Elbe River.

The 9th Army's destruction was both a military disaster and a humanitarian catastrophe, with estimates of total deaths (including civilians) ranging from 30,000 to 40,000 in the fighting and breakout attempts. The operation ultimately failed to relieve Berlin as Hitler had ordered, but Wenck and Busse prioritised rescuing as many survivors as possible, focusing their efforts on opening a corridor for escape rather than launching futile offensives.

By early May, the remnants of both the 9th and 12th Armies, along with thousands of civilians they had helped rescue, made their way across the Elbe and surrendered to American forces. The 9th Army ceased to exist as an effective fighting force, marking one of the final, most desperate episodes of the war in Europe

After leaving Hitler Weidling issued combat orders to his divisions and chose the Tempelhof airfield for his command post.

About 10pm I left the Reich Chancellery and went to the commanders of the defence sectors who had been newly placed under me to see what the situation was on the ground. After speaking to the commanders, this is how I saw it:

Berlin was defended not by organised armies but by loosely-connected units and small groups. More-or-less suitable officers had been brought in as commanders, but the first thing they had to do was form their staffs. There were no means of communication. The infantry was made up of Volkssturm battalions, artillerymen and Hitler Youth units. The only anti-tank weapons were grenade-launchers [Panzerfaust].

The artillery was equipped with captured guns, and there was no overall command. The backbone of the defence was the fixed anti-aircraft batteries, and although it had a centralised command these were rarely useful in ground combat due to the scarcity of motor transport.

The chain of command was confused. Orders came not only from the defence command, but also from many Party officials, such as the Defence Commissioner and the Deputy Gauleiter. What shocked me most was the fate of the civilian population, whose sufferings Hitler ignored. Any sane person could easily see what a horrifying drama was unfolding.

Late at night on 24 April, my Deputy Commander arrived at the Corps command post and informed me that the Corps' movements that night had generally gone according to plan. Soon after, I was again summoned to the Reich Chancellery. I arrived there about midnight that night.

Krebs told me that due to the impression I had made yesterday on the Führer, he was appointing me Commander of the Berlin fortified region. He told me to go immediately to the command post of the fortified region in the Hohenzolerndam and report to him when I had taken command.

I only replied that it would be better if Hitler enforced the order for my execution, at least this chalice would pass me by.

But the real reason for my appointment was not the impression I had made on Hitler. The first commander of the fortified region, Lieutenant-General Reymann, had been dismissed earlier that day after a confrontation with Goebbels, the Berlin Defence Commissioner. His immediate successor was Colonel Kaether, Chief-of-Staff to the Wehrmacht's Chief National-Socialist Officer, who, on being appointed to this position, was simultaneously promoted to Lieutenant-General.

But because Kaether was not trained for this leading position, and I was the only commander of combat troops available, I was assigned this task.

Taking command of the defence area, I understood that the real commander was the Defence Commissioner of Berlin, Dr Goebbels and his retinue. The headquarters of the defence area region were used mainly as an inquiry office (due to contradictory orders) and that interfered considerably with the new commander's efforts to control the actual fighting.

I received no precise information on the strength of the defence forces, either at the moment of my appointment or later. I now believe it was between 80–100,000 men. Neither in numbers, training nor available ammunition was this force capable of defending a city of several million from a modern army.

In mid-April, 30 well-armed 'Volkssturm' battalions had been formed in Berlin, which were attached to the 9th Army. The previous commander, Lieutenant-General Reymann, had protested at this military nonsense, and was, as I have already mentioned, dismissed.

Gathering up the reins of this more-than-complicated command took me half the day of 24 April, and only at 19:00 was I able to report to Krebs that I had assumed command.

On 25 April, I was on the road almost all day, to see for myself the readiness of my sector for defence. I happened to discover some interesting details. First of all, no arrangements had been made to evacuate the civilian population from the central districts of the city, which might become a battlefield at any moment. The civilian population was left to itself to decide when to escape. Second, none of the bridges had been prepared for demolition. Goebbels had entrusted a 'Spur' company with this task, because demolition carried out by combat units damaged surrounding property. But it turned out that all the materials prepared for blowing up the bridges as well as explosives stored for that purpose had been removed from Berlin when the 'Spur' offices were evacuated.

In the evening, I was invited to the Reich Chancellery to discuss the situation. At 21:00, I met Krebs. Not long before, Air Force General Ritter von Greim had arrived at the Reich Chancellery on a stretcher. He had flown into Berlin with a woman pilot, Hanna Reitsch, and had been wounded in the leg while landing. Hitler appointed Ritter von Greim Supreme Commander of the German Air Force and gave him the rank of Field-Marshal. Göring was dismissed. Before the meeting, Hanna Reitsch passed by me several times, once walking arm-in-arm with Frau Goebbels. The rest of the time she was in Hitler's private apartments. I heard that Hanna Reitsch later got Field-Marshal von Greim out of Berlin.

As for Frau Goebbels, I later saw her every evening in Hitler's bunker.

Almost all the officers had gathered in the Führer's reception-room. I was introduced to Goebbels, who greeted me with exceptional courtesy. He seemed to me to be Mephisto personified. Goebbels' aide-de-camp, State Secretary Naumann, was tall and thin, but in other respects resembled his master. Reichsleiter Bormann, as I was later told in the Reich Chancellery, was Hitler's evil genius. With his close friend Burgdorf, he gave himself up to the earthly joys of life, the main ones being cognac and port. Ambassador Hewel hid himself in a corner and it seemed to me that he had renounced everything. I did not see Ribbentrop again; they said that he had left Berlin.

The Deputy Gauleiter of Berlin, Dr Schach, almost crawled before his master, Goebbels. The Hitler Youth Leader Axmann looked modest and reserved. Himmler's liaison officer, Gruppenführer Fegelein, was a typical arrogant, swaggering and self-assured SS officer. [A few days later Fegelein was executed for treason on Hitler's orders.] There were also Hitler's adjutants: Major Johannmeier from the Army, Colonel von Below from the Air Force and Sturmbannführer Günsche from the SS. There was only one Naval liaison officer, Vice-Admiral Voss.

When Krebs arrived with a battle map, we all entered the Führer's study. Hitler greeted me with a handshake. Goebbels immediately took a seat opposite Hitler by the wall where he usually sat during meetings. Everyone else sat wherever they could.

Krebs stood at Hitler's right, with Burgdorf and Bormann, and myself on his left, ready to report. I had to make an effort not to stare at Hitler, bent over in his armchair, his arms and legs trembling constantly.

I began my report by describing the enemy's situation, illustrating it with a large map I had prepared with the enemy positions marked on it. Hitler showed particular interest in this map. Several times he asked Krebs if my estimate of the enemy's strength corresponded with the truth. Each time, Krebs confirmed my information.

Then I reported on the situation of our forces. Apart from two deep penetrations, one near Spandau and the other in the northern sector of Berlin, it was still possible to hold the main front line. At the same time, I described the situation in the defence sectors to which my Corps was being despatched. Hitler forced me to tell him about it in detail.

Turning to the state of the civilian population, I immediately noticed that I had touched on a matter that disturbed them. Goebbels began to feel uneasy and took the floor without asking permission from Hitler. According to Goebbels, everything was completely in order, and his deputy was keeping him informed about this in regular reports. I had to restrain my indignation.

At the end of my report I pointed out the great threat to all our supply lines. All the warehouses were in the outer ring of the city and they were already in imminent danger. Goebbels was about to intervene again but Krebs interrupted and started to report on the general situation.

It became clear to me how tightly this camarilla was bound up with each other. They ignored anything that was unpleasant to them. It seemed to me that Hitler's role was already finished. This physically and morally broken man was only an instrument in the hands of the courtiers.

I remember the following incident in Krebs' report of 25 April. He said the 9th Army had reported that it was moving in the direction of Luckenewald. i.e. in a westerly direction. Hitler excitedly rapped on the table with the three pencils he constantly held in his left hand to stop his fingers trembling. Perhaps he realised that his plan of operations to relieve Berlin had gone off course? But Krebs knew how to calm him, despite it being obvious to any sane man that after the withdrawal of the 56th Panzer Corps the 9th Army would be unable to attack the powerful Russian forces.

The 9th Army's real job was to avoid being encircled and to join up with General Wenck's 12th Assault Army, but Krebs reported that Wenck's army had begun an offensive to lift the blockade of Berlin. These were what Germany was holding in reserve! Wide and deep penetrations by the Russian forces through the 'Weichsel' Army Group would not have an influence on the defence of Berlin, Krebs said.

It was already one o'clock in the morning. After the meeting everyone, including the secretaries, had a brief conversation. Here I got to know some of the people better.

On 26 April, the situation of Berlin's defenders became more critical. Deep penetration took place in all sectors. Krebs telephoned almost every hour and tried to make the overall situation as favourable as possible. First of all, according to his information, the 12th Assault Army was advancing and its vanguard patrols were approaching Potsdam. Despite repeated requests, Krebs said nothing about the movements of the troops to the north of the city, whose attack was very necessary. In fact these two groups never even began to advance.

One more episode should be mentioned that is characteristic of the Chancellery group's behaviour. Goebbels telephoned me late at night and asked, most politely, to let one of the commanders of a sub-sector in northern Berlin Lieutenant-Colonel Bärenfänger go to the Reich Chancellery for a few hours. Before my Corps arrived, Bärenfänger had been the independent commander of the defence sector, but later he was demoted to sub-sector commander. As a former Hitler Youth leader, he was a fanatical supporter of Hitler. His pride had been wounded and he appealed to Goebbels, whom he knew well.

About 2 or 3 hours after my conversation with Goebbels General Burgdorf called me and said that Lieutenant-Colonel Barenfänger had been given the rank of Major-General and Hitler wanted to appoint him commander of an independent sector. It seemed to me that the fortified region had turned into a lunatic asylum!

I reported to Krebs daily. I was relieved of having to attend the nightly general situation conferences at the Reich Chancellery because of the amount of work I had to do.

On 27 April, the enemy's encirclement of Berlin was complete and the city was surrounded. In a concentrated attack, the Russian tank and infantry divisions were moving closer and closer to the centre of the city. In those tragic days of April, the horrified civilian population saw everything that had managed to survive the Anglo-American bombing destroyed in heavy fighting. The inhabitants huddled in bomb-shelters and in the underground like cattle. Life no longer had meaning for them. There was no electricity, no gas, no water!

The worst situation was in the hospitals. Professor Sauerbruch, in his letter to the Commandant of Berlin, described the terrible fate of the wounded. Being a combat veteran I know how cruel modern warfare is, but what Berlin experienced surpassed everything.

In the early morning, our command post in the Hohenzollerndam came under fire, and we had to move to the Bendlerstrasse. In the evening of 27 April, it became absolutely clear to me that there were only two options available: to surrender or break out. Further fighting in Berlin would be criminal.

During the next situation meeting at the Reich Chancellery, my task would be to portray to Hitler the futility of further fighting and to get permission to surrender Berlin.

At 22:00 on 27 April, another meeting took place in Hitler's office. I began by explaining the enemy's strategic situation. According to my Corp's intelligence, a Russian tank corps, which had been operating to the south of Berlin, had been relieved by an infantry corps. Presumably the Russian Command had thrown this tank corps against [our] 12th Assault Army. After his initial success, General Wenck was bogged down in heavy defensive fighting to the south-west of Potsdam. Berlin was surrounded, but there was no sign of a diversion of the besieging forces in response to the four attacking groups. We could not depend on the siege of Berlin being lifted.

In this respect, I indicated a dangerous threat to the troops' morale, due to our own propaganda. Right up to the last, newspapers had been published in Berlin with the headlines 'Numerous armies are speeding to lift the blockade of Berlin'. Soon the troops would know what was true and what was fiction.

Goebbels interrupted, saying indignantly: 'You're going to blame me for this, aren't you?' I had to control myself to answer quietly that being the commander of the troops I considered it my duty to point this matter out. Martin Bormann calmed Goebbels.

This confrontation took place in Hitler's presence but he did not say anything.

At that moment, State Secretary Naumann burst into the room and, interrupting me, reported in great agitation: 'My Führer, a Stockholm radio station has broadcast that Himmler has made a proposal to the British and the Americans for the capitulation of Germany and received an answer from them that they would agree to hold talks as long as the third partner, Russia, were invited.' There was silence in the room. Hitler was tapping on the table with his pencils. His face was distorted and there was fear and alarm in his eyes. Voicelessly he mouthed a word like traitor to Goebbels.

For some time there was a heavy silence, then Krebs quietly advised me to continue with my report. I reported that both Berlin airfields, Templehof and Gatow, were lost. An emergency airstrip that had been built in the Tiergarten could only be partially used by single aircraft because it was so heavily cratered by enemy fire. Supplying Berlin was only possible now by air. Almost all of the large supply depots, including that in the Western Port, had been captured by the enemy on 26 and 27 April. The shortage of ammunition was already being felt.

I had earlier experienced the defeat of an entire army in a small area in East Prussia, so it was not difficult for me to picture what the next few days would be like. This time, the situation was even more terrible, because the civilian population would share the same fate as the troops. I pictured the terrible fate awaiting the wounded and read Professor Sauerbruch's letter aloud. As I was about to sum up, I was interrupted by Hitler, who said 'I know what you are driving at', and then delivered a lengthy explanation as to why it was necessary to defend Berlin to the last. His speech was punctuated by frequent pauses, during which Goebbels interrupted more than once, supporting what Hitler had said.

All of Hitler's speech boiled down to this: 'If Berlin falls into the hands of the enemy, the war will be lost. That is why I am here and why I firmly reject any capitulation.' I therefore decided not to propose a break-out from the encirclement at this time. Because it was 2am, we were dismissed. Goebbels and Bormann stayed with Hitler in his study.

We all sat in the next room and discussed Himmler's betrayal. At the end of the conversation, I explained the plan for a break-out from Berlin. Krebs showed great interest in it. He entrusted me with the task of developing a plan for a break-out and to report on it at the next conference. His interest was so great that he asked for a draft of it to make his own amendments.

The break-out was to be in three waves from two sides across the Havel bridge. Work on the plan was performed on the morning of 28 April at the command post in the Bendler Block. It was to take place in three waves from two sides, using bridges over the Havel south of Spandau. Hitler and his headquarters would be in the third wave.

At noon, my Chief-of-Staff Colonel von Dürfing went to the Reich Chancellery and presented the plan to General Krebs. Krebs approved it.

Meanwhile the situation was getting more and more desperate. The ring around Berlin was getting tighter and tighter.

At 22:00 on 28 April 1945 there was another situation meeting in the Reich Chancellery. Fewer people were there this time. Two of the adjutants, Colonel von Below and Major Johannmeier, were absent. It was said that they had been sent out of Berlin with important documents. How and by what route they had left Berlin I was unable to discover. I cannot be sure if I saw Gruppenführer Fegelein on 28 and 29 April. I only heard about his execution on Hitler's orders several months later in Moscow.

This time, because of the increasing shortage of ammunition and the impossibility of aerial resupply, it was not difficult for me to propose a break-out.

Hitler thought for a very long time, then, in a tired, hopeless voice, he said: 'What good would this break-out do? We'd just go from one cauldron to another. Should I wander around, waiting for the end in some peasant's house or other such place? It is better for me to stay here.' Now it was all clear. It was all about himself, about '*I the ego*'. Goebbels' interjection was the same: 'Certainly, my Führer, absolutely right!'

I was prepared for anything but this. For security in the bunker for as long as possible, many thousands of people on both sides were to make the ultimate sacrifice in this criminal fighting. I left the Reich Chancellery in an embittered mood.

The drama was swiftly coming to its end. The airborne supply on the night of 29 April had brought almost nothing – only 6 tons of supplies were delivered, including 8–10 boxes of small arms ammunition, 15–20 artillery rounds and a small quantity of medical supplies.

The troops' demands for ammunition became more and more insistent. Communication between the separate sectors was possible only by messengers, who had to go on foot because the Berlin streets were impassable to vehicles.

In our command post, we were on the front line. Facing us, on the other side of the Landwehr canal, was the enemy. The Reichstag was lost. The enemy's machine-guns were concentrated on the Potsdammerplatz.

Under fire from machine-guns and grenade-launchers, I reached the Reich Chancellery covered in mud. It was 22:00 on 29 April. The atmosphere in the bunker was like that of our command post. All who gathered there for the situation report were in despondent mood. Hitler, even more haggard, was looking fixedly at the map spread before him.

I persistently asked Hitler to permit a break-out as soon as possible, saying that, as was well known, no soldier can fight without weapons. I finished with the words: 'The break-out will be a success if an assault group comes to meet us.'

Hitler, with bitter irony in his voice, said 'Look at my map. Everything shown on it is not based on information from the Supreme Command, but from foreign radio station broadcasts. No one reports to us. I can order anything, but none of my orders is carried out anymore.'

Krebs supported me in my attempts to get permission for a break-out, but in very cautious form. At last it was decided that, as there were no airborne supplies, the troops could break out in small groups, but on the understanding that they should continue to resist wherever possible. There was to be no talk of capitulation.

Although I had failed to get Hitler to call a final halt to the bloodshed, I had managed to persuade him to end resistance in Berlin. Where Hitler would be during this break-out was not mentioned. This struck me only when I got to my command post. But Hitler's personal safety was outside my responsibility.

I ordered all the sector commanders to assemble at the Bendlerstrasse at 10:00 on 30 April. They were instructed as to what small groups meant, and the time for the break-out was decided.

Because the previous night's airborne supply drop had almost completely ceased, I set the time for the breakout at 22:00 on 30 April. The commanders agreed with me that the units under their command should remain under their command, and so 'small groups' was to mean their units. This was against Hitler's orders but it was impossible to consult with Krebs, as all telephone communication had been cut since early that morning.

About 13:00, the commanders went to their units. They felt a sense of moral relief, because they would not have to continue senseless fighting in Berlin. The future did not seem so gloomy for them.

I intended to reach the Reich Chancellery in the afternoon, but at 15:00, a Sturmführer arrived from there to see me having been ordered to deliver a personal letter from Hitler to me. I thought I might be going to be held to account for disobeying Hitler's orders as to the meaning of 'small groups'. My officers only let the Sturmführer come to my room alone after they had disarmed him.

Very tensely, I opened the letter. It was dated 30 April 1945. Hitler repeated exactly what had been said at the last meeting, namely that due to continuing lack of airborne supplies, a break-out in small groups was permitted. These groups must continue fighting wherever possible. Any capitulation must be decisively rejected. The letter was signed in pencil.

About 5pm, I was about to return to the Reich Chancellery when the Sturmführer returned. He was brought to me and handed me a note with the following contents: 'General Weidling must come immediately to the Reich Chancellery to see Krebs. All actions planned for the evening of 30 April must be postponed.' The signature was illegible.

From the Sturmführer, I learned that this note had been signed by the adjutant of Brigadenführer Mohnke, who commanded the defence of the government district and reported directly to Hitler.

Again, I was faced with a difficult decision. Was this all right? Was this order a trick by fanatics, who intended to fight in Berlin until the last bullet? Or maybe something had happened that put things in a completely different light? If I stayed here for one more night then there would be only one way out – surrender.

Taking all this into consideration, I decided to obey the order and go to the Reich Chancellery. The Bendlerstrasse was some 1200 metres from the Reich Chancellery. Usually it took a quarter of an hour to walk there, now it took five times as long, as I had to make my way through debris, cellars and gardens. Sweating, I reached the Reich Chancellery sometime around 6 or 7 pm. 'I was immediately taken to the Führer's study. Goebbels, Bormann and Krebs were already seated at the table. As I entered, they all stood up. Krebs solemnly stated the following:

1. Hitler had committed suicide at 3pm.
2. His death should be kept secret for the time being. Only a small circle of people knew about it. We were made to promise to keep the secret.
3. Hitler's corpse, according to his last will, had been soaked with petrol and burnt in a shell-hole in the grounds of the Reich Chancellery.
4. In his last will Hitler had appointed the following government:
5. Reichs president – Grand-Admiral Dönitz, Reichs Chancellor – Reichsminister Dr Goebbels.
6. Party Minister – Reichsleiter Bormann, Defence Minister – Field-Marshal Schörner, Interior Minister – Seyss-Inquart. Other ministerial posts were unoccupied, because they had no significance.
7. Marshal Stalin had been informed of this by radio.
8. Attempts had been made for the last two hours to contact the Russian High Command to arrange for a cease-fire in Berlin. If these were successful, the German government legally appointed by Hitler would begin talks with Russia concerning surrender. I was to be sent as a negotiator.

The mood of those present and the businesslike manner of Krebs' speech seemed strange. I had a feeling that all three of them were shaken by the death of Hitler, who had been their God until now. It seemed to me as if I were among a group of businessmen who were conferring after their boss had departed and despite myself I said: 'First I must eat. Do any of you have a cigarette? Now one can finally smoke in this room.'

Goebbels took out a pack of English cigarettes and offered them to all of us.

I used these few minutes to consider what Krebs had said. My first thought was: So we have been fighting for five and a half years for someone who committed suicide. Having drawn us into this terrible disaster, he himself chose the easy way out and left us to fend for ourselves. We must now end this madness as soon as possible.

I addressed Krebs as follows: 'Krebs, you lived in Moscow for a long time and should know the Russians better than anyone else. Do you believe they would agree to an armistice? Whatever happens, tomorrow or the day after, Berlin will fall into their hands like a ripe apple. The Russians know it as well as we do. In my opinion the Russians will only accept unconditional surrender. Shall we go on with this senseless fighting?'

Instead of Krebs, Goebbels answered. In powerful words he insisted that any thought of Berlin's capitulation must be rejected. 'Hitler's will is still compulsory for us'. Then, having calmed down, he said 'The traitor

Himmler tried and failed to hold talks with the English and Americans. The Russians would sooner agree to negotiate with a legal government than with a traitor. It is possible that we shall succeed in reaching a separate peace with Russia. It all depends on the rapid formation of a legal government, and for that we need a cease-fire.'

I replied 'Mr. Reich Minister, do you really think that Russia will enter into negotiations with the government in which you sit, the most ardent representative of National Socialism?' It was all I could manage to say.

Goebbels was offended and wanted to object but Krebs and Bormann intervened. Both tried to convince me of the need to make every effort to conclude a separate peace with Russia.

My opinion that only an unconditional surrender would be acceptable was not supported.

As for Krebs, I felt that he personally he agreed with me in many ways because he asked me to name someone with whom the Russians would agree to negotiate. For some reason, the name of Professor Sauerbruch came to mind. [Professor Ernst Sauerbruch was one of Germany's most famous and influential surgeons, renowned as a pioneer of thoracic surgery. He served as head of surgery at Berlin's Charité hospital, and continued performing operations there throughout the battle of Berlin when he worked from an underground bunker.]

Krebs did not dare to come up with his own opinion, as like the other two he supported the idea of a cease-fire. I was held in the Reich Chancellery, and had to wait for Krebs' return.

I managed to find out from Burgdorf and Bormann the details of Hitler's last hours. Lately, Hitler's fear of death had become noticeable. They said that if, for example, a shell hit the bunker, he gave orders to find out if anything was damaged. Generally, shells exploding above the bunker severely irritated Hitler.

On the night of 29–30 April, Hitler told those closest to him of his decision to commit suicide. Frau Goebbels apparently went on her knees before him, begging him not to abandon his people in this difficult hour.

Hitler took poison and shot himself. His wife Eva Braun also poisoned herself.

According to Hitler's last will, the corpses were to be burnt. Hitler had apparently said that he didn't want his body put on show in Moscow.

I was told that three SS men placed the bodies of Hitler and Eva Braun in a shell crater, doused them with gasoline and set the bodies on fire, then covered with earth.

That night of 30 April – 1 May was the first time I had heard that Hitler had lived with Eva Braun for the past 15 years. On 28 April Hitler, wearing a Volkssturm uniform, married Eva Braun in the Reich Chancellery. Through this marriage, Hitler sought to legalise his 15-year cohabitation.

I did not see Hitler's last will, and I don't know what he wrote. At 13:00 on 1 May, General Krebs returned to the Reich Chancellery. The Russians, as expected, had rejected the cease-fire proposal and demanded the unconditional surrender of Berlin.

My point of view again failed in the face of Goebbels' stubbornness, and the loyal Krebs and Bormann supported him. Capitulation was rejected. I received permission for the break-out I had planned earlier for the evening of 30 April, and I was released from my promise to keep silent about Hitler's death.

Meanwhile, as could be expected, the situation became so bad that a break-out could no longer be contemplated. On the night of 1/2 May, I surrendered to the Russians together with the units of which I was still in communication.

While in captivity, I heard that Hitler's body had not been found. This made me wonder whether Hitler's death was a sham.

I was badly shaken by the events of 30 April to 1 May, and believed the news of Hitler's death was the truth. At the time, it did not occur to me that Hitler's associates would abuse my trust and lie to me. I believed that Hitler was dead, and because of that, on the evening of 30 April, I had dared to tell Goebbels: 'Will History blame us, if we do not obey the will of a suicide?' (by this I meant Hitler's absolute refusal to surrender). Hitler deserted us in a terrible situation and because of that we have the right to act as we see fit.

On 2 May Weidling surrendered Berlin.

General Weidling remained in Soviet captivity for the rest of his life. He was detained at Vladimir Central Prison, in the Russian SFSR, Soviet Union. In 1952 he was sentenced to 25 years' imprisonment by a Soviet tribunal for alleged war crimes. He died on 17 November 1955 at the age of 64. According to KGB records the official cause of death was listed as heart failure ('arterial and cardiac sclerosis along with circulatory collapse'). He was buried in an unmarked grave at the prison cemetery

Chapter 10

HANNA REITSCH

It is not possible to determine the manner of Hitler's death with any certainty. There are too many conflicting accounts.

One of the most remarkable accounts of the last days in the bunker came from another outsider who provided a valuable insight into Hitler's mental state. Hanna Reitsch was a famous test pilot with numerous awards – the Iron Cross First Class during the Second World War – known for her pioneering achievements in aviation during the 1930s and 1940s. She was the first woman to pilot a rocket-powered aircraft (Messerschmitt Me 163) and a jet fighter (Messerschmitt Me 262). She was also an ardent Nazi and devoted admirer of Hitler.

On 24 April 1945, Hitler telegraphed Luftwaffe Lieutenant-General Ritter von Greim in Munich ordering him to report to the Reich Chancellery on a very urgent matter. This was an almost impossible task as the city was surrounded by the Russians. However, von Greim decided that it was possible to get through to the city with Hanna Reitsch's help as a pilot in an autogyro which could land in the streets or in the gardens near the Reich Chancellery.

The nearest gyrocopter, however, was at Rechlin, 750km away. By the following night, after a seven-hour journey by road, they reached the historic airfield, which served as the main testing site for the Luftwaffe, and were ready to fly to Berlin immediately.

But the only autogyro available had been damaged that day, so it was decided that von Greim would be flown by the sergeant-pilot who two days previously had taken Albert Speer to Hitler and thus had experience of the flight. Out of a sense of responsibility to von Greim as his personal pilot and friend, Reitsch asked to be taken along. A Focke-Wulf Fw 190 with only one passenger seat behind the pilot's seat was chosen for the flight. Reitsch clambered into the fuselage through a small emergency hatchway.

Forty fighters were detailed to escort them. Almost as soon as they took off, they encountered Russian fighters. After a low-level flight, they reached Gatow airfield, south-west of Berlin, and the only one still held by the Germans. Their plane made it with only a few minor hits to the wings, although the escort had suffered heavily.

The landing at Gatow took place during a Russian air raid, and the remaining escort fighters engaged the attackers while von Greim's plane landed safely. Immediately, an attempt was made to establish telephone contact with the Reich Chancellery, but all the lines had been cut.

It was decided to fly the rest of the way there in a Fieseler-Storch that was at the airfield and land close enough to Hitler's bunker to be able to walk there. Von Greim took the pilot's seat, with Reitsch as a passenger. The plane took off amid dog-fighting Russian and German aircraft. Von Greim managed to clear the airfield and flew at treetop height to the Brandenburg Gate.

Von Greim was wounded in the right leg by ground fire. Reitsch took the controls, reaching over von Greim's shoulders, and managed to land the plane on the East-West axis road. The moment they landed, heavy Russian artillery and small-arms fire rained down on the landing site. A passing car was commandeered to take them to Hitler's bunker. Von Greim received first aid on the way.

Von Greim and Reitsch arrived at the bunker between 6:00 and 7:00 on the morning of 26 April. Magda Goebbels was the first to meet them, rushing up to Reitsch with tears and kisses, expressing surprise that there still were people of courage and honesty to come to the Führer – unlike all those who had deserted him. Von Greim was immediately taken into an operating room where Hitler's doctor bandaged his wounded leg.

Reitsch recounted this dramatic event to an incredulous Captain Robert Work, Chief Interrogator of the United States Air Corps, three months later after she surrendered to the Americans. Work wrote in his report that according to Reitsch, Hitler came to the injured man's room, expressing his deep gratitude to von Greim for his arrival. He was saying something to the effect that even a soldier had the right not to obey an order if it was obvious that the fulfilment of such an order was useless and hopeless. After that, von Greim made an official report of his arrival.

Hitler then said to him: 'Do you know why I summoned you?

Von Greim: 'No. I don't, my Führer.'

Hitler: 'Because Hermann Göring betrayed and deserted me and the Fatherland. Behind my back, he established contact with the enemy.

His actions were a manifestation of cowardliness. And, contrary to my orders, he escaped to Berchtesgaden. From there, he sent me a disrespectful telegram. He said that some time ago I had appointed him as my successor and that now, when it was impossible for me to govern from Berlin, he was ready to rule instead of me from Berchtesgaden. He concluded the telegram with the statement that if he did not receive a reply from me by 9:30 today by telegraph, he would consider that I had agreed to this.'

Work said this scene was described by Reitsch as touchingly dramatic. She says that when the Führer was speaking about Göring's betrayal there were tears in his eyes, his head was bowed, his face was deathly white and when he handed this message to von Greim the paper shook in his trembling hand.

Reitsch said 'While von Greim was reading, the Führer's face was very gloomy. Then its every muscle started to twitch, and his breathing became intermittent. With an effort, he regained enough control to shout: "An ultimatum! Harsh ultimatum! Now there is nothing left. Nothing was spared me. There is no one faithful, no honesty left. There is no disillusionment that has not befallen me, no treacheries I have not endured and now – this on top of all. There is nothing left. All the evil has been already done to me."'

According to Reitsch's description, it was a classical 'Et Tu, Brute' scene, full of lamentations and self-pity. For a long time, Hitler couldn't continue. With a harsh look in his half-closed eyes and in an unusually low voice he said: 'I shall immediately arrest Göring as a traitor to the Reich. I stripped him of all ranks and removed him from all his positions. That's why I summoned you. By this, I proclaim you the successor to Göring as Air Force Supreme Commander. In the name of the German people, I give you my hand.'

Hitler's adjutant, Otto Günsche, while in Russian captivity, later described this scene when Hitler received news of Göring's betrayal. Günsche said he took Göring's radio message directly to Hitler in his study. The Führer was sitting with Eva Braun on the sofa facing the door. When Günsche told him that he must speak urgently to him, Hitler looked at him suspiciously. He nodded at Eva who immediately left the room. At Hitler's signal Günsche read out the message. He had not come to the end of the first sentence, however, before Hitler jumped up and tore the message out of his hand.

With trembling fingers he put on his spectacles. His face puffed up. It turned as red as a turkey from fury. 'Oh this Göring!' he groaned. 'Responsibility of internal and external affairs! To make me an ultimatum!' He crumpled up the radio message in his fist, dropped into a chair and, moaning, covered his face with both hands. A minute later, he blurted out, 'Send a message to Göring at once! Write this down!' Hitler began to dictate in clipped phrases: 'I am as ever in possession of all power and do not feel in any way limited in my freedom of movement. I forbid you to assume power in any way. Adolf Hitler.' He fell silent and stared into the middle distance.

Feverishly, Hitler commanded, 'Get me Bormann immediately!' Günsche left the study and told Bormann about Göring's radio message. Bormann hurried off to see Hitler, while Günsche went off to the room containing the radio station and ordered Hitler's message to be sent to Göring immediately.

Linge was standing in the antechamber when Bormann, red as a beetroot, tumbled past him and headed into Hitler's study. 'That toe-rag Göring', he muttered in passing. Bormann stoked up Hitler's anger yet more and drove him to the point of incandescence: 'That pig Göring. He knows full well that your answer cannot arrive before 10.00 p.m.!' he screamed.

Reitsch continued that Hitler threw a tantrum. Pummelling the table with his fists, he yelled, 'Bormann, issue orders to our criminal police on the Obersalzberg to arrest Göring immediately! Send the message at once! If he tries to run away he must be shot on the spot!' Bormann ran out with great zeal. As he dashed past Linge he called out to the duty officer of the bodyguard to send him Högl straightaway. (Peter Högl was an SS-Obersturmbannführer, who served as deputy commander of the Reichssicherheitsdienst (RSD), Adolf Hitler's personal security and bodyguard service during World War II. He was killed by the Russians while trying to escape the bunker.) Then he went to Goebbels. When Högl appeared in the bunker, Bormann went with him to the radio station to have Hitler's order transmitted. The commander of the Obersalzberg, SS-Obersturmbannführer Frank, was given the order to arrest Göring.

Von Greim and Hanna Reitsch were deeply shocked by the news of Göring's betrayal. As if by some previous arrangement, both of them grabbed Hitler's hands, asking to be allowed to stay in the bunker and to sacrifice their lives for the great sin that Göring had committed against the Führer, the German people and the Air Force itself. They asked to be allowed to stay to preserve the honour of the fallen pilots, to restore the honour of the Air Force, profaned by Göring, and to guarantee the honour of their Fatherland in the eyes of the whole world. Hitler agreed and said that they might stay and that their decision would be remembered in the history of the Air Force for a long time. But back in Rechlin it had been decided that, the next day, a plane would arrive to remove von Greim and Reitsch from Berlin. Now that they had decided to stay, there was no way to tell anyone that their plans had changed. Aircraft after aircraft was sent from Rechlin but they were shot down one by one by the Russians. At last, on 27 April, a Ju 52 carrying SS personnel and ammunition managed to land on the east-west axis road, but because von Greim and Reitsch had decided to stay, it was sent away empty. (The order for Göring's dismissal had been issued from the underground Supreme Headquarters on approximately 23 April.)

Later, on this first evening, Hitler summoned Reitsch to his room. She recollected that his face was deeply wrinkled and there was always a misty film over his eyes. He said in a very low voice: 'Hanna, you are one of the people who want to die with me. Each of us has a small bottle of poison like this.' And he gave her a bottle for herself and another for von Greim. 'I don't want any of us to fall into the hands of the Russians and I don't want them to find our corpses. Everyone is responsible for the annihilation of their bodies so that nothing is left for identification. Eva and I will burn our bodies. Find your own means for yourself. Would you give a bottle to Greim?'

Reitsch slumped into a chair in tears. Not because, she says, that she now knew she was finished, but because for the first time realised that the Führer considered the game lost. Weeping, she asked: 'My Führer, why are you here? Why are you robbing Germany of your life? If it were known that you were staying in Berlin to the very end, the people would be struck with horror. "The Führer must live to enable Germany to live", the people will say. Save yourself, my Führer, this is the wish of every German.'

Hitler replied 'No, Hanna, if I die, it will be for the honour of our Nation, because being as a soldier I must obey my own orders according to which I would defend Berlin to the end. My dear girl, I didn't expect this. I strongly believed that Berlin would be saved on the banks of the Oder. We sent all we had to hold that position. Believe me, when our greatest effort brought no results, I was more horrified than anyone else. Later, when the city was being surrounded, the thought that there still were 3 million of my compatriots. But, my Hanna, I still cherish one hope. General Wenck's Army is coming from the South. He must stand and he will drive the Russians back far enough to save our nation. Then we will rise again.'

Reitsch went on 'It almost seemed as if he believed it himself, and when he had finished, he paced the room with long, quick, uneven strides, clenching his hands behind his back, his head shaking with every step. Although his words expressed hope his appearance showed that the war was ended.'

She returned to von Greim and gave him the poison, and they decided that if the end came, they would quickly drink the contents of the bottles and then each clutch a hand grenade to their chests and pull the pin.

Late on the night of 26–27 April the first heavy shelling of the Chancellery began. The explosions of heavy artillery and the crash of collapsing buildings directly above the bunker caused everyone such nervous strain that through the doors someone could be heard crying. Hanna spent the night looking after von Greim, who was in considerable pain, and she kept hand grenades ready in case the Russians reached the Chancellery that morning.

Next morning, she was introduced to the other people in the bunker and for the first rime found out who would be facing death with the Führer. She said that in the bunker on 27 April were: Goebbels and his wife and six children; State Secretary Naumann; Hitler's right-hand man Reichsleiter Martin Bormann; Hewel from Ribbentrop's Chancellery; Admiral Voss, Dönitz's representative; General Krebs and his aide-de-camp Burgdorf; Hitler's personal pilot Hans Baur; Beetz, another pilot; Eva Braun; SS Obergruppenführer Fegelein (later executed for treason), who was Himmler's liaison officer and the husband of Eva Braun's sister; Hitler's personal physician Dr Stumpfegger; Colonel von Below, Hitler's Air Force aide-de-camp; Dr Lorenz, the representatives of the Press Chief Dr Dietrich; two of Hitler's secretaries – Frau Christian, the wife of Air Force General Christian and Fraulein Krüger; and assorted orderlies and SS messengers. Reitsch says that was everyone.

Reitsch says she did not have much contact with most of those staying in the bunker, being mainly engaged in looking after von Greim. But she had opportunities to talk to many of them and to observe their reactions to the state of affairs in the bunker during those last days.

According to Work's report, 'She appears to try to describe her observations truthfully and sincerely. It should be remembered that before Reitsch reached the bunker, she had had little contact with the majority of those people and she had rather a low opinion of them. Among those whom she could closely observe, the Goebbels couple possibly stand apart.'

She described Goebbels' terrible shock at Göring's betrayal. 'He paced his small, luxurious room with long strides like an animal, murmuring malicious accusations about the Air Force commander and what he had done. The desperate military situation – was Göring's fault. Their current suffering – was Göring's fault. If the war were lost, as seemed inevitable, then it would also be Göring's fault.'

'That swine', Goebbels said, 'who always presented himself as the Führer's main helpmate, now hasn't the courage to be beside him. Moreover, he wants to replace the Führer as Head of the State. He, who understands nothing, who destroyed the Fatherland by his mistakes and stupidity, now wants to rule the Nation. That is enough to prove that in fact he never was truly one of us, that deep in his heart he was always weak and a traitor.'

All this, according to Hanna, was performed theatrically with extravagantly waving hands and complicated gestures. His nervous loping about the room made the spectacle even funnier. When he was not attacking Göring, he was addressing the world, praising those who were providing an historic example by staying in the bunker. As if he were on a platform, grasping a chair as if it were a lectern, he declaimed: 'We show to the world how people can die for their honour and our deaths will be an eternal example for all the Germans, both friends and enemies. One day, the whole world will recognise that we were right, that we thought to defend the world from Bolshevism with our lives. Someday this will be written down in history forever.'

Obviously, Goebbels practised his greatest talent to the end. His room was next to Reitsch's and the doors were usually open. Through them, Goebbels could be heard speaking at all hours of the day and night. And all the time he spoke of 'honour, of how to die, of how to stay loyal to the Führer till the end, of the example that will shine as a sacred thing in the tablets of History'. One of the last phrases that Reitsch heard from the master of propaganda was: 'We shall die for the glory of the Reich, so that Germany will live forever.'

Robert Work's report said even Reitsch had to come to the conclusion that Goebbels' performance, notwithstanding the desperate situation, was a little exaggerated and completely theatrical. She says it seemed to her that Goebbels usually behaved as if he were addressing a legion of attentive historians who were writing down his every word. She adds that her own opinion of Goebbels' pretentiousness, his superficial knowledge and artificial oratory, was completely confirmed by these tricks. She also says that, having listened to these tirades, she and von Greim often asked themselves sadly, shaking their heads: 'And these are the people who ruled our country?'

Magda Goebbels, according to Hanna Reitsch, often thanked God that she was alive and could kill her children to save them from any 'evil' which would follow defeat. She said to Reitsch: 'My dear Hanna, when the end comes, you must help me with the children if I lack strength. You must help me to leave this life. They belong to the Third Reich and the Führer and if both go, there will be no place here for the children. But you must help me. Most of all I am afraid that at the last moment I won't have the strength.' Hanna thought that at the last moment she did have the strength.

Robert Work said Hanna's notes 'lead us to the conclusion that Frau Goebbels was just one of the most convinced listeners to the highly skilful speeches of her own husband and presented the most extreme example of the Nazi influence on German women'.

Hanna Reitsch also had a firm opinion about Eva Braun, and did not believe that she and Hitler would marry. According to Reitsch's impressions, the Führer's girlfriend was strictly faithful to her ornamental role in the Führer's circle. She spent most of the time polishing her nails, changing her dress every hour and having her hair done etc. She obviously took the prospect of death with the Führer for granted and behaved as if she were saying: 'Has not our affair lasted for 12 years and did I not threaten to commit suicide when Hitler once wanted to get rid of me. It would be a much simpler death and cleaner.' Reitsch said she repeatedly said. 'Poor, poor Adolf, everyone left him, everyone betrayed him. Better ten thousand others die than he is lost to Germany.'

Reitsch said that in Hitler's presence, she was always charming and cared for his needs in every way. But only when she was with him did she keep this performance up. Once he had left the room and could not hear her, she would start talking about the ungrateful swine who had abandoned their Führer and that they should all be killed.

'These remarks sounded childish', Reitsch said, 'and it seemed that at that moment the only good Germans were those in the bunker and all the others were traitors, because they were not here to die with him. The reason for her willingness to die with the others was the same as that of Frau Goebbels: after the Third Reich, Germany would not be fit for true Germans to live in. Often, she expressed her sorrow that there were people who could not kill themselves and who would have to live without "honour, like human beings without a soul".'

Reitsch emphasised Braun's obviously limited intellectual abilities, but says that she was a very beautiful woman. 'Reitsch thinks it hardly possible that Braun had any wide-ranging influence on Hitler. The rumours of a last-minute marriage ceremony Reitsch considers highly unlikely not only because, according to her, Hitler did not have such, but because the situation in the bunker at the time would have made such ceremony ridiculous. Up to the moment when Reitsch left the bunker, only a day before the announcement of Hitler's death, there was no talk of such a marriage. She quickly rejects rumours that there were children from the affair as fantastic.'

During Hanna's stay in the bunker, Hitler's behaviour and his physical state deteriorated even further. At first, it seemed that he played his part, defending Germany and Berlin, and at the beginning this was still possible to a certain extent, because communications were still fairly reliable. Information reached them through the telephone in the flak-tower and also from a radio with a portable antenna attached to a balloon. But each day it was getting more difficult and finally by the evening of 28 April and all day on the 29th it was almost impossible to maintain communications.

She said the 20 April conference, during what seemed to be the last meeting of the War Council held by Hitler in Reich Chancellery, the Führer, it was reported, was so depressed by the hopeless situation that he expressed his complete despair in front of the whole Council. In the bunker, Hanna heard that after this, even the greatest optimists in Hitler's entourage believed that the war was truly lost. According to Reitsch, after this shock in the conference-room, Hitler never recovered either physically or morally.

'Sometimes it seemed that he still counted on the success of General Wenck, who was trying to break through from the south. He spoke of little else and throughout the 28th and 29th he was making tactical plans that Wenck could use to liberate Berlin. He paced the bunker, waving a road map, which almost disintegrated in his clammy hands, and described plans for Wenck's campaign to anyone who would listen. When his excitement reached its peak, he grabbed the map and paced the room with quick, nervous steps, directing the defence of the city with armies that no longer existed' (because even Wenck's army had been defeated, something that Hitler did not know).

Reitsch describes a pathetic picture of a complete ruin of a man. A tragicomedy of disillusionment, fruitlessness and futility 'to see a man, running blindly from one wall to another in his last retreat, brandishing papers that shook in his trembling hands or sitting at his table, moving the sweat-slicked counters on the map that showed his non- existent armies, like a boy playing war games'.

Reitsch's account to the Americans of the final hours in the bunker shows that she had great respect for the Führer. It says 'What she says about her opinion of him suffering considerably in the last stages of the war could be true. She described obvious mistakes by the leadership, which she saw or heard about in the bunker. For example, Berlin did not have enough ammunition to secure the German position on the Oder. When this defensive line was penetrated, it turned out that there were no proper plans for the defence of Berlin itself, nor the proper means to command that defence from the bunker. There were no external communications apart from the telephone in the flak-tower. It is possible that Hitler only decided at the last moment to command the fighting from the bunker, so he lacked the necessary means to do so. There were no maps, no battle plans and no radio, only hastily-established messenger communications and one telephone. The fact that several days after the defeat of Wenck's army, Hitler was unaware of it, is only one example of the results of this poor organisation. Consequently, the Führer of Germany remained helplessly in his bunker, playing war games on the table.'

At the end of the report on her stay in the bunker Reitsch repeats that 'such a man should never be allowed to rule Germany, or any other nation, again'. But strangely she doesn't seem to blame him personally for all the evil that was done, which she completely recognises and readily points out. She says: 'The responsibility is largely that of the people who manipulated him, misled him, criminally misdirected and misinformed him. But he can't be forgotten because it was he who chose those who manipulated him.'

'Hitler finished his life as a criminal before the world', she says in the report, but is quick to add 'He began differently. At the beginning, he thought only of how to re-vitalise Germany, how to give his people a life without economic hardship and inadequate social protection. To achieve this, he played a big game, bragging that there was no one who could control the life of his people (except for him?). It was his first big mistake, his first major shortcoming. But when the initial risks brought success, he repeated the mistake of all gamblers – he started to risk more and more, and winning each time, it was easy for him to risk bigger stakes each time.'

According to Reitsch, this all started with the occupation of the Ruhr. It was the first and most difficult gamble of all, and when the world did not respond with war to his Ruhr bluff, all of the subsequent stakes were easily won.

Every new success increased the enthusiasm of the people, and that gave him support for the next step. In the end, as Reitsch says, Hitler himself changed, turning from an idealistic benefactor into a greedy and cowardly despot. He fell victim to his own megalomania. 'It should never again be allowed in the history of the world', she concludes, 'for one man to have such power.'

There was no event called 'Hitler's occupation of the Ruhr'. It most likely refers to the 1923–5 period when French and Belgian troops occupied Germany's Ruhr industrial region in response to

Germany defaulting on First World War reparations payments – not an occupation initiated or led by Adolf Hitler.

However, this occupation was highly significant in Hitler's political rise. The French-Belgian occupation, combined with the economic crisis and hyperinflation it triggered, fuelled anger and nationalism in Germany. Hitler and the Nazi Party exploited this resentment, using the occupation and Germany's humiliation as key justifications for their own attempted coup – the Beer Hall Putsch in November 1923. Although Hitler was not in government and had no military control in 1923, he used the events surrounding the Ruhr occupation to gain national attention for the Nazi party and to position himself as a defender of German interests against foreign occupation.

Reitsch's account of the events continued: 'On the night of 27/28 April, the Russian shelling of the Chancellery reached its peak. The accuracy seemed amazing to those of us who were underneath. It seemed that every shell landed exactly where the previous one had, centring on the Chancellery building. It demonstrated that the Russians might arrive at any moment, so the Führer assembled the second suicide council. Again, all the plans to destroy the bodies of everyone in the bunker were repeated. It was decided that as the Russians entered the grounds of the Chancellery, the mass suicide would begin.'

The last instructions were given on how to extract the poison from the vials. Everyone was in a kind of trance after this meeting about suicide, and a general discussion started on how to completely destroy human bodies. After that, some people made short speeches swearing allegiance to the Führer and Germany, which were repeated again and again. But there was still a glimmer of hope that Wenck would hold out long enough to let them escape. Even on the 27th, Reitsch says, they were only repeating this in imitation of the Führer. Almost all had lost their hope of salvation and they talked about it when Hitler was not around.

Concluding their discussions on annihilation of the bodies, it was decided that the SS should receive orders to make sure there was no trace of them. All day on the 28th, the heavy shelling continued and discussions about suicide were held in the bunker to the accompaniment of exploding shells.

Then, on the 29th, the heaviest blow fell. A telegram was received to the effect that Hitler's bulwark, Himmler, had joined Göring on the list of traitors. For everyone, it was like a deadly blow. Reitsch says that all the men and women cried and shouted in fury, fear and desperation, everything mixed up in one crazy convulsion. Himmler, the Protector of the Reich, is a traitor! It was impossible. The telegram said that

Himmler had contacted the American and British authorities through Sweden and proposed surrender at the conference in San Francisco. Hitler raved like a man possessed. His face was red and virtually unrecognisable. The additional proof of Himmler's betrayal was that he had asked not to be named in connection with the proposal. They said that the American command was satisfied with this proposal but the British were not.

After a long paroxysm of rage, Hitler sank into a torpor and for the time being all in the bunker were silent. Information arrived subsequently that the Russians would launch an all-out attack to take the Reich Chancellery on the morning of the 30th. At the same time, small-arms fire was heard above the bunker. According to reports, the Russians were approaching the Potsdamer Platz, killing thousands and fanatically preparing for the attack which was to start the next morning.

Reitsch says that everyone once again looked to their poison vials. Then came the order to evacuate the bunker. At 1:30 in the morning of 30 April, Hitler entered von Greim's room, his face white as chalk, and sat heavily on the edge of his bed. He said: 'Our only hope is Wenck, and to make it possible for him to arrive we should summon the Air Force to protect his advance.' Then Hitler said he had been informed that Wenck's artillery was shelling the Russians in the Potsdamer Platz.

'All available aircraft', Hitler said, 'should be summoned at daybreak, so I order you to return to Rechlin and to send your planes from there. The mission of your air force is to pound the positions from which the Russians want to start the attack on the Chancellery. With the help of the Air Force, Wenck will come. This is the first reason why you should leave the bunker. The second is that it is necessary to stop Himmler.' And as he named the Führer of SS, his voice became less confident, and his hands and lips trembled . . . Von Greim was ordered to arrest Himmler immediately if he had really contacted the enemy and could be found.

'Never should a traitor be my successor as Führer! You have to leave here to prevent it.'

Von Greim and Reitsch protested energetically, saying that the attempt would be fruitless, that it was impossible to reach Rechlin and that they preferred to die in the bunker, that the plan would fail and that it was crazy.

'Your sacred duty as soldiers of the Reich', replied Hitler, 'is to do everything possible. This is the only chance for success. Your duty and mine is to take it.'

Hanna was not convinced. 'No, no' she shouted. 'What can be done now even if we do break through? All is lost; it is crazy to try to change anything.' But von Greim thought differently. 'Hanna, we are the only hope for those staying here. Even if there is only a tiny chance, we must take it. If we don't go, we'll deprive them of the only ray of hope left. Maybe Wenck is there. Maybe we can help. Whether we can help or not, we'll go.'

Hanna, still convinced that the attempt was senseless, went alone to the Führer while von Greim was getting ready. Sobbing, she asked: 'My Führer, why, why don't you allow us to stay?' He looked at her and said only: 'May God preserve you.'

All the preparations were made very quickly, and Reitsch describes their parting in every detail. Göring's former liaison officer to the Führer, now von Greim's, said: 'You should go. It is up to you to tell the truth to our people, to save the honour of the Air Force, to save the image of Germany for the world.' Everyone gave them something to take away with them into the world they were about to leave. Everyone quickly wrote final short letters. Reitsch says that she and von Greim delivered all of them, except for two letters from Goebbels and his wife to their eldest son by Frau Goebbels' first marriage, who was in an Allied prisoner-of-war camp. These letters were found with Reitsch. Magda Goebbels gave her a diamond ring from her finger to wear in remembrance of her.

The whole city was engulfed in flames and rifle fire could be heard very close by. The SS troops who guarded Hitler until the end were being forced back into a circle. These soldiers provided a small armoured car to take von Greim and Reitsch to the Brandenburg Gate where an Arado Ar 96 was hidden. The air was full of the sound of exploding shells, some of them falling so close that their car was damaged several yards from the shelter in which the Arado was hidden.

Reitsch says she is sure that it was the last plane available. She says the rumours that there was another airworthy plane available that could have flown Hitler out are highly improbable because von Greim would certainly have known about it. She knows that there was no such aircraft. She also knows that von Greim sent other planes but all of them were shot down. And because the city was already completely surrounded by the Russians, she is sure that Hitler remained in Berlin.

A wide street leading from the Brandenburg Gate was to be their runway. They had 40m of flat, undamaged road to use. They took off in a hail of bullets, and when the plane reached rooftop height it was caught by many searchlights and shot at. The plane was tossed about like a feather by the shell-bursts, but only a few splinters hit it. Reitsch circled up to an altitude of 20,000ft, from which the city below looked like a sea of fire. From up there, the extent of the destruction seemed immense and fantastic. Heading north, they reached Rechlin in 50 minutes, again landing under fire from Russian fighters.

Von Greim immediately ordered all available planes to be sent to help Berlin. Having fulfilled Hitler's first order, he decided to fly to Plön near Kiel to find our if Dönitz had any news about Himmler. He flew there in a Junkers Ju 181. As they took off, German pilots were already arriving in response to von Greim's order. The skies were practically full of German and Russian aircraft. To escape detection, Reitsch flew as low as 1–2m above the ground, and even then they were attacked twice.

After they landed in Lübeck, they had to go by car to Plön and again they were under constant Russian air attack. On arrival, they learned that Dönitz knew nothing about Himmler's activities. The next trip they made was to Keitel to organise any necessary changes in air tactics to support Wenck's entry into Berlin. They found Keitel early on the morning of 1 May and he told them that Wenck's army had already been defeated or captured and that he (Keitel) had sent a report about it to Hitler (on 30 April). Now von Greim and Reitsch knew that Hitler had probably given up hope, and they were both sure that the well-laid plans for suicide had been put into effect.

The advance of the British troops forced von Greim and Reitsch to retreat to Schleswig on the evening of 1 May. Here, Reitsch and von Greim learned that Hitler's death had been announced and that his successor was Dönitz. On 2 May, the new Government was called to Floen. Von Greim and Reitsch, to receive orders from Doenitz as to the immediate Luftwaffe activities, had the additional purpose of meeting Himmler and confronting him with the betrayal story.

Reitsch says Himmler arrived late so that all the others were in the conference room, leaving Reitsch alone when he walked in.

'One moment, Herr Reichsführer, I have a question of great importance. Do you have any time?' Reitsch asked.

Himmler looked almost playful as he answered: 'Yes, sure.'

'Is it correct, that you, Herr Reichsführer, contacted the Allies offering peace without Hitler's orders?'

'Why, sure.'

'You betrayed your Führer and the people at the worst moment. It is high treason, Herr Reichsführer. You did it when your place was in the bunker with Hitler.'

'High treason? No! You'll see that History will see it in a proper perspective. Hitler wanted to go on with the struggle. He was driven mad by his arrogance and his sense of honour. He still wanted to shed German blood when there was no blood left. Hitler was insane. This should have been stopped long ago.'

'Insane? I left him less than 36 hours ago', Reitsch replied 'He died for the cause he believed in. He died bravely and full of the honour you are talking about, and as for you, Göring and the others, you shall live branded as traitors and cowards.'

Himmler: 'What I did, I did to save German blood, to save what was left of our country.'

'You talk about German blood. Herr Reichsführer? You talk about it now? You should have thought about it years ago, before you were associated with this useless bloodshed.' A sudden air raid interrupted this conversation.

Von Greim said that in the first war council at Dönitz's headquarters little was decided, but all agreed that it was possible to hold out for only a few days more, while the commanders on the Russian front were ordered to stand firm until the end so as to enable as many people as possible to escape. Reitsch says that von Greim, despite the deteriorating condition of his wounded leg, insisted on immediately flying to see Field-Marshal Schörner, commander of the forces in Silesia and Czechoslovakia, to instruct him to continue resistance, even after the order to surrender.

During the flight to Schörner, the pain of von Greim's wound was so bad that sometimes he lost consciousness. On arrival, Schörner informed them that he had already decided to hold out as long as possible and had already ordered this before von Greim's arrival.

It was then decided to fly to Kesselring with the same message, but von Greim's leg was in such a state that it was impossible to move him. From 3 to 7 May they had to stay at Schörner's headquarters in Königgratz where Reitsch cared for von Greim until he was able to be moved again.

On the night of 7 May, they flew in a Dornier Do 217 to Graz, where Kesselring was reported to be. When they were directly over the airfield, German anti-aircraft guns damaged their plane and it crash-landed at the end of the runway. Reitsch and von Greim learnt that the capitulation would take place on the night of 9 May and hearing that Kesselring had left Graz for Zell-am-Zee, they flew there to give him his instructions.

They arrived at Zell-am-Zee in a Fieseler Storch and reached General Koller, Chief of the General Staff of the Air Force, who could tell them where Kesselring was. Here, they learnt that the capitulation would take place on the 8th, not the 9th. They still wanted to see Kesselring, but Koller preferred not to say where he was, either because it was too late or he did not know that Kesselring was in the village of Almdorf, several miles to the north of Zell-am-Zee. On hearing this, Reitsch and von Greim decided that any further efforts on their part would be absolutely fruitless. Before the capitulation, they left Zel-am-Zee for Kitzbühl to see a famous doctor who had just opened a clinic there. Reitsch says that if it had not been for von Greim's weakened state, she would not have been be able to force him to save his leg; to the end, he wanted to support resistance against the Russians.

In answer to the question why the last redoubt in Austria and Southern Germany was not used, Reitsch has little to add to what is already known. She says that as early as 15 April it seemed that everything had been prepared to move the government and the military headquarters to Berchtesgaden. All the offices and headquarters in Berlin were on constant two-hour alert at that time. It seems from the account of Colonel Below and others that the meeting mentioned above was intended to work out this proposal in detail. She says that the reports Hitler received were so dire that he was convinced it was impossible to complete the preparations for a successful defence from the redoubt in time. It was believed that Hitler's loss of confidence was caused by the realisation that this 'redoubt' project, which had been expected to be so successful, had finally been abandoned. It was also said that Göring and Hitler had a serious argument about it. Göring insisted on an early evacuation to the 'redoubt' but Hitler refused, in the hope that the line on the Oder would hold.

Supposedly, Göring argued that the redoubt was completed while Hitler preferred to wait until its readiness was proved at the above-mentioned conference. Later, at a war council at Dönitz's headquarters, they said that Göring's departure could be explained by the fact that he knew that the Oder line would not hold and hoped in vain that only the partly-finished redoubt would do so. The failure of the 'redoubt' was due first to Göring's failure to complete it, and Hitler's belief that continued resistance in Berlin would be more effective than a retreat to a partially-completed redoubt.

Von Greim and Reitsch arrived in Kitzbühl on the morning of the 9th and were brought before the American military authorities. Von Greim was under interrogation until 23 May and then brought to Salzburg before being sent to Germany as a prisoner of war. On the night of 24 May, he committed suicide in Salzburg, using the poison capsule Hitler had given him.

Although he was far less well-known, both in Germany and abroad, than his corpulent predecessor, Hanna believes he should have had

Göring's job years ago. She considers the fact that he disagreed with Göring about almost everything was sufficient proof of his abilities.

The American interrogation report by Robert Work concludes that the information 'presented above was given in good faith and with a sincere wish to speak correctly and accurately'.

> The suicide of her family, the death of her closest friend, von Greim, the physical sufferings of Germany and all she experienced in the last days of the war led her to also seriously contemplate suicide. She says that she lives now only for the truth, to tell the truth about Göring, a petty showman, to tell the truth about Hitler, criminally incapable and to tell the truth to the German people about that dangerous form of rule that created the Third Reich. She believes that by answering the investigator she has fulfilled a major part of her mission. For this reason, we consider that her account can be taken as a profound effort to be truthful and honest. She is now experiencing a difficult inner struggle, trying to reconcile her understanding of 'honour' with her evidence concerning Göring, Himmler and Hitler himself. These difficulties, it seems, are not so great when she talks to the investigator as when she talks to private individuals.
>
> But according to information which the investigator has received from private individuals whom she has contacted and with whom she was not previously acquainted, it can be seen that she has tried to influence her compatriots in a more progressive and democratic way.

The report is dated 8 October 1945, and signed by Robert E. Work, Captain, Air Corps Chief Investigator.

By the third week of May Elena Rzhevskaya and her team believed they had completed their work in establishing that Hitler and his cohorts were dead.

Their official report reads:

> After completion of the forensic medical examination and the carrying out of all operational measures for their identification, all the bodies were buried in the area of the city of Buch.
>
> In connection with the relocation of the counterintelligence department 'SMERSH' in Berlin, the bodies were exhumed and transported first to the area of the city of Rathenow, (about 90 kilometres north-west of Berlin) The bodies are in wooden boxes, in a grave at a depth of 1.7 meters.

The report then gives a detailed description of the location at Rathenow:

> Along the road from Rathenow toward Pritzerbe, before reaching the railway line of Friedersdorf, that is, 825 metres from the railway bridge,

along the forest clearing, from the stone marker with the number 111; north-east to the next wooden boundary marker with the same number 111; 635 metres from this marker in the same direction to the next stone (wooden) boundary marker with the same number 111; – 55 metres from this 8th marker, strictly to the east – 26 metres.

And then, on 3 June 1945, the bodies were once more moved to a location near the city of Stendal, before once again being exhumed at a later date and moved to the city of Magdeburg.

But everything was not finished. Suddenly, 'Operation Myth' began, which Rzhevskaya believes was the start of the cover-up. While the official report says the bodies were initially buried in the area of the City of Buch, the actual location was Finow, about 8km away.

She recounted how this operation started:

On 18 May, a general appeared from General Headquarters, flanked by Lieutenant General Alexander Vadis [Chief of SMERSH Counter-Intelligence for the Central, Belorussian, and 1st Belorussian Fronts], Andrey Miroshnichenko and other bigwigs from our army headquarters, with, we were told, instructions from Stalin to check everything relating to Hitler's death and return with a report.

Miroshnichenko could have been in big trouble for failing to realise that Stalin's reluctance to make Hitler's death public, or indeed to let anyone else know about it, did not indicate that he was prepared to take the fact on trust, without having everything thoroughly verified by his personal representative. Stalin wanted to 'own' this secret all by himself.

Something major was afoot. Käthe Heusermann and dental technician Fritz Echtmann had been arrested and brought in; SS bodyguard Harry Mengershausen, whom we had questioned, reappeared. A new investigation began. The whole identification and interrogation process restarted and was referred to as a repetition.

In these interrogations, Käthe Heusermann and Fritz Echtmann are referred to as 'detainees'. This time, each interrogation was preceded by an official warning to me, as the interpreter, of my potential liability under Article such-and-such. At no time during the war, no matter what level I was translating for, had there been anything of that kind. This was new. In part, no doubt, it reflected the special burden of responsibility I bore in the interrogation, but it reflected no less the coming of a new, post-war era.

During the war there had been more trust and less formality but, of course, a full seventeen days had elapsed since victory had been celebrated in Berlin. The general studied everything, asked questions and listened attentively.

He did not sign the records, but during breaks their text was forwarded verbatim to General Headquarters over the government's special high-security communication lines. The records were signed by the assembled top brass and, in front of my eyes, I witnessed the brazen falsification of history.

Anyone reading those documents would suppose Miroshnichenko was the leading figure in the investigation, the man who made history. It was straightforward fraud. Gorbushin [Rzhevskaya's boss and friend] is nowhere in the records. The historian commentators, bless them, are unaware that he had been sent off to Flensburg as a member of the Allied Commission.

[Gorbushin was involved in liaising with the Allies about the death of Heinrich Himmler, who had poisoned himself with a cyanide pill after being recognised following his arrest by Allied soldiers. He received their official reports and passed it on to Moscow.]

At the end of the second day, this terribly senior investigation reached its climax. Picture the scene: a small town, the gentle light of evening, and a strange procession on its way to the city outskirts. There, in sparse woodland, during the curfew to ensure no snoopy spy among the local townsfolk should witness the deed, the crates containing the remains brought from Buch had been committed to the earth and a covert 24-hour guard deployed.

Now Major Bystrov again walks ahead, showing the way. Behind him, the general, the Supreme Government Inspector, so to speak. Next, the military. Next, Hitler's dentists Heusermann and Echtmann. Next the Führer's bodyguard, Mengershausen, then some others.

Hardly speaking among ourselves, we walk slowly, oppressed by knowledge of what is imminent, our approaching confrontation of the mystery that always surrounds death. Finally we enter the woodland. The crates have already been exhumed.

Another report is compiled. All present, the Germans as well as the Soviet military (except for the general), sign. This report, compiled in the presence of his nuncio, is for Stalin himself.

The materials discovered by the investigation, the irrefutable proof of Hitler's death, namely his jaw and his denture, are readied before my eyes to be sent to front headquarters and thence, presumably, to Moscow with the general, who departs shortly afterwards.

Judging by the documents soon after the general left Finow there was an influx to 'the heights' of top secret information concerning the discovery of Hitler's body'. The Council of Ministers Archive preserves a 'Note' via the top-security line, sent by Lieutenant General Vadis to Beria (Chief of the NKVD) and Abakumov on 23 May 1945, 'detailing the circumstances of the discovery of the bodies of Hitler and Eva Braun; the testimony of Kunz and Schneider, the former having heard about Hitler's suicide from Goebbels, while the latter reported the request for petrol; the interrogations of Günsche and Linge confirming the fact of the suicide and burning of the bodies; and the identification of Hitler's teeth by Fritz Echtmann and Käthe Heusermann'.

And the note from Beria to Comrade Stalin and to Comrade Molotov, passing on the information. Everyone was very busy, but what would Stalin do? Would he announce the discovery?

Next, Colonel Gorbushin was summoned to Moscow to report on Hitler to Stalin. Gorbushin had just returned from Flensburg. When he returned from Moscow, he told Bystrov and myself he had been ordered not to leave his hotel room and to await a call from Stalin, which never came. Instead, he was summoned by Abakumov, who said, 'Comrade Stalin has familiarised himself with the entire course of events and the documents relating to the discovery of Hitler, and he has no questions. He considers the matter closed. At the same time, Comrade Stalin said, 'but we shall not make this public. The capitalist encirclement continues.'

Vasiliy Gorbushin told me and Bystrov now to forget what he had said.

A tyrant is always a mystery and that is his strength. Everything emanating from him is imbued with a secret significance hidden from the eyes of his subjects. Stalin's pragmatic motivations are easier to work out, but not sufficient to explain why he would conceal such an important historical fact.

The answer is largely hidden away in his inscrutable personality, in his ambiguous attitude towards Hitler, in the way he measured himself against certain analogous situations in which Hitler found himself, in the devastating sense of loss he may have experienced with the death of the hated, alluring enemy he had spent the days and nights of the war opposing, and in Stalin's many psychological complexes. These depths I will not attempt to plumb.

The foreign enemy and, no less, the domestic enemy, were an essential component of the system Stalin created. He loathed the idea of detente, and there would be less pressure for it if Hitler was still alive and secretly hiding somewhere. If Hitler was alive, Nazism was not yet vanquished and the world was still in danger. Stalin saw that as tactically important in the imminent discussions with the Allies about the nature of the post-war world.

So in Potsdam, when he was asked whether anything was known about Hitler, he was evasive. With a knack for dealing unceremoniously with inconvenient facts that by rights belonged to history and hence to the people, Stalin sat on the truth.

If, when Stalin was asked about Hitler at the Potsdam Conference, he had announced he was ready to provide proof that Hitler had been found, imagine the impact! A total triumph for Stalin! For the Red Army!

And his work at the conference would have benefited from that far more than it did from galvanising a corpse.

But I wonder whether Stalin was already sensing a growing tension between himself and his Allies, and concealing a truth that was their common achievement was perhaps his first move in the approaching Cold War.

Transcripts of the formal re-interrogations of the bunker survivors, and interviews with the Americans, together with autobiographies form the basis of what we know about the actual death of Hitler.

In general, their stories coincide, but divert at crucial moments. When seen side by side the inconsistencies and contradictions become obvious.

Chapter 11

HANS RATTENHUBER

Gruppenführer Hans Rattenhuber fills in the hours after the departure of Hanna Reitsch up to the final moment. Rattenhuber was Hitler's principal bodyguard and head of the Reichssicherheitsdienst (RSD), the Reich Security Service, with authority over all major security operations for the Nazis' top leadership. His career spanned police, military service, and SS leadership, and he had been close to Hitler since 1933 he Hitler rose to power. His military rank was equivalent to a Lieutenant General.

He said that after the assassination attempt in 1944 Hitler was overwhelmed with fear and was consumed by mistrust. He said he became hysterical about his security and demanded that Rattenhuber take decisive measures to protect it. Hitler hated the 'rabble', as he called the 'good Germans' within his own circle, and trusted them only slightly more than his enemies.

He said Hitler was given daily injections until his death to maintain energy and also to prevent sudden impact. The injections were given so often that the 'quack' doctor, Professor Morell, who Hitler trusted implicitly, never left his side

Rattenhuber said his right hand was shaking after the assassination attempt then transferred to the left hand soon after, and in recent months he had been noticeably dragging his left leg.

'All this led to the fact that he became very swollen and turned grey and grew old, and in the last days he trembled more and more. At every explosion of shells he would jump out of the room shouting "What happened?"'

After giving an account of the events in the bunker during April, which ended with the military defeat, he offered his own thoughts about the treachery of Göring.

'I think it should be emphasised that Göring's betrayal was quite logical', he said,

because it was the result of all his previous behaviour in his post as second-in-command of the Reich. The war had shown that Göring was unable to maintain the combat abilities required of the German Air Force. For a number of years, Göring had been exploiting his high status, by engaging mostly in improving his own situation, and after the German Army's success in Europe, this peculiarity was taken to almost incredible lengths.

He mainly used his visits to Italy, France and occupied regions of Russia to shamelessly plunder these countries' valuables. It could be said that the catastrophe that Germany was suffering hardly troubled Göring. Just as before the war, he continued hunting in his clownish attire – a red jacket and high green boots – and spent his time with his family in his palaces in Karinhal and Berchtesgaden. At home, he wore a white or pink satin robe with gold fastenings and had his nails manicured.

In autumn 1944, Göring cynically said in my presence: 'There is nothing left in life to gain for me, my family is already provided for.' Thus he completely revealed his character.

On 27 or 28 April, Deputy Reich Press Chief Lorenz reported to Hitler that according to the Reuters Press Agency, Himmler had approached the governments of the US and Britain with a proposal to conclude a separate peace agreement with them. In despair, Hitler threw this telegram on the table and said: 'Now, even Himmler has betrayed me. I'd rather die here in Berlin than lose my life somewhere in a street.' On the same day, he expelled Himmler from the Party.

Hardly had Hitler regained his spirits after Göring and Himmler's betrayal, when a telegram from Field-Marshal Keitel was received, saying that the 12th Army was under heavy attack by Russian troops and was unable to continue with its offensive to Berlin.

The 9th Army was completely surrounded by the Russians and Holste's Corps had gone on the defensive. Thus, all our hopes for salvation collapsed. Our troops' breakthrough had been unsuccessful.

The drama of the situation was aggravated by the fact that Hitler received all these reports to the accompaniment of heavy Russian artillery shells bursting in the grounds of the Reich Chancellery. It was scary looking at Hitler that day. He could barely speak and rarely moved. Going from a military meeting to his room Hitler said to me: 'I cannot live any longer, I am sick of life.'

But even on that tragic day Hitler, being a superstitious man, conducted a farce by marrying Eva Braun. Hitler had had an affair with her for 12 years but, for a long time, the name of his 'girlfriend' was not known in Germany.

Eva Braun was the daughter of a teacher at the Munich School of Applied Arts, and when she met Hitler she was working in the photo studio of Hoffmann, who later became Hitler's personal photographer. At first, as Hitler's 'girlfriend', she was a housekeeper in his residence in Berchtesgaden, where she played the mistress of the house. Later, Eva Braun lived in the Munich suburb of Bogenhausen, in a villa bought for her and luxuriously furnished by Hitler.

When Hitler lived in Munich, where he had his own flat in a private house, he kept his visits to Eva Braun secret even from his immediate circle. It should be emphasised that Eva Braun played a prominent part in Hitler's private life and influenced him very strongly. Many persons close to Hitler were afraid of her, including even Martin Bormann, who was feared and hated by everyone.

Braun did not interfere in politics or public life. She was an 'empty' woman interested only in fine clothes and looking after her appearance. The fate of the German people did not affect her at all. 'Our Führer', she used to say, 'is a true sufferer. All have betrayed and abandoned him. It's better for thousands of Germans to die, but Hitler's life is priceless and must be saved.'

It was 29 April. The whole area around the new Reich Chancellery was under heavy shelling and bombing by the Russians, Hitler's personal garage and the cars in it were destroyed by a direct hit.

The Russian forces advanced towards the Potsdam Station and the Headquarters continued its feverish existence.

Everyone was confused. Everyone thought only of saving their own lives. I still remember the treachery of a person very close to Hitler – his brother-in-law (Hermann) Fegelein, a Gruppenführer and Hitler's SS adjutant. He was married to Eva Braun's sister. On that day, it was discovered that Fegelein had gone to his flat, changed into civilian clothes and was planning to flee Berlin. On Hitler's orders, he was arrested and shot in the grounds of the Reich Chancellery.

There was also news of other people's betrayals, but it could not have been any other way, because treachery and hypocrisy had been cultivated among Hitler's associates long before the time I describe. In those critical days for the German people, the ruling clique displayed all its putrid venality, because it consisted of people who had abandoned all their morals.

The rich, who had made large fortunes by robbing the German people and later looting the occupied countries, spent their days in drunken orgies, bathed in luxury and wealth and exploited their close relationship with Hitler only for their own interests.

Hitler was fully aware of the shameless behaviour of his henchmen because he was repeatedly informed of it by many people, including myself. But his delusions of grandeur meant that he averted his eyes from it, as these were the people who hypocritically sang his praises and created the fame he craved. During my long service to Hitler, I came to understand the nature of many of the high-ranking officials close to him.

Professor Hoffmann, Hitler's personal photographer, was possibly his best friend. Having acquired a monopoly as Hitler's personal photographer, Hoffmann amassed such wealth that he became one of the richest men in Germany. Hoffman was an alcoholic and when drunk created disturbances that were known to the public. Hitler knew of this but went on treating him as his friend.

Hitler's personal aide-de-camp, Obergruppenführer Schaub, was his most trusted aide. In 1923, they were in Landsberg prison together. It was no secret that Schaub had drunken orgies with ballerinas. It was also known that he used his position close to Hitler only for his self-interest.

From 1938, Reichsleiter Martin Bormann was one of those closest to Hitler – one of the very few people who could influence him. He was an exceptionally cruel, cunning, callous and egotistical man. His long drunken parties with Fegelein, Admiral Puttkamer and others were indescribable.

Others close to Hitler were not much better; Julius Streicher, the Gauleiter of Franconia, for instance and [Adolf] Weber, the Munich District President, as well as Gauleiter [Wilhelm] Kube, who later became a Reich viceroy in Belorussia, and many others. Kube boasted of nightly drunken parties with prostitutes which were the talk of Berlin. Terboven [Josef Terboven, Reichskommissar for Norway, who had taken over the royal palace] got drunk every night and started drunken brawls. Before the war, all of Munich had talked about the 'nights of the Amazons', organised by Weber. In his park, he rode horses with naked women accompanied by naked SS officers. Hitler knew all about it.

At the end of the day on 29 April, in the presence of General Krebs, Goebbels and Bormann, Hitler asked General Mohnke, the commander of the troops defending the government district, how long he could hold out. Mohnke replied that with the weapons and ammunition he had, he could hold out for two or three days more. Hitler said nothing and went to his room.

In the evening, all those who gathered for the regular meeting were in low spirits. Hitler, his face more pinched than before, stared dully at the battle map before him. General Weidling, the Commandant of Berlin, repeatedly asked Hitler to permit the breakout from Berlin to begin. Hitler replied, with bitter irony: 'Look at my map. Everything marked here is not based on the reports of the Supreme Command but comes from foreign radio station broadcasts. No one reports to us. I can order whatever I want but none of my orders is fulfilled anymore.'

Finally, it was decided that because of the complete failure of airborne resupply, the troops were to be allowed to break out in small groups, on condition that they would continue the fight where possible. Capitulation was impossible.

29 April was really a fateful day! About 10 o'clock at night, Hitler called me to his room and ordered me to gather the leading personnel of the Headquarters and his close collaborators in his reception room by 10 o'clock. I remember that at that moment Hitler looked like a man who had taken a very significant decision. He sat on the edge of a desk, his eyes fixed on one point, his gaze concentrated.

I went to the door to carry out his order. Hitler stopped me and said, as far as I remember, the following: 'You have served me faithfully for many years. Tomorrow is your birthday and I want to congratulate you now and to thank you for your faithful service, because I shall not be able to do so tomorrow . . . I have taken the decision . . . I must leave this world . . .'

I went over to Hitler and told him how necessary his survival was for Germany, that there was still a chance to try and escape from Berlin and save his life. 'What for?' Hitler replied, 'Everything is ruined, there is no way out, and to flee means falling into the hands of the Russians . . . Never would there have been a moment, Rattenhuber', he continued, 'that I would have spoken to you about my death, if not for Stalin and his army. It was only Stalin who prevented me from carrying out the mission entrusted to me from heaven.'

Eva Braun came in from the next room. For several more minutes, Hitler talked of himself, of his role in history that had been prepared for him by destiny, and shaking hands with me asked me to leave them alone.

Notwithstanding all my loyalty to Hitler, it was extremely unpleasant for me to see that even at the last moment he could not help making high-flown speeches about his 'higher mission' and so on. I was overcome with laughter.

At 10 clock, in Hitler's reception room, everyone gathered together – Generals Burgdorf and Krebs, Vice-Admiral Voss, Hitler's personal pilot General Baur, Standartenführer Beetz, Obersturmbannführer Hegel, his personal servant Sturmbannführer Linge, Günsche and me.

He said the following, exactly: 'I have decided to abandon this life. Thank you for your honest and conscientious service. Try to escape from Berlin with the troops. I am staying here.'

Saying goodbye he shook hands with each of us and, dragging his feet and with his head bowed, he went to his room.

A few minutes later, Hitler called me, Linge and Günsche in, and in an almost inaudible voice told us to burn his body and that of Eva Braun. 'I don't want', Hitler had said, 'the enemy to display my body in a freak show.'

By nightfall about 200–300 wounded had gathered at the bunker, where they were cared for by the nurses. Reich Youth Leader Axmann came to the bunker and asked Bormann to let him introduce to Hitler fifty-two girls, the best nurses in the Reich Chancellery's hospital. Hitler agreed.

About 2am, the girls were lined up along both sides of the lobby on the top floor of the shelter. Soon Hitler appeared. He slowly went up the stairs and shook hands with each of the girls. Then with the traditional raised arm he saluted all the others who were in the bunker and returned to his room.

That night, Hitler ordered Professor Haase, who was working as a surgeon at the Reich Chancellery's hospital, to be summoned to him. When Haase arrived, Hitler showed him three small glass capsules which he had received from Dr Stumpfegger, each of them in a metal case resembling a rifle cartridge-case. Hitler said at these capsules contained an instantaneous deadly poison.

Hitler asked the Professor how the efficacy of the poison could be tested. He replied that it could be tested on animals, for example on a dog. Then Hitler ordered Sergeant-Major Tornow, who cared for Hitler's favourite dog, Blondi, to be called. When the dog was brought, Haase crushed the ampoule with pliers and poured the liquid into the dog's mouth, which was held open by Tornow. Several seconds later, the dog started to tremble and 30 seconds later it died. After that Hitler told Tornow to check if the dog was really dead.

When we left Hitler's room, I asked Haase what kind of poison was in the ampoules and if it guaranteed instant death. Haase replied that there was cyanide in the ampoules, and that its action was immediate and deadly.

That was the last time I saw Hitler alive. It was 30 April. About 10am, I went to check the sentries. Upstairs, I approached the SS guard on duty, Mengershausen, who was standing at the exit from the Reich Chancellery to the garden. Mengershausen reported to me that about 8 o'clock in the morning Eva Braun came up from the shelter, said good morning and went out into the garden, returning about 15 minutes later.

She explained her visit to the garden by saying: 'I want to see the sun for the last time.' Then she said goodbye to him and, upset, went down into the bunker. At the time the grounds of the Reich Chancellery were exposed to Russian gunfire.

I went to Hitler's reception room several times and went out to carry out my duties. The situation was very tense and I considered it my duty to provide suitable protection for the bunker because at any moment we expected the Russians to reach the grounds of the Reich Chancellery.

Between 3 and 4 o'clock that afternoon I returned to Hitler's reception room and was struck by a powerful smell of bitter almonds. My deputy, Hegel, reported excitedly that the Führer had just committed suicide.

I must say that although I had expected this, the news still shook me greatly and I slumped into an armchair in despair. At that moment, Linge came in and confirmed that Hitler was dead, saying that he had had to carry out the hardest order the Führer had ever given him. I looked at Linge in surprise. He explained to me that before his death, Hitler ordered him to leave the room for 10 minutes, then to return, wait 10 minutes more and then carry out the order.

Having said that, Linge quickly went to Hitler's room and returned with a Walther pistol which he placed on the table before me. By its special external finish, I recognised it as the Führer's personal pistol. Now it was clear to me what Hitler's order had been. Obviously Hitler, doubting the effectiveness of the poison after all the injections he had been given for such a long time, ordered Linge to shoot him after he had taken the poison. Linge had shot Hitler.

Reich Youth Leader Axmann, who was present, took Hitler's gun from him and said that he would hide it for better times. For some time I was unable to stir myself because of nervous stress and depression. My life passed before my eyes as if on a screen.

I was shaken out of my stupor by a noise in the room. I saw Linge, Günsche, Hitler's personal driver Kempka and two or three more SS officers, accompanied by Goebbels and Bormann, carrying the corpses of Hitler and Eva Braun out of Hitler's private room, wrapped in grey military blankets. I pulled myself together and followed them to accompany to his final destination the man to whom I had given 12 years of my life.

The SS men placed the corpses in a small hole not far from the entrance to the shelter. The fierce shelling of the area did not allow for even minimal honours to Hitler and his wife. The bodies were doused with gasoline and set on fire. We could not even find the national flag to cover the remains.

Returning to the shelter I learned that Goebbels intended writing a letter to the Soviet High Command telling them that Hitler had committed suicide and had appointed Admiral Dönitz as Reich Chancellor.

On the night of 1 May, with Goebbels' permission, there was a breakout attempt, but nothing worked. I was wounded and captured by the Russians.

Rattenhuber's testimony seems to make clear that Linge shot Hitler post mortem, although he does not mention hearing a shot. But even after 80 years there is no conclusive answer.

While still a prisoner of the Soviets, Rattenhuber was arrested on 28 August 1951 by the MGB on charges that 'from the first days of the establishment of the fascist dictatorship in Germany in 1933 and until the defeat of the latter in 1945, he had carried out Hitler's personal protection as well as other leaders of the Reich'. He was sentenced to 25 years' imprisonment. In October 1955, following a decree of the Supreme Soviet, he was released from prison, and handed to authorities of the GDR (East Germany).

Chapter 12

TRAUDL JUNGE

Traudl Junge was Hitler's personal typist.

Hanna Reitsch and General Greim prepared to fly out. . . . After a long conversation with Hitler, they left the bunker.

We women took refuge in Eva Braun's room with the children and the dogs. Decision was in the air now. Our nerves were stretched to breaking point. Eva told Frau Christian and me, 'I bet you'll be shedding tears this evening'. We looked at her in alarm. 'Has the time come?' No, she said, we would see something else, something really touching, but she couldn't tell us any more yet.

I don't know now how we passed all those hours. It was like a nightmare. I don't remember any more conversations or other details. What was there to talk about? Only the hellish noise made by the bombs, grenades, artillery and tanks spoke now. Soon the Russians would have reached the Potsdamer Platz, perhaps in a few hours' time, and then they would be nearly at our door. Nothing happened in the bunker. The nation's leaders sat there inactive, waiting for the decision, the last that Hitler would make. Even for the ever-zealous Bormann and the industrious Goebbels there was nothing more to do. Axmann, Hewel, Voss, the servants and adjutants, the orderlies and staff, they were all waiting for a decision. No one expected victory now. We all just wanted to be out of this bunker at last.

It seems to me almost incredible that we could still eat and drink, sleep and talk. We did it mechanically, and I have no memory of such things.

Goebbels made long speeches about the disloyalty of his colleagues. He was particularly indignant over Göring's behaviour. 'That man was never a National Socialist', he claimed. 'He just basked in the Führer's glory, he never lived by idealistic, National Socialist principles. It's his fault that the German Luftwaffe failed, we have him to thank for it that we're sitting here now about to lose the war.' You suddenly realised that these two great figures had been bitter enemies and rivals. Frau Goebbels joined her husband in accusing the Reich Marshal.

We had become perfectly indifferent in those hours. We'd given up waiting. Time dragged wearily by while bedlam raged outside. We sat about talking, smoking, vegetating. You get tired doing that. The tension of the last few days now relaxes. There is only a great emptiness in me. I find a camp bed somewhere and sleep for an hour. It must be the middle of the night when I wake up. Servants and orderlies are busily coming and going in the corridor and in the Führer's rooms. I wash, change my clothes, it must be time to drink tea with the Führer. We still drink tea with him. And death is always an invisible guest at the tea-party. But today something unexpected awaits me when I open the door to Hitler's study. The Führer comes towards me, shakes hands and asks, 'Have you had a nice little rest, child?' When, surprised, I say yes, he adds, 'There's something I'd like you to take down from dictation later.'

I had entirely forgotten that this weary, weak voice sometimes used to race through dictation so energetically that I could hardly keep up. What was there to be written now? My glance passes Hitler and is attracted to the festively laid table. It is laid for eight tonight, with champagne glasses. And the guests are already arriving, Goebbels and his wife, Axmann, Frau Christian, Fräulein Manziarly, General Burgdorf and General Krebs. I can't wait to know why they have all been summoned. Is Hitler going to make a big occasion of his farewell? Then he beckons me over. 'Perhaps we could do it now. Come along', he says, leaving the room. Side by side we go to his conference room. I am about to remove the cover from the typewriter, but the Führer says, 'Take it down on the shorthand pad'. I sit down alone at the big table and wait. Hitler stands in his usual place by the broad side of the table, leans both hands on it, and stares at the empty table top, no longer covered today with maps or street plans. For several seconds, if the concrete didn't act like a drumskin, mercilessly amplifying the reverberations of every bomb blast and every shot, you could have heard only the breathing of two human beings.

Then, suddenly, the Führer utters the first words. 'My political testament'. For a moment my hand trembles. Now, at last, I shall hear what we've been waiting for days: an explanation of what has happened, a confession, even a confession of guilt, or perhaps a justification. This final document of the 'Thousand-Year Reich' should contain the real truth, told by a man with nothing more to lose.

But my expectations are not fulfilled. In tones of indifference, almost mechanically, the Führer comes out with the explanations, accusations and demands that I, the German people and the whole world know already. I look up in surprise as Hitler names the members of the new government. I really don't understand what's going on. If all is lost, if Germany is destroyed, if National Socialism is dead forever, and the

Führer himself can see no way out but suicide, what are the men he is appointing to government posts supposed to do? I can hardly grasp it. Hitler goes on speaking, scarcely looking up. He pauses for a brief moment, and then begins dictating his private will. And now I discover that he is going to marry Eva Braun before they are united in death. I fleetingly remember what Eva said, about the tears we'd shed today. But I can't summon up any tears.

The Führer lists his legacies, but here, suddenly, he does mention the possibility that there may be no German state left after his death. Then the dictation is over. He moves away from the table on which he has been leaning all this time, as if for support, and suddenly there is an exhausted, hunted expression in his eyes. 'Type that out for me at once in triplicate and then bring it in to me.' There is something urgent in his voice, and I realise, to my surprise, that this last, most important, most crucial document written by Hitler is to go out into the world without any corrections or thorough revision. Every letter of birthday wishes to some Gauleiter, artist, etc., was polished up, improved, revised – but now Hitler has no time for any of that.

The Führer returns to his party, which will soon be a wedding party. As for me, I sit in the waiting-room outside Goebbels' room and type out the last page in the history of the Third Reich. Meanwhile the conference room has been turned into a registry office, a registrar fetched from the nearby front has married the Hitlers, Eva has begun to write her surname with a B when signing the register, and has had to have it pointed out that her new name begins with H. And now the wedding party is sitting in Hitler's room. What will they raise their champagne glasses to? Happiness for the newly married couple?

The Führer is impatient to see what I have typed. He keeps coming back into my room, looking to see how far I've got, he says nothing but just casts restless glances at what remains of my shorthand, and then goes out again.

Suddenly Goebbels bursts in. I look at his agitated face, which is white as chalk. Tears are running down his cheeks. He speaks to me because there's no one else around to whom he can pour out his heart. His usually clear voice is stifled by tears and shaking. 'The Führer wants me to leave Berlin, Frau Junge! I am to take up a leading post in the new government. But I can't leave Berlin, I cannot leave the Führer's side! I am Gauleiter of Berlin, and my place is here. If the Führer is dead my life is pointless. And he says to me, "Goebbels, I didn't expect you to disobey my last order too . . ." The Führer has made so many decisions too late – why make this last one too early?' he asks despairingly.

Then he too dictates me his testament, to be added as an appendix to the Führer's. For the first time in his life, it says, he is not going to carry out an order by the Führer because he cannot leave his place in Berlin at the Führer's side. In later times, an example of loyalty will be more valuable than a life preserved . . . And he too tells the world that he and his whole family prefer death to life in a Germany without National Socialism.

I type both documents as fast as I can. My fingers work mechanically, and I am amazed to see that they make hardly any typing errors. Bormann, Goebbels and the Führer himself keep coming in to see if I've finished yet. They make me nervous and delay the work. Finally they almost tear the last sheet out of my typewriter, go back into the conference room, sign the three copies, and that very night they are sent off by courier in different directions. Colonel von Below, Heinz Lorenz and Bormann's colleague Zander take Hitler's last will and testament out of Berlin.

With that, Hitler's life is really over. Now he just wants to wait for confirmation that at least one of the documents has reached its destination. Any moment now we expect the Russians to storm our bunker, so close do the sounds of war seem to be. All our dogs are dead. The dog-walker has done his duty and shot our beloved pets before they can be torn to pieces up in the park by an enemy grenade or bomb.

Any of the guards or soldiers who have to go out in the open now are gambling with their lives. Some of our people have already been wounded. The leader of the escort commando has been shot in the leg and can't move for pain.

Almost no one stops to think of the five blonde little girls and the dark-haired boy still playing in their room, enjoying life. Their mother has now told them it's possible they may all have to be inoculated. When there are so many people living together in a small space you have to take precautions against disease. They understand that, and they're not afraid.

30 April begins like the days that went before it. The hours drag slowly by. No one knows just how to address Eva Braun now. The adjutants and orderlies stammer in embarrassment when they have to speak to the 'gnaüdiges Fraülein'. 'You may safely call me Frau Hitler', she says, smiling.

She asks me into her room because she can't spend the whole time alone with her thoughts. We talk about something, any-thing, to distract ourselves. Suddenly she opens her wardrobe. There hangs the beautiful silver fox fur she loved so much. 'Frau Junge, I'd like to give you this coat as a goodbye present', she says. 'I always liked to have well-dressed ladies around me – I want you to have it now and enjoy wearing it.' I thank her with all my heart, much moved. I am even glad to have it although I've no idea how, where and when I can wear it. Then we eat lunch with Hitler. The same conversation as yesterday, the day before yesterday, for many days past: a banquet of death under the mask of cheerful calm and composure. We rise from the table, Eva Braun goes to her room, and Frau Christian and I look for somewhere to smoke a cigarette in peace. I find a vacant armchair in the servants' room, next to the open door to Hitler's corridor. Hitler is probably in his room. I don't know who is with him. Then Günsche comes up to me. 'Come on, the Führer wants to say goodbye.'

I rise and go out into the corridor. Linge fetches the others. Fraülein Manziarly, Frau Christian, I vaguely realise there are other people there too. But all I really see is the figure of the Führer. He comes very slowly out of his room, stooping more than ever, stands in the open doorway and shakes hands with everyone. I feel his right hand warm in mine, he looks at me but he isn't seeing me. He seems to be far away. He says something to me, but I don't hear it. I didn't take in his last words. The moment we've been waiting for has come now, and I am frozen and scarcely notice what's going on around me. Only when Eva Braun comes over to me is the spell broken a little. She smiles and embraces me. 'Please do try to get out. You may yet make your way through. And give Bavaria my love', she says, smiling but with a sob in her voice. She is wearing the Führer's favourite dress, the black one with the roses at the neckline, and her hair is washed and beautifully done. Like that, she follows the Führer into his room – and to her death. The heavy iron door closes.

I am suddenly seized by a wild urge to get as far away from here as possible. I almost race up the stairs leading to the upper part of the bunker. But the Goebbels children are sitting halfway up, looking lost. They felt they'd been forgotten in their room. No one gave them any lunch today. Now they want to go and find their parents, and Auntie Eva and Uncle Hitler. I lead them to the round table. 'Come along, children, I'll get you something to eat. The grown-ups have so much to do today that they don't have any spare time for you', I say as lightly and calmly as I can. I find a jar of cherries, butter some bread and feed the little ones. I talk to them to distract them. They say something about being safe in the bunker, and how it's almost fun to hear the explosions when they know the bangs can't hurt them. Suddenly there is the sound of a shot, so loud, so close that we all fall silent. It echoes on through all the rooms. 'That was a direct hit', cried Helmut, with no idea how right he is. The Führer is dead now.

I want to be on my own. The children, satisfied, go back to their room. I stay sitting by myself on the narrow bench at the round table on the landing. There is a bottle of Steinhäger standing there, with an empty glass beside it. Automatically, I pour myself a drink and swallow the strong liquor. My watch says a few minutes after three in the afternoon. So now it's over.

I don't know how long I sit like that. Men's boots have passed me by, but I didn't notice. Then the tall, broad figure of Otto Günsche comes up the stairs, and with him a strong smell of petrol. His face is ashen, his young, fresh features look gaunt. He drops heavily to sit beside me, reaches for the bottle too, and his large, heavy hand is shaking. 'I've carried out the Führer's last order … his body is burned', he says softly. I don't answer, I don't ask any questions.

He goes down again to make sure that the bodies are burned without trace. I stay sitting there for a while motionless, trying to imagine what will happen now. Then, after all, I suddenly feel an urge to go down to those two empty rooms. The door to Hitler's room is still open at the end of the corridor. The men carrying the bodies had no hands free to close it. Eva's little revolver is lying on the table with a pink chiffon scarf beside it, and I see the brass case of the poison capsule glinting on the floor next to Frau Hitler's chair. It looks like an empty lipstick. There is blood on the blue-and-white upholstery of the bench where Hitler was sitting: Hitler's blood. I suddenly feel sick. The heavy smell of bitter almonds is nauseating. I instinctively reach for my own capsule. I'd like to throw it as far away as I can and leave this terrible bunker. One ought to be able to breathe clear, fresh air now, feel the wind and hear the trees rustling. But freedom, peace and calm are out of reach.

Suddenly I feel something like hatred and helpless anger rise in me. I'm angry with the dead Führer. I'm surprised by that myself, because after all, I knew he was going to leave us. But he's left us in such a state of emptiness and helplessness! He's simply gone away, and with him the hypnotic compulsion under which we were living has gone too.

Monday evening, 30 April. Traudl Junge describes her escape from the bunker.

It could be about eight-thirty in the evening. We are to be the first group leaving the bunker. A few soldiers I don't know from the guards battalion, we four women, Günsche, Mohnke, Hewel and Admiral Voss make our way through the many waiting people and go down underground passages. We clamber over half-wrecked staircases, through holes in walls and rubble, always going further up and out. At last the Wilhelmsplatz stretches ahead, shining in the moonlight. The dead horse still lies there on the paving stones, but only the remains of it now. Hungry people have come out of the U-Bahn tunnels to slice off pieces of meat . . .

Soundlessly, we cross the square. Sporadic shots are fired, but the gunfire is stronger further away. Then we have reached the U-Bahn tunnel outside the ruins of the Kaiserhof. We climb down and work our way on in the darkness, over the wounded and the homeless, past soldiers resting, until we reach Friedrichstrasse Station. Here the tunnel ends and hell begins. We have to get through, and we succeed. The whole fighting group gets across the S-Bahn bend uninjured. But an inferno breaks out behind us. Hundreds of snipers are shooting at those who follow us.

For hours we crawl through cavernous cellars, burning buildings, strange, dark streets! Somewhere in an abandoned cellar we rest and sleep for a couple of hours. Then we go on, until Russian tanks bar our way. None of us has a heavy weapon. We are carrying nothing but pistols. So the night passes, and in the morning it is quiet. The gunfire has stopped. We still haven't seen any Russian soldiers. Finally we end up in the old beer cellar of a brewery now being used as a bunker. This is our last stop. There are Russian tanks out here, and it's full daylight. We still get into the bunker unseen. Down there Mohnke and Günsche sit in a corner and begin to write. Hewel lies on one of the plank beds, stares at the ceiling and says nothing. He doesn't want to go on. Two soldiers bring in the wounded Rattenhuber. He has taken a shot in the leg, he is feverish and hallucinating. A doctor treats him and puts him on a camp bed. Rattenhuber gets out his pistol, takes off the safety catch and puts it down beside him.

A general comes into the bunker, finds the defending commander Mohnke and speaks to him. We discover that we are in the last bastion of resistance in the capital of the Reich. The Russians have now surrounded the brewery and are calling on everyone to surrender. Mohnke writes a last report. There is still an hour to go. The rest of us sit there smoking. Suddenly he raises his head, looks at us women and says, 'You must help us now. We're all wearing uniform, none of us will get out of here. But you can try to get through, make your way to Dönitz and give him this last report.'

I don't want to go on any more, but Frau Christian and the other two urge me to; they shake me until I finally follow them. We leave our steel helmets and pistols there. We take our military jackets off too. Then we shake hands with the men and go.

An SS company is standing by its vehicles in the brewery yard, stony-faced and motionless, waiting for the order for the last attack. The Volkssturm, the OT men and the soldiers are throwing their weapons down in a heap and going out to the Russians. At the far end of the yard Russian soldiers are already handing out schnapps and cigarettes to German soldiers, telling them to surrender, celebrating fraternisation. We pass through them as if we were invisible. Then we are outside the encircling ring, among wild hordes of Russian victors, and at last I can weep.

Where were we to turn? If I'd never seen dead people before, I saw them now everywhere. No one was taking any notice of them. A little sporadic firing was still going on. Sometimes the Russians set buildings on fire and searched for soldiers in hiding. We were threatened on every corner. I lost track of my colleagues that same day. I went on alone for a long time, hopelessly, until at last I ended up in a Russian prison. When the cell door closed behind me I didn't even have my poison any more, it had all happened so fast. Yet I was still alive. And now began a dreadful, terrible time, but I didn't want to die anymore; I was curious to find out what else a human being can experience. And fate was kind to me. As if by a miracle, I escaped being transported to the East. The unselfish human kindness of one man preserved me from that. After many long months, I was at last able to go home and back to a new life.

Chapter 13

REICHSJUGENDFÜHRER ARTUR AXMANN

Artur Axmann was the leader of the Hitler Youth and present in the bunker on 30 April. The following day he joined a breakout group which included Martin Bormann and Ludwig Stumpfegger. After witnessing the death of Bormann and Stumpfegger, he successfully evaded the Soviets, living under the alias 'Erich Siewert' for several months.

In December 1945, Axmann was arrested in Lübeck by US Army counterintelligence, who had uncovered a Nazi underground movement he was organising. He was tried by a denazification court in 1949, sentenced to three years and three months in prison as a major offender, but was not convicted of war crimes. In 1958, a West Berlin court fined him for indoctrinating youth with Nazism but again cleared him of direct war criminality.

Axmann's sworn testimony was given at Nuremberg on 10 October 1947, before Walter Rapp, Director, Evidence Division US Office of the Chief Counsel for War Crimes. Note that this statement was made more than two years after Hitler's death, yet Axmann, and presumably the American interrogator, did not know that Hitler's body had been discovered. His description of Hitler's body is radically different to that of the other witnesses.

On 30 April 1945, Axmann again went to the Bunker to see the Führer. It was about three in the afternoon when he arrived. Goebbels told him that the Führer had decided to see no one so he waited in one of the waiting rooms at the Bunker together with Goebbels, Bormann and the others and was told that Hitler and his wife had retired to their sitting room and wished to be left alone. Although no one spoke much, there was a general feeling that this was it.

Around four o'clock Hitler's Adjutant, Günsche, entered the waiting room where Axmann and the others were gathered waiting to see Hitler and said 'The Führer is dead'. Everybody, including Axmann, then got up and walked slowly to the sitting room where Hitler and his wife were. As they entered they saw the Führer sitting on a small divan, Eva Braun at his side with her head resting on his shoulder. The Führer was only slightly slumped forward and everyone recognised that he was dead. His jaw hung somewhat loosely down and a pistol lay on the floor. Blood was dripping from both temples and his mouth was bloody and smeared but there was not much blood spattered around.

There was no outward sign of death on Eva Braun's face and it was immediately assumed that she had taken poison. Axmann stated that he also believed that Hitler took poison first and then shot himself through the mouth and that the concussion of such a blast resulted in the blood on the Führer's temples. They all stood there in awe for a few minutes and then decided to carry the Führer outside into the small courtyard where in accordance with his wishes he wanted to be burned.

A blanket was thrown over his face to prevent detection by the outside guards while he was being burned and buried. Kempka and Günsche carried the body into the courtyard with Hitler's feet in black boots dangling free from under the blanket. Eva Braun was also carried out and was laid alongside of the Führer. Previous arrangements had been made to procure approximately 180 litres of gasoline and with the help of some soaked rags the bodies were set afire.

Axmann did not personally witness the burning saying it was too horrible for him to witness but he knows as a matter of fact that it did take place. The amount of gasoline used was not sufficient enough to destroy the bones of the two dead people and therefore they were then put into one of the many bomb craters which exist around the Reichs Chancellery and he was carefully buried.

Axmann believes that one of the reasons Hitler's body was never discovered is because the impact of the shot fired into his mouth destroyed his dental fixtures and also lots of people in the last few days of Berlin were killed and burned around the Reichs Chancellery and the bodies thrown indiscriminately into these bomb craters. Hitler did not want to have dead bodies lying around the courtyard when he ventured forth for his half-hour strolls in the yard between the 20 and 30 April 1945.

Axmann fixes the death of Hitler at four in the afternoon of the 30 April 1945. There is not the slightest doubt in his mind that the body he saw was that of his beloved Führer and that he was dead.

Walter H. Rapp
Director Evidence Division

Three months later, Axmann was interrogated again, this time by Judge Michael Musmanno, presiding judge for the Einsatzgruppen trial in the US military court at Nuremberg. 'Einsatzgruppen trials', of which there were twelve, were subsequent Nuremberg Trials for 'War Crimes' and 'Crimes against Humanity' after the end of the Second World War. In 1950, he published a book based on his research and personal interviews with witnesses, in which he argued that Hitler had indeed committed suicide in Berlin in 1945, confirming that Western leaders had not been told by Stalin that Hitler was dead.

Chapter 14

ERICH KEMPKA

Erich Kempka, Hitler's chauffeur, was interrogated by US Judge Michael Musmanno, Member of the Nuremberg Commission, on 7 January 1948 in Munich.

Kempka said he was not in the bunker at the time but he helped Günsche and others to carry the bodies into the garden. He told Musmanno that Hitler had shot himself in the mouth, but conceded this was only what he had heard from Günsche and Axmann.

He did, however, go into the room. He continued:

In the room where he had shot himself a blood stain was on the carpet near the place where the pistol had been lying. This carpet was burnt afterwards so that no traces could be found later. In front of the sofa there was a small round table and there he shot himself into the mouth so that his head fell on to the small table and then the blood ran down on the carpet.

The pistol, that is the 7.65 [mm] one was lying next to the blood stain, right in the middle in front of the sofa, and the 6.35 pistol, Eva Braun's, was lying before the right front leg of the sofa.

Asked whether he examined the pistols to see whether they had been fired, Kempka said Günsche and he did have them in their hands, but they did not examine whether shots had been fired from them.

His account was relatively consistent with other bunker witnesses who escaped Berlin. However, Kempka later admitted that he was willing to tell Western interrogators 'just about anything . . . I thought they wanted to hear' to protect himself, so his testimony may have been coloured by self-preservation.

Kempka escaped Berlin initially disguised in civilian clothes with the help of a Yugoslav woman who claimed to Soviet soldiers that

Kempka was her husband, allowing him to evade immediate capture. He eventually made his way to Wittenberg and then Munich, where he obtained false identification papers from a German woman who worked for the Allies as an interpreter.

From Munich, Kempka continued south to Berchtesgaden, Hitler's mountain retreat in Bavaria. There, on 20 June 1945, he was captured by US Army troops. Kempka was held by the American authorities until October 1947. He became the first direct witness in Allied hands able to confirm the details of Hitler's death in the bunker.

It is clear from these testimonies that the Russians knew everything there was to know about the events in the bunker, but the Americans, in particular, were still asking questions three years later. Stalin's plan to deceive the Allies appeared to be working.

Chapter 15

SS MAJOR OTTO GÜNSCHE

Written statement in German translated into Russian by Assistant Chief of Investigation Section Intelligence Department of the Red Army General Staff Captain of the Guards Shirokov.

At 3:00 in the morning of 30 April, 1945, I went to my concrete shelter under the Reich Chancellery and went to bed. I left orders to be woken at 10:00. When I woke I went for breakfast in the officers' mess in the Führer's bunker, which was next to the Führer's living-room. There I met Reichsleiter Bormann, General Krebs and General Burgdorf. They were discussing the situation in Berlin. I was with them for some time, then I left. When I returned to this room around 12:00–13:00, the three of them were still there in a highly emotional state, and from what they said I understood that the Führer had said goodbye to them. Then they left the room and I alone there. After some time, the Commander of the Reich Security Service Gruppenführer and Police Lieutenant-General Rattenhuber and the Führer's pilot Gruppenführer and Police Lieutenant-General Baur came in. A little later, the Führer entered the room and said: 'After my death, my corpse must be burnt for I don't want my corpse to be exposed for show later, for an exhibition.' After that he looked at us steadily and then returned to his room. I went to Major-General Mohnke and told him that Hitler now intended to take his own life.

At 14:30, I went to the conference room and met Reichsleiter Bormann, Dr Goebbels, General Krebs, General Burgdorf and Reich Youth Leader Axmann, who in my absence had also arrived at the Führer's bunker. They talked about the Führer's saying goodbye and were in a very agitated state.

At 15:15, I left this room and in another met the Chief of the Führer's SS Guard Sturmbannführer Schedle and the Führer's driver Obersturmbannführer Kempka. I told them what the Führer had said to me, Rattenhuber and Baur. After that, we remained in the same room for some time. Suddenly, the door to the lobby half-opened and I heard the Führer's valet, Sturmbannführer Linge, say: 'The Führer is dead'. Though I had not heard a shot, I immediately went through the lobby to the conference room and told the leaders who were gathered there: 'The Führer is dead'. They got up and walked out with me to the lobby and there we saw two bodies being carried out; one of them was wrapped in a blanket, the other was also wrapped in a blanket but not completely covered. The corpses were carried by Sturmbannführer Linge, Hauptscharführer Kruge, Obersturmführer Lindloff and another SS officer whom I did not recognise.

Then Obersturmbannführer Kempka and Sturmbannführer Medle joined them. From one of the blankets, the Führer's legs were visible. I recognised them by the boots and socks he always wore; out of the other blanket the feet and head of the Führer's wife protruded. Both bodies were carried out through the emergency exit of the Führer's bunker to the garden. There they were doused with petrol prepared beforehand by Reichsleiter Bormann and set alight. That happened at 16:00. Both corpses were accompanied by Reichsleiter Bormann, General Burgdorf, General Krebs., Reich Youth Leader Axmann, Dr Goebbels and myself. Then I helped to carry the body of the Führer's wife away from the door of the bunker. I am not sure if Rattenhuber and Baur were present, but it is quite possible because it was very crowded on the staircase and rather dark.

After the petrol-soaked corpses were set alight, the door to the shelter was closed because of the fierce fire and fumes.

After that, all who were present went to the front room, and from there Dr Goebbels, Reichsleiter Bormann, General Burgdorf, General Krebs, Axmann and later State Secretary Dr Naumann went into the conference room.

The door to the Führer's private room was open and there was a very strong smell of almonds (cyanide) coming from it. I looked inside but did not go in, and I then returned to the conference room. SS General Mohnke was already there. They discussed the current situation and the Führer's order that after his death they should immediately escape from Berlin in small groups. I heard that Reichsleiter Bormann wanted to get to Grand-Admiral Dönitz by any means, so as to inform him about the Führer's last instructions before his death. I don't know what these were. After that, I again left the room and went next door to have a little rest.

Then General Mohnke came to me and said that, according to what the Führer had said, now that he was gone, only co-operation with Russia could even partially save Germany. General Krebs had been ordered to open negotiations with the Russian General Zhukov for a cease-fire. Thus, the breakout from the bunker was postponed. Then I returned to my room and after that went to one of General Mohnke's combat groups.

During the night, I learnt that General Krebs' terms had been rejected, and on the night of 1 May 1945 we were ordered to break out. I was to head north, with Mohnke's group and the Führer's secretaries, Frau Christian and Frau Junge, his dietitian Fraulein Manziarly and Reichsleiter Bormann's secretary Fraulein Krüger.

At 22:00, the breakout began. Our group reached the vicinity of the Wedding railway station without loss, but there we met enemy resistance. After regrouping, we reached the Schultheiss brewery near Monhauseralde railway station at midday on 2 May. Among the soldiers who were there, rumours were circulating that Berlin had capitulated and one could see that they were demoralised.

After that, the four women who were with us were dismissed by General Mohnke and they immediately left the brewery. I do not know where they went. At 18:00 that evening, General Mohnke, the newly-arrived General Rauch and his orderly and I went with a Russian interpreter to the commander of one of Russian Corps. Upon our return to the Schultheiss brewery, I was taken prisoner-of-war.

SS Sturmbannführer Otto Günsche
17 May 1945. Moscow

Note that although Günsche says he looked inside the room where Hitler committed suicide he did not say he saw any guns.

Chapter 16

HEINZ LINGE

The one man most closely associated with Hitler personally was his valet, Heinz Linge. His association with Hitler began through a mix of military service, personal reliability and proximity to the SS elite guard units. He was the son of a restaurateur and trained as a bricklayer. He completed secondary education and took courses in construction.

In 1933, after Hitler came to power, Linge joined the SS and the Leibstandarte SS Adolf Hitler (LSSAH), the elite unit responsible for the Führer's personal protection. While serving in Berlin-Lichterfelde, in late 1934 Linge was assigned with about two dozen comrades to Hitler's mountain retreat at Obersalzberg.

In January 1935, Linge was officially made a valet, one of three men responsible for Hitler's daily routine, personal quarters and travel arrangements. He took care of Hitler's wardrobe, meals, daily schedule, and managed all domestic staff. He was 'household manager, traveling companion, butler, and maid-of-all-work combined'.

Linge became chief valet in 1939, replacing Karl Wilhelm Krause. He remained in close contact with Hitler in Berlin, at the Wolf's Lair in Rastenburg, at the Obersalzberg, and on all trips. Linge was also a member of the Führerbegleitkommando (FBK), the close-protection security detail for Hitler, and by 1944 managed the entire personal service staff.

Hitler's secretary Traudl Junge described him as ' . . . an extraordinarily clever, able man. He never lost his temper and had a good sense of humour . . . No wonder, even Hitler's most distinguished colleagues would ask Linge, out in the ante-room, whether this was a good time to give Hitler bad news.'

Linge and Kempka joined one of several groups who broke out of the bunker. Kempka managed to get out of Berlin but was captured a month later by United States forces at Berchtesgaden in southern Germany. Linge only got as far as the entrance of the Chancellery before being captured by Russian troops and handed over to SMERSH officers.

Strangely, although he was a key witness to what had happened in the bunker Linge appears not to have been taken to the team searching for Hitler's body. Instead he was taken, initially, to a detention and interrogation point for high-profile prisoners at Poznan, then transferred through several camps, eventually ending up in Soviet NKVD camp No. 326 in Tallin (Estonia) and later in Moscow.

Soviet records reveal that he first faced NKVD officers at Tallin on 22 November 1945, where he made a formal written statement. Writing specifically about the events of 30 April, he said:

> Around 16:00, Hitler went to Dr. Goebbels' study, supposedly to rest. Dr. Goebbels tried to persuade him to leave Berlin and save his life, but Hitler refused and announced his final decision to commit suicide.
>
> Then Hitler shook Goebbels's hand and went to his room. At that time, I, along with senior servant Krüger, was following him, since I, too, wanted to say goodbye to Hitler. He told me that he wanted his corpse to be thoroughly burned, since he was afraid his body might end up in Moscow on display.
>
> Eva Braun entered Hitler's room. After a short time, I heard a shot. I informed Reichsleiter Bormann, who was in the hallway. Then, together with him, I entered Hitler's office. There, we found Hitler lying with a gunshot wound to his right temple and on the sofa, next to him were two pistols. Next to him sat his wife, who had no gunshot wounds. She had committed suicide by cyanide. Helped by guards, we put the bodies in the blankets. After this the corpses were taken to the park where gasoline was poured over them and set on fire. We waited until only the charred bones and ashes remained.

Two weeks later, on 8 December, he was cross-examined about this statement by the head of the Tallinn NKVD operations department, Captain Kapigan. After briefly giving his background the questioning turned to the death of Hitler.

> QUESTION: Who, besides you, knew about Hitler's intention to commit suicide?
> ANSWER: Besides me, General Mohnke knew about it; he told me that Hitler himself also ordered him to burn his body. Also Goebbels knew of Hitler's intention to commit suicide; he discussed this with me personally. I was present during this conversation.

QUESTION: After Hitler's death, who specifically was in charge of burning his body?
ANSWER: Reichsleiter Bormann was in charge of burning the bodies of Hitler and Eva Braun.

QUESTION: Tell in detail who was present when the bodies of Hitler and Eva Braun were burned.
ANSWER: When Hitler's and Eva Braun's bodies were burned, present together with me were Reichsleiter Bormann and three or four unidentified men from the offices of the Reich Chancellery. We all poured gasoline on the bodies; I personally threw a piece of burning paper onto the blanket that covered the corpses.

QUESTION: Could you still recognise the Führer's face after burning his body?
ANSWER: Yes, after the burning I could still recognise the Führer's face, as the facial features remained, only the corpse took on a dark-brown coloration.

QUESTION: Why were you not present during the burial of the bodies?
ANSWER: I was not present during the burial of the bodies, because of an order of Reichsleiter Bormann. We all, except for the guard on duty at the entrance to the bunker, left the command post. Besides, we were so upset that we were not thinking even about the bodies.

QUESTION: What do you know about the fate of the corpses of Hitler and Eva Braun?
ANSWER: On May 1, 1945, at 22:00, during an assembly in the bunker of the Reich Chancellery, one of my comrades (I don't remember who) told me that General Mohnke had ordered the burial of the bodies in the park of the Reich Chancellery. I do not know exactly where, but I assume that the bodies were buried in a pit in the park near the bunker.

He then described the breakout from the bunker and his capture.

Linge, together with Otto Günsche, was later transferred to Moscow where they underwent severe coercive questioning over a number of years by the NKVD as part of 'The Hitler Book' operation, described in a later chapter

After his eventual release and return to Germany, Heinz Linge wrote his autobiography *With Hitler Till the End* and gives the following account of the final day:

In captivity the Russians asked me why Hitler had married on the last full day of his life. In this they saw proof for their theory that Hitler was a typical middle-class citizen who required everything to be rubber-stamped and 'official' for it to have any validity.

'You Germans', an NKVD intelligence officer remarked to me disparagingly in this connection, 'are only revolutionaries if you have a piece of paper authorising it.' There was no point in explaining to him that Hitler's decision to marry Eva Braun 'properly' resulted from quite different motives. It is certain that the ceremony and its consequences meant nothing at all to him. He merely wanted to fulfil Eva's wish that after coming to him in Berlin, she should die at his side as his lawful wife. In principle this is put another way in his Last Will and Testament of 29 April 1945. 'Since I believed during the years of struggle that I should not accept the responsibility of marriage, I have decided before ending my earthly span to make that girl my wife who, after long years of loyal friendship, came of her own free will into an almost besieged city in order to share her fate with mine. It is her wish that she should accompany me into death as my wife. Death will replace for us that of which my work robbed us both in the service of my people.'

Linge said Eva Hitler's composure after her marriage proved Hitler right. For a while she seemed to have forgotten the catastrophe and her environment.

When I saw her afterwards, instead of addressing her as gnädiges Fräulein as I always had done, or gnädige Frau as she now was. I preferred the emphatic 'Frau Hitler'. Her eyes lit up. She gave me a happy smile and for a moment laid her hand on my forearm. Eva Hitler. She had dreamed of this for more than ten years. Instinctively I thought of what Kurt Tucholsky had written, according to which one gets one's heart's desire, but always a day too late and always a size too small. This seemed coined for Eva Hitler, who went off to bed with her husband after drinks. We, 'the most intimate circle', stayed behind and celebrated the marriage 'deep below the ground' while the Russian artillery churned up the parkland around the Reich Chancellery.

The next day, 30 April 1945, I went to Hitler in the early morning. He was opening the door as I arrived. He had lain on the bed fully dressed and awake as he had done the night before. While Bormann, Krebs and Burgdorf kept loaded pistols within reach, safety catches off, and dozed on sofas near his door, and the female secretaries made themselves as comfortable as possible while awaiting the events that must soon come (at any moment the Russians could reach the bunker entrance), he signalled to me to accompany him, finger to his lips, indicating I should be careful not to disturb the sleeping figures.

We went to the telephone exchange, where Hitler rang the commandant, who told him that the defence of Berlin had already collapsed. The ring which the Russians had laid around the city could no longer be penetrated, and there was now no hope of relief. Arthur Axmann did offer to 'bring the Führer out of Berlin' using about 200

Hitler Youth volunteers and a panzer, but Hitler declined, murmuring quietly: 'That is no longer an option, I am remaining here!'

The 'hour of truth' had come. Firstly however, there was a last midday meal to be taken together. Hitler delivered a monologue about the future. The immediate post-war world would not have a good word to say for him, he said: the enemy would savour its triumph, and the German people would face very difficult times.

Even we, his intimate circle, would soon experience things that we could not imagine. But he trusted to 'the later histories' to 'treat him justly'. They would recognise that he had only wanted the very best for Germany. Not until after my release from captivity did I understand what he meant when he said: 'You will soon experience things that you cannot imagine.'

After the meal Eva Hitler came to me to take her leave. Pale, having remained awake all night but careful to maintain her composure, she thanked me for 'everything you have done for the Führer'. With a sad look she begged me at the finish: 'Should you meet my sister Gretl, do not tell her how her husband, Hermann Fegelein, met his death.' I never saw Gretl Fegelein again. Next she went to Frau Goebbels while Hitler retired to his study. Magda Goebbels wanted another 'personal conversation with the Führer', as Günsche told me. I approached Hitler and he allowed her to come.

They were alone for a while. When I entered, Hitler was thanking her for her commitment and services. He asked me to remove the gold Party badge from one of his uniforms and pinned it on her in 'especial recognition'. Immediately after this Hitler and I went into the common room where Goebbels appeared and begged Hitler briefly to allow the Hitler Youth to take him out of Berlin. Hitler responded brusquely: 'Doctor, you know my decision. There is no change! You can of course leave Berlin with your family.' Goebbels. standing proudly, replied that he would not do so. Like the Führer he intended to stay in Berlin – and die there.

At that Hitler gave Goebbels his hand and, leaning on me, returned to his room. Immediately afterwards followed the last personal goodbyes.

Flugkapitän Baur and SS-Sturmbannführer Otto Günsche came, two men who had dedicated their lives to Hitler. My mouth was dry. Soon I would have to carry out my last duty. Anxiously I gazed at the man whom I had served devotedly for more than ten years. He stood stooped, the hank of hair, as always, across the pale forehead. He had become grey. He looked at me with tired eves and said he would now retire. It was 15:15 hours. I asked for his orders for the last time.

Outwardly calm and in a quiet voice, as if he were sending me into the garden to fetch something, he said 'Linge, I am going to shoot myself now. You know what you have to do. I have given the order for the break-out. Attach yourself to one of the groups and try to get through to the west.' To my question what we should fight for now, he answered 'For the Coming Man'. I saluted. Hitler took two or three tired steps towards me and offered his hand. Then for the last time in his life he raised his right arm in the Hitler salute. A ghostly scene. I turned on my heel, closed the door and went to the bunker exit where the SS bodyguard was sitting around.

As I assumed that Hitler would put an end to his life at any moment I did not stay there long, but returned to the anteroom. I smelt the gas from a discharged firearm. Thus it had come to pass. Although I was beyond surprises, everything in me resisted opening the door and entering alone. I went to the map room where a number of people were gathered around Martin Bormann. What they were discussing I have no idea. They had no knowledge of what had happened. I gave Bormann a signal and asked him to come with me to Hitler's room, which he did.

I opened the door and went in, Bormann following me. He turned white as chalk and stared at me helplessly. Adolf Hitler and Eva Braun were seated on the sofa. Both were dead. Hitler had shot himself in the right temple with his 7.65mm pistol. This weapon, and his 6.35mm pistol which he had kept in reserve in the event that the larger gun misfired, lay near his feet on the floor. His head was inclined a little towards the wall. Blood had spattered on the carpet near the sofa. To his right beside him sat his wife. She had drawn up her legs on the sofa. Her contorted face betrayed how she had died. Cyanide poisoning. Its bite was marked in her features The small box in which the capsule had been kept lay on the table. I pushed it aside to give myself room.

In a later interrogation in Moscow, Linge expanded slightly on this narrative:

In Hitler's right temple gaped a bullet wound the size of a Pfennig and two streams of blood ran down his check. On the carpet next to the sofa a puddle of blood the size of a plate had formed. The wall and the sofa were bespattered with blood. Hitler's right hand lay palm uppermost on his knee. The left hung at his side. Next to Hitler's right foot lay a 7.65mm Walther pistol, and next to his left foot a 6.35mm of the same make. Hitler wore his grey tunic emblazoned with the Gold Party Badge, the Iron Cross First Class and the Wounded Badge of the First World War – as he had done constantly in recent days. He was wearing a white shirt with a black tie, black trousers, black socks and black leather slippers. Eva Braun's legs were drawn up under her on the sofa. Her brightly coloured high-heeled shoes lay on the floor. Her lips were firmly pressed together. She had poisoned herself with cyanide.

While Bormann went outside to fetch help to remove the bodies. I spread out the blankets. laid the cadavers on them and wrapped them round. It did not strike me until later, when the Russians asked me about it, that I did not see Hitler's face closely, and I was unable to say what damage the bullet had inflicted to his head. My main aim was to finish and get away.

Eva Hitler was carried out first. Erich Kempka lifted her up but then replaced her on the floor so that Günsche could take over because he found it awkward to carry her alone. Bormann picked her up in his arms and brought the body out of the room where Kempka took over again because he did not like the idea of the man she had despised in life carrying her now to the grave.

I reached below Hitler's head, two officers from his SS bodyguard lifted the body, wrapped in a grey blanket, and we carried him out. Immediately in front of the bunker door, in the Reich Chancellery garden, his body was laid next to Eva's in a small depression where gasoline was poured over the cadavers and an attempt was made to set light to them. At first this proved impossible. As a result of the various fires in the parkland there was a fierce wind circulating which smothered our attempts to set the bodies alight from a few metres distance. Because of the relentless Russian artillery we could not approach the bodies and ignite the petrol with a match.

I returned to the bunker and made a thick pile of some signal papers. Bormann lit it and I threw it onto Hitler's petrol-soaked body which caught fire immediately. Standing at the bunker entrance we, the last witnesses – Bormann, Goebbels, Stumpfegger, Günsche, Kempka and I – raised our hands for a last Hitler salute. Then we withdrew into the bunker.

Since Hitler had given me the additional task of burning everything that remained of him, I had no time to concern myself with the bodies. These were still burning towards 19:30 hours. I destroyed the bloodstained carpet, Hitler's uniforms, his medicines, documents etc. While I was doing this a squad under the command of an SS bodyguard officer buried the carbonised bodies in a shell crater.

Everything had to be done quickly and secretly, for if the fighting troops in the Reich Chancellery and defending the government district knew what had transpired they were likely to abandon their weapons. I realised at the time that that must not happen, because Hitler had arranged for a government to continue the struggle.

Bormann, Goebbels and a few military men went to the conference room to decide how to proceed in Hitler's absence. When I met the new Reich Chancellor Dr Joseph Goebbels next morning, he stopped me to ask why I had not made Hitler change his mind about committing suicide. 'Herr Doktor, if you were unable to do it, how should I?' I replied. 'Yes, Linge', he admitted, 'last night I also intended shooting myself, but it is a very difficult thing to do. I simply could not do it.'

Now we sat in the bunker and hoped in vain that the Russians would agree to the terms that General Krebs offered them on Dr Goebbels's behalf on the morning of 1 May 1945. In captivity Soviet officers told me why the meeting between Krebs and the Russian generals Chuikov and Sokolovski had a negative outcome. The Russians wanted capitulation. Krebs did not have the authority.

Chapter 17

OPERATION 'DECEIT'

The Russian military had full control of Berlin until mid-July 1945, when British, American and French forces moved in. Allied leaders had agreed at the Yalta Conference in early 1945 to divide Germany into four military occupation zones, each managed by one of the victorious Allied powers: the United States, the United Kingdom, France, and the Soviet Union. This division was formalised at the Potsdam Conference (July–August 1945), following Germany's unconditional surrender.

The Soviet Union controlled the Eastern zone; the United States the Southern zone; the United Kingdom the North-western zone, with the South-western zone, controlled by France. This zone was carved mostly from US and British areas at their concession. Although located deep within the Soviet zone, Berlin was also divided into four sectors (one for each Allied power). Austria was also divided into four occupation zones.

The Allies, through the Allied Control Council, were supposed to jointly govern Germany. In practice, each zone was run separately by its occupying power, with different policies, especially regarding economics and politics. The intention was for Germany to remain a single country under joint authority, but growing Cold War tensions led to increasing separation.

After Russian forces captured Berlin in late April 1945, they had unfettered control over the city until Western military forces moved into their respective zones in mid-July. Each power controlled its own sector, but all four occupying forces maintained joint authority over Berlin through the Allied Control Council. This arrangement was unique to Berlin; while the rest of Germany was also divided into four occupation zones, only Berlin, fully surrounded by the Soviet zone, was jointly administered by all four powers.

Because of the uncertainty which had been deliberately created by Stalin, British Military Intelligence, MI6, decided to conduct their own investigation into Hitler's 'supposed' death shortly after taking over the British Zone following rumours that Hitler might be hiding there. They, and the Americans, had been unnerved by contradictory Russian statements, including by Marshal Zhukov himself.

Zhukov and General V. D. Sokolovsky, the deputy commander in chief of Soviet forces in the Russian zone, informally told several Western military men and diplomats in May that they had identified a body believed to be that of Hitler through dental identification. And on 5 June when the Supreme Allied Commanders met in Berlin in order to organise the establishment of the Four-Power Government, responsible Russian officers told officers from Eisenhower's staff that Hitler's body had been discovered and 'identified with almost completely certainty'. They said the body was found in the bunker together with three others. It had been badly charred, attributed to the flamethrowers with which their troops had advanced.

They said, disingenuously, that if the Russians were not officially announcing Hitler's death, it was only due to their reluctance to commit themselves as long as there was the 'slightest room for doubt'. On 6 June Zhukov's staff officers told Eisenhower's staff officers that Hitler's body had been discovered, exhumed and scientifically identified.

On the same day the day the Soviet Military Administration in Germany was set up, the Russians held an unofficial press conference in Berlin at which correspondents from the United States, Great Britain and France were present. An officer from Zhukov's staff disclosed details of the search for Hitler's corpse and authorised the correspondents to report, without naming him as the source, that it had been found and identified with a high degree of probability.

He said Hitler's smoke-blackened and charred corpse was one of four that had been discovered in the bunker on 3 and 4 May. They had been burnt in the corridor by a flamethrower, but despite this, after careful examination of teeth and other characteristics the Russians singled out one body which they believed almost certainly was that of Hitler.

They said that after examination by chemists from the Red Army, there were indications that Hitler most probably died of poisoning. This clearly referred to the autopsy conducted at Berlin-Buch by Scharavsky's team of pathologists.

American journalist Joseph Grigg, Jr., of United Press suggested that 'This probably will remain a secret for all time to guard against the possibility of Nazi fanatics trying to recover the bodies'.

While the Soviets in Berlin on 6 June were saying that they believed with a high degree of certainty that Hitler was dead, Stalin was saying just the opposite. On the same day in Moscow when high-ranking American diplomates met with Stalin, he said he was sure that Hitler was still alive. Thus, it is not surprising that after the 6 June press conference, Stalin immediately sent Andrei Vyshinsky (later prosecuting attorney at Nuremberg) to Marshal Zhukov in Berlin as his 'political representative to the Chief of the Soviet Military Administration'.

Then on 9 June a major press conference was held in Berlin, with one of Stalin's senior aides, Andrei Vyshinsky and Zhukov, gave a new 'official' Russian version. Zhukov disclosed for the first time that Hitler had married Eva Braun, adding that the references to the marriage had been found in the diaries of Hitler's personal adjutants.

But then he pointedly said 'We have found no corpse that could be Hitler's' and added that Hitler and Braun had good opportunities to get away from Berlin; 'He could have taken off at the very last moment, for there was an airfield at his disposal. The circumstances are highly mysterious. We did not identify Hitler's body and I cannot say anything about his fate . . . now it is up to you British and Americans to find him.'

Colonel General Nikolai Berzarin, Soviet commander of Berlin, turning to the question of whether Hitler had died in Berlin, said 'There are all sorts of people who were close to him who say that he killed himself. Still others say he was killed by an exploding shell but no body has been found. My personal opinion is that he has disappeared somewhere into Europe.' Berzarin said 'Perhaps he is in Spain with Franco. He had the possibility of getting away.'

On 10 June American Major General Kenneth Strong asked a Soviet intelligence officer regarding Zhukov's statement that Hitler was still alive. The Soviet officer replied that the Russians had revised their earlier opinion that Hitler was dead, and that none of the evidence at present in their possession indicates definitely that this was so. This Russian Intelligence officer was not named, but was most likely one of the SMERSH officers who had been involved in the search. This was Elena Rzhevskaya's 'cover up' in action.

On 31 October, as a goodwill gesture, the record of the interrogation of Hanna Reitsch was sent by US intelligence to Major General Sidney. Following that, on 1 November, Brigadier General Ford sent a circular to Brigadier General Conrad (USA), Major General Sidney (USSR) and Colonel Poulu (France), proposing that the next meeting of the Intelligence Committee should discuss the various claims about Hitler's death.

The first paragraph of that text read: 'The only conclusive proof of Hitler's death would be the finding and definite identification of the body.' It was, however, just this conclusive proof that was being denied, concealed both from the Allies and from Russians themselves. Brigadier General Ford continues, 'In the absence of this proof, the only positive proof consists of the detailed accounts of particular witnesses who were either acquainted with his intentions or were eyewitnesses to his fate.' 'As we have seen' Rzhevskaya said, 'there really was no shortage of such witnesses.'

The British intelligence officer Hugh Trevor-Roper summarises:

Analysing the testimony of those witnesses who fell into the hands of the Allies, and the information that had leaked from our side, it is impossible to suppose that the accounts of the various eyewitnesses are a fabricated story. They were all too busy planning their own escapes to . . . have any inclination to memorise a fictional charade that they would maintain for five months in isolation from each other under detailed and persistent cross-examination.

However, the evidence about the last days and death of Hitler is 'not yet complete', and Brigadier General Ford appeals to his colleagues on the quadripartite Intelligence Committee for information about the whereabouts of, and a request to be allowed to interrogate, Günsche and Rattenhuber (who are in captivity according to the Russian communique of 7 May), Traudl Junge (Gertraud but called Gertruda in our records) and Hans Baur, Hitler's personal pilot, who had been seriously injured and, according to unconfirmed reports, was in hospital, again in the Russian sector.

At the end of this message to his colleagues is the most important point: 'A rumour came from the Russian side that a body had been found that was identified, or was believed to have been identified, as Hitler's body from the teeth. Could they perhaps report the results of that investigation to establish the extent to which that can be relied on?'

There was no response. 'Evidently, Rzhevskaya said 'it had not proved possible to conceal the facts completely, and perhaps nobody had tried all that hard. The main thing was to keep everybody guessing.'

Chapter 18

HUGH TREVOR-ROPER

In the British investigation of the death of Hitler Hugh Trevor-Roper's name looms large. Allied Commander-in-Chief Dwight Eisenhower was one who appears to have been convinced by the Soviet story that Hitler was still alive, but was dissuaded after a conversation with Trevor-Roper.

Trevor-Roper, then a young intelligence officer attached to MI6 in Berlin, was asked by the chief of British counter-intelligence in Berlin, Brigadier Dick White, to investigate what happened to Hitler. Using the alias 'Major Oughton' he interviewed as many people as he could, including witnesses to the burning of the bodies who had managed to evade Russian capture, but received no co-operation from the Russians. In less than six months he was able to piece together an accurate account of what had happened. His report was submitted to MI6 and the findings were summarised to the press at the British press headquarters in Berlin in November 1945.

An extended book version of the report was subsequently published in 1947 called *The Last Days of Hitler*. Trevor-Roper concluded, unequivocally, that Hitler was dead, not 'possibly alive' as the Russians kept insisting. But he acknowledged that his investigation was severely hampered by Soviet obfuscation.

In the preface to the 3rd edition, published in 1956, Trevor-Roper wrote:

The principal witnesses whom I sought and failed to find in 1945 were five. They were Otto Günsche, Hitler's SS adjutant, and Heinz Linge, his personal servant, both of whom undoubtedly saw Hitler dead and took part in the burning of his body; Johann Rattenhuber, who commanded Hitler's detective bodyguard and who, I believed, knew the place of his burial; Hans Baur, Hitler's personal pilot, who was with him to the end; and Harry Mengershausen, an officer of the bodyguard who was reported to know about the burial of the bodies.

There were of course other important witnesses whom I had missed, but it was these five whom I particularly sought because I had positive evidence that they were still alive. Günsche and Linge had both been seen and identified among Russian prisoners in Berlin, and the Russians had themselves included the names of Baur and Rattenhuber among their prisoners in an official communiqué which they had published on 6 May 1945. However, as I have said, these requests were unavailing: the Russians declined to answer any questions and in the end I wrote my book without the help of these missing witnesses.

Elena Rzhevskaya herself told me in 1991 that she and the rest of the SMERSH team were aware of Trevor-Roper's investigation and praised him for his diligence in difficult circumstances. And she was saddened that she could not help him. She intimated that it would have saved an awful lot of trouble.

Trevor-Roper's book, banned in the USSR, quickly became the accepted version of what happened in the bunker, and how Hitler had died. It went through seven editions over the next 45 years. His conclusion as to Hitler's death, published in the first edition, 1947, never wavered up to an including the seventh edition in 1995.

But it is diametrically opposed to the Russian version, hence the dilemma, and is one of the reasons for the lingering mystery in the West about Hitler's death. Who do we believe? It is not helped by Trevor-Roper's own personality. He became an authoritative historian, and was later appointed Regius Professor of Modern History at Oxford University, but his polemical stance on historical subjects made him controversial. For instance, he was critical of the official version of the assassination of President John F. Kennedy in November 1963, saying the (Warren) Commission employed a 'smokescreen of often irrelevant material' and 'accepted impermissible axioms, constructed invalid arguments, and failed to ask elementary and essential questions'. His reputation was severely dented in 1983, when as a director of *The Times* newspaper he authenticated the so-called '*Hitler Diaries*' which turned out to be forgeries.

Trevor-Roper's account of Hitler's death in the first edition is clear and succinct:

About two o'clock (30 April) he took lunch. Eva Braun was not there; evidently she did not feel hungry, or ate alone in her room; and Hitler shared his meal, as usual in her absence, with his two secretaries and the cook. The conversation indicated nothing unusual. Hitler remained quiet, and did not speak of his intentions. Nevertheless, preparations were already being made for the approaching ceremony.

In the morning, the guards had been ordered to collect all their rations for the day, since they would not be allowed to pass through the corridor of the Bunker again; and about lunch-time Hitler's S.S. adjutant Sturmbannführer Günsche, sent an order to the transport officer and chauffeur, Sturmbannführer Erich Kempka, to send 200 litres of petrol to the Chancellery garden. Kempka protested that it would be difficult to find so large a quantity at once, but he was told that it must be found. Ultimately he found about 180 litres and sent it round to the garden. Four men carried it in jerricans and placed it at the emergency exit of the Bunker. There they met one of the police guards, who demanded an explanation. They told him that it was for the ventilating plant. The guard told them not to be silly, for the plant was oil-driven. At this moment Hitler's personal servant, Heinz Linge, appeared. He reassured the guard, terminated the argument, and dismissed the men. Soon afterwards all the guards except those on duty were ordered to leave the Chancellery, and to stay away. It was not intended that any casual observer should witness the final scene.

Meanwhile Hitler had finished lunch, and his guests had been dismissed. For a time he remained behind; then he emerged from his suite, accompanied by Eva Braun, and another farewell ceremony took place. Bormann and Goebbels were there, with Burgdorf, Krebs, Hewel, Naumann, Voss, Rattenhuber, Hoegl, Günsche, Linge, and the four women, Frau Christian, Frau Junge, Fraulein Krueger, and Fraulein Manziarly. Frau Goebbels was not present. Unnerved by the approaching death of her children, she remained all day in her own room. Hitler and Eva Braun shook hands with them all, and then returned to their suite.

The others were dismissed, all but the high-priests and those few others whose services would be necessary. These waited in the passage. A single shot was heard. After an interval they entered the suite. Hitler was lying on the sofa, which was soaked with blood. He had shot himself through the mouth. Eva Braun was also on the sofa, also dead. A revolver was by her side, but she had not used it; she had swallowed poison. The time was half-past three.

The account then continues with the removal of the bodies and cremation in the garden. Trevor-Roper never wavered from his determination that Hitler shot himself in the mouth. The account makes no mention of cyanide, except for Eva Braun.

Fifty years later, in the preface to the 7th edition, Trevor-Roper wrote:

I have said that the Russian version is 'substantially' the same as mine, for in one small detail I must admit that we differ. Both in their early admissions and in their later film the Russians suggested that Hitler had killed himself by taking poison. On 5 June 1945, Zhukov's staff officers stated that Russian doctors had established, by an examination of Hitler's body, that he had died of poison. In their film Hitler is shown swallowing a poison-capsule. On the other hand I have stated that he shot himself through the mouth. Since the Russians had possession of Hitler's body and I had not, they were obviously in a more favourable position than I was to determine the cause of his death. On the other hand none of their pronouncements has been authoritative, reasoned, or even circumstantial. Their early statements, before 9 June 1945, were unofficial and second-hand. In some respects they were certainly inaccurate – at least in the form in which they were reported, and their film was unashamed propaganda full of tendentious inaccuracies: it cannot be taken as scientific documentation. In these circumstances perhaps it is best to go behind their loose statements and re-examine the available evidence.

The first witness who was available in 1945 was Erich Kempka, Hitler's chauffeur. He had escaped from Berlin and had been captured by the Americans. Under interrogation he stated that immediately after Hitler's death, Günsche, who had inspected the body, had told him that Hitler had shot himself through the mouth. This of course is only second-hand evidence; but Kempka added that after helping to carry Eva Braun's body out to the burning, he himself had gone into the 'death room' and seen, lying on the floor, two revolvers, one a Walther 7.65, the other a Walther 6.35. Seven months later this evidence was confirmed and completed by the Hitler Youth Leader, Artur Axmann, who had been at large in the Bavarian Alps and who is thus independent of Kempka.

Axmann said that he had been one of those who entered the 'death room' immediately after Hitler's suicide. 'As we entered, we saw the Führer sitting on a small divan, Eva Braun at his side, with her head resting on his shoulder. The Führer was only slightly slumped forward and everyone recognised that he was dead. His jaw hung somewhat loosely down and a pistol lay on the floor. Blood was dripping from both temples, and his mouth was bloody and smeared, but there was not much blood spattered around . . . I believe that Hitler took poison first and then shot himself through the mouth, and that the concussion of such a blast resulted in the blood on the Führer's temples.'

Such was the evidence available to me in 1946. Now it is supplemented by the evidence of Linge and Mengershausen who, having spent the intervening decade in Russian prisons, have had no opportunity of collusion with either Kempka or Axmann. Linge is a first-hand witness: he too went into the 'death room' immediately after Hitler's suicide, and it was he who carried the body out into the garden. According to his account, when he went into the room, 'there, almost upright in a sitting position on a couch, was the body of Adolf Hitler. A small hole, the size of a German silver mark, showed on his right temple and a trickle of blood ran slowly down over his cheek.'

After this statement, which exactly confirms the entirely independent account of Axmann, Linge goes on to confirm the details given by Kempka: 'one pistol, a Walther 7.65 lay on the floor where it had dropped from his right hand. A yard or so away lay another gun of 6.35 calibre.' To this must be added the evidence of Mengershausen, who states that when he was shown the remains of Hitler's body about a month later, the head had a bullet hole in the temple. Mengershausen adds that he believes, from the state of the head when he inspected it, that Hitler had shot himself through the head, not through the mouth as I had written. The hole in the temple seemed to him to be the hole of an in-going, not an outgoing bullet. Had Hitler shot himself through the mouth, Mengershausen says, the air pressure would surely have broken the jaws; which, however, were intact. I am not competent to judge this matter, and the experts whom I consult give me such different answers that I am content to leave the matter in suspense. But the evidence seems clear that although Hitler may conceivably, as Axmann surmised, have taken poison as well, he certainly killed himself with a revolver shot.

In 1968 the Russians, under Leonid Brezhnev, appear to have tried to make amends for Stalin's deception by allowing Elena Rzhevskaya's fellow wartime interpreter, Lev Bezimensky, to inspect the records of Faust Scharavasky's autopsy at Berlin-Buch. He subsequently wrote a book, *The Death of Adolf Hitler*, first in German, then translated into English.

Western historians and reviewers were both interested in and critical of his account. *The Spectator* magazine criticised it as 'utter, unmitigated rubbish' and pointed out that its central claims, far from solving the mystery, reflected Soviet political interests and contradicted already-accepted Western research (notably Hugh Trevor-Roper's 1947 work, which had established Hitler's suicide as the consensus in the West).

'Bezymenski always was a humorous and cynical fellow', it said, 'but this is going a bit too far. Soviet doctors bound by the Hippocratic Oath? Really! What will he think of next! The history of the USSR presents a long procession of "internationally recognised" authorities lying their heads off about medical evidence.' The review further noted that the book was curiously never published in Russian – only for Western audiences, suggesting a propagandistic motive rather than a genuine effort at historical transparency.

Critics dismissed the forensic details provided by the book (such as the claim that Hitler died by cyanide instead of gunshot, or suggestions of a coup de grâce) as unconvincing, ideologically motivated and scientifically questionable. The autopsy's assertion that Hitler had only one testicle was also met with scepticism – the report was called 'ridiculous' and 'intolerably bad work' by German pathologist Otto Prokop, with recent historians labelling it as 'riddled with scientific inconsistencies and tainted by ideological motivations'.

Because this was the first time anyone in the West had heard of an autopsy, some reviewers used the phrase 'supposed autopsy', casting doubt on its authenticity. Despite this, Western scholars did accept the value of some documents, such as the publication of photographs of Hitler's dental remains, which matched known dental records and have since been considered reliable forensic evidence.

Trevor-Roper noted the peculiar aspects of its publication: the autopsy report had been kept secret in the USSR for decades, fuelling speculation, and was published belatedly 'for Western consumption only', he said, 'which raised doubts about its intended purpose'.

He noted Elena Rzhevskaya's involvement for the first time, commenting on her first work *Berlin Notes*. He noted that the early stages of the Russian inquiry had confirmed his own conclusions. Understandably perhaps, because her name was Lieutenant Kagan at the time, Trevor-Roper appears not to have identified her role in finding Käthe Heusermann and identifying Hitler's corpse through the dental records.

> The fact of the inquiry in Berlin, and of its suppression by Stalin, had been confirmed. So had my account of the method of identification (by the teeth) and of the conclusion of the inquiry (the death by poison). The only discrepancy lay still in the difference between that conclusion and my own. I had concluded that Hitler had shot himself, though he might conceivably have taken poison too; the Russians had concluded that he had poisoned himself, though he might conceivably have been shot as well. This difference is not very great or important, and even if it were to be resolved one way or another, such resolution (we may think) would hardly constitute a 'sensation', radically altering the received version of events.

Again, the only unanswered question, according to Trevor-Roper, was who fired the shot?

Following that criticism the book seems to have failed to gain traction and more or less disappeared. The Soviets made no further attempts to set the record straight, which is not surprising considering the Cold War tensions at the time, especially after the Soviet invasion of Czechoslovakia in the same year.

In the 1990s, Bezymenski 'partially recanted' some the accounts in his book, stating he had been given only limited and possibly altered information by the Soviet authorities. He admitted he was a tool of the state's disinformation apparatus and that his book may not represent objective historical truth. While not intimately involved in the capture of Germans in the bunker he was a member of Zhukov's headquarters staff and had high-level access to 'classified Soviet post-war investigations' especially involving the Hitler case. He likely worked under the broader structure of SMERSH or GRU's special operations division.

Chapter 19

THE HITLER BOOK

By June 1945 the SMERSH team had finished its task of resolving the 'real' Hitler story, even as the 'official' story was still being concocted.

All the captives from the bunker were transported to Russia, where they were farmed out around various prisons and prisoner of war camps. Some, including General Weidling, never saw freedom again. Some of the prisoners had a harder time than others, namely Heinz Linge, Otto Günsche, Hans Rattenhuber and, surprisingly, Käthe Heusermann, whose only 'crime' was to be a dental assistant to Hitler's dentist. Linge and Günsche spent many years being interrogated, sometimes under harsh conditions, as the Russians tried to get a full picture of the mind of Adolf Hitler, as part of the ongoing 'Operation Myth'. It culminated in a remarkable document, unearthed in the Russian Archives more than 50 years later – Document 462a. It was found by chance when Matthias Uhl, a German historian and researcher specialising in twentieth-century German and Soviet history came across it. Uhl was a research fellow at the Deutsches Historisches Institut (German Historical Institute) in Moscow, and was undertaking a systematic examination of the papers of the Archives in the course of carrying out a research project for the Institute for Contemporary History in Munich.

A Russian colleague who had access to the presidential archive compared the copy to the original and confirmed the authenticity of the document – file no. 462a was a word-for-word copy of the 1949 NKVD/MVD dossier, known as *The Hitler Book*. Uhl published the book in German, called, appropriately, *The Hitler Book. The Secret Dossier Prepared for Stalin*, later translated into English.

Uhl explained that members of the NKVD (which later became the KGB) hunted down all the available documents on Hitler and his regime, while officers in the department searched prisoners of war camps for Hitler's helpers, who had to undergo endless interrogations, so that they could provide Stalin with a history of Adolf Hitler. Eventually, on 29 December 1949, the dictator received something like a final report of 413 typed pages covering Hitler's life between 1933 and 1945. After he had read it, Stalin had the text placed in his personal collection of documents, the General Secretary's Archive. This copy is today preserved in the personal archive of the Russian President and may not be consulted by foreigners. The copy, presumably, is still in the archives and available, subject to permission, to researchers.

The purpose of this investigation on Stalin's behalf is not completely clear, but it's been suggested that he was haunted by how Hitler double-crossed him after signing the non-aggression treaty between Nazi Germany and the Soviet Union in 1939. Stalin was lulled into a false sense of security by this pact, which rebounded on him when Germany suddenly attacked Russia in 1941.

The two Germans who suffered most for this dossier were Linge and Günsche. The NKVD interrogations used their usual techniques of torture – beatings, sleep and food deprivation, threats against their families – and simultaneously offers of reward for co-operation. According to Uhl's account initial resistance on the part of the witnesses was quickly broken. The most effective means by far was the removal of the prisoners' POW status on 27 February 1946 and their classification as war criminals. After being robbed of their uniforms and dressed in the standard prisoners' clothing, with their rations reduced to the appropriate Soviet levels, most of them submitted.

After being released in 1955 Linge wrote of his treatment in Russia.

I was thrown into the notorious Lubianka Prison. There in a filthy bug-infested cell I waited, expecting the worst. It came in the form of a large GPU lieutenant-colonel who spoke good, cultivated German. He interrogated me with a monotonous patience which brought me to a state of sheer despair. Over and over he asked the same questions, trying to extract from me an admission that Hitler had survived.

My unemotional assertion that I had carried Hitler's corpse from his room, had poured petrol over it and set it alight in front of the bunker was considered a cover story. In order to lull me into a false sense of security he occasionally told me that before the war he had been in Germany, and he chatted with me as though he were an old war comrade. I remained as alert as I could, no easy task for the bedbugs gave me no respite and only rarely did I sleep. Finally the bugs were even too much for the officer who had to watch me constantly.

'Tell the commissar', he advised me. When I replied with a cynical grin that 'if I did that they would increase the bug population', he countered:

'Tell him!' I did so, and could scarcely believe the result. I was moved to a 'lavish cell' with parquet flooring. Slowly it dawned on me why. It had been expected that I would complain.

Now came the carrot-and-stick treatment. Since I would not confirm what the commissar wanted to hear I had to strip naked and bend over a trestle after being warned that I would be thrashed if I did not finally 'cough up'. Naked and humiliated I persisted with my account: 'Adolf Hitler shot himself on 30 April 1945. I burned his body!' The commissar ordered a powerfully-built lieutenant holding a whip with several thongs: 'Give it to him.' As I cried out like a stuck pig, he observed cynically: 'You ought to know about this treatment better than us. We learned it from your SS and Gestapo!'

Nevertheless I kept to the facts. He changed the procedure only inasmuch as he had me brought to a sound-proofed room – dressed again – where seven or eight commissars were waiting. The ceremony began once more. While somebody roared monotonously: 'Hitler is alive, Hitler is alive, tell the truth!' I was whipped until I bled. Near madness I yelled until my voice failed. Still bellowing the torturers in officers' uniform stopped for a rest. I was allowed to dress and returned to my cell where I collapsed. That was the beginning of an intensive interrogation strategy which even today gives me nightmares.

About a year after the end of the war I was thrust into a barred railway wagon and transported like some wild animal back to Berlin. My daily rations were a salted herring, 450 grams of damp bread and two cubes of sugar. In Berlin I was put into a jail. What the Russians wanted was to be shown where – according to me – Hitler had shot himself. I was taken to the ruins of the New Reich Chancellery where a number of commissars and Marshal Sokolovski awaited. I showed them the sofa on which Hitler had shot himself, still where we had left it, but meanwhile ripped by 'souvenir hunters'. After this local visit, for which the Russians seemed to have little enthusiasm, I was returned to the prison for more interrogations.

These Berlin interrogations were carried out in a different way to those in Moscow. A female interpreter asked politely, I responded in like manner. The only thing certain was that the Russians did not believe me. In 1950 they were still doubtful that Hitler was dead.

Accordingly, the question-and-answer game in Berlin went round in monotonous circles. 'How much blood sprayed on the carpet?' 'How far from Hitler's foot did the pool of blood extend?' 'Where was his pistol exactly?' 'Which pistol did he use?' and 'How and where was he sitting exactly?' These were some of the stereotype, endlessly repeated questions I was obliged to answer. The interpreter was hearing these details for the first time and they interested her, but even so it was not hard to see that she would have preferred be doing something else. The questioning usually went on without interruption until the bread trolley was heard.

One day when I had had just about enough of the same stupid questions I reacted stubbornly as the trolley passed. 'That is the end of it', I said, 'I am hungry and cannot go on.' The interpreter reacted with a friendly smile and the observation that she was from Leningrad and knew 'what hunger really was'.

'When you tried to starve us out', she went on with a blush, 'we ate mice and rats.' I was ashamed of my outburst and fell silent. The interrogation ended.

Measured by the term of my imprisonment, Berlin was only a flying visit. Soon I was back in the Moscow prison where, a long time later, I met Otto Günsche again. In the prison hospital we were treated with kid gloves in order to show us how good things could get.

One day it was revealed to us that we were to have the opportunity to write our 'memoirs'. We were released from hospital and given rooms in a Moscow villa in which the widow of a general lived. After she had got to know and trust us, she told me that her son had often been seen in public with Stalin. Under guard we now set down on paper, day in, day out, our experience of Hitler. Then before we had really got used to the house and surroundings, it was time to move on. We arrived at a villa outside Moscow.

German soldiers served us as they had General Seidlitz, captured at Stalingrad, and who had been our predecessor in this dacha. It was not a bad life. The food was good and we were decently treated. Suddenly it was not so important to the Russians where Hitler might have gone. They wanted manuscripts which proved that his main aim had been to play the Russians for fools – if necessary with the Western Powers.

According to the Soviets we knew more about this than was in the official documents. Our career as historians came to an end when the Russians realised that we were not prepared to portray Molotov's negotiations with Hitler falsely. Without blinking an eye they denied that for a period Stalin and Hitler had made common cause and shared out Poland between them.

Our 'memoirs' were archived. We became normal POWs and were put into a camp for generals. It contained forty-two generals and three staff officers. Although we lived well there, the other inhabitants made us sick. Looking at these idlers, pedlars swapping little boxes and other nonsense, I asked myself how the 'Boss' could have expected to win the war with them.

The generals went home to Germany. We, the two 'Hitler people', were put on trial in 1950 and received twenty-five years' hard labour in the Soviet Union.

Käthe Heusermann, Blashcke's dental assistant, was also treated harshly. Elena Rzhevskaya writes 'After rendering a uniquely important service to history, Heusermann was held as a dangerous criminal first in the Lubyanka, then in Lefortovo Prison in solitary confinement for six years!'

In August 1951 Heusermann was finally charged with being a 'voluntary participant in Hitler's dental treatment, and therefore she had helped the German state to prolong the war. While attending to Hitler's teeth she could have killed him with a bottle of water and thereby done the world a favour.'

She was sentenced to ten years in severe-regime labour camps, less the six and a half years she had already spent in solitary confinement. She went to a 'corrective' forced labour camp along with other women. In December 1951, along with three other German women and several men she was despatched in a cattle truck to Siberia.

In the camp in Taishet (700km north-west of Irkutsk), lacking the strength to fulfil the labour quota, Heusermann was put on penal rations. She received no parcels because her relatives knew nothing about her. She would have died of starvation had it not been for another prisoner who became her lifelong friend, a Carpathian Jew, Heusermann called her, who spoke German. This woman was able to meet the quota and, earning a little money, had a few rubles to spend when the mobile food store came round. She shared her food and, when released before her, memorised the addresses of her relatives. She let them know about her and Käthe began receiving parcels. Käthe Heusermann was in prison for ten years.

In September 1955, Konrad Adenauer, the first Chancellor of West Germany, negotiated a landmark agreement with the Soviet Union to secure the release of the last German prisoners of war (POWs) and civilian internees detained in Soviet captivity since the end of the Second World War.

Millions of German soldiers were captured by the Soviets, with hundreds of thousands held for years as forced labourers in camps under harsh conditions. By the early 1950s, most POWs held by the Western Allies had been released, but about 10,000–15,000 Germans remained in Soviet camps, fuelling deep anxiety and public pressure in West Germany.

Adenauer travelled to Moscow and engaged in tough negotiations with Soviet leaders Nikita Khrushchev and Nikolai Bulganin. The Soviets demanded the Federal Republic of Germany (West Germany) establish official diplomatic relations with the Soviet Union – something that did not then exist due to Germany's East-West division and Cold War tensions.

Adenauer's delegation prioritised the humanitarian goal: bringing home POWs missing for a decade. The talks were difficult and at times near collapse, but a diplomatic breakthrough came after personal appeals by Adenauer and his colleague Carlo Schmid emphasising the suffering of German families. Ultimately, Adenauer agreed to establish diplomatic relations with the USSR, while the Soviets made an oral commitment to release the remaining German prisoners. Approximately 10,000 surviving German POWs and about 5,000 civilian internees were released from Soviet captivity and returned to Germany between late 1955 and early 1956. This arrangement was celebrated in West Germany as 'The Homecoming of the Ten Thousand', for many families, it marked the true end of the war.

Adenauer's success in securing their release was a major domestic and diplomatic victory and helped legitimise West Germany's new post-war status. The agreement was seen as a pragmatic, humanitarian achievement that improved the lives of thousands and marked a shift in East-West relations, even as political differences remained unresolved.

Within months, the prisoners most closely aligned with the death of Hitler were released. In Käthe Heusermann's case it involved transfers between prisons, before arrival at Moscow's Bykovo Airport. In a typewritten unpublished biography written in the late 1950s she recounted being provided a well-furnished house near Moscow with a garden and a library of German books. Now she was leaving, she described 'amazing courtesies' – after all her torment, a sightseeing bus trip round Moscow, the Kremlin, the University and, above all, the Moscow Metro 'with its artistically designed stations'. She specially liked Mayakovsky Station. All that was in the run-up to her departure by train for Germany. 'And then we were off, in sleeping compartments with white bedlinen and silk lampshades, to Berlin.' She discovered that her fiancé, not receiving news or even knowing if she was alive, waited five years before marrying and raising a young family. Käthe was 45 when she returned.

The treatment of Käthe Heusermann was in stark contrast to that given to her wartime 'boss' Hugo Blaschke, who was intimately involved in the Nazi programme to extract gold teeth from concentration camp victims, and illustrated the differences in treatment between the Russians and the Western Allies. In the final days of the War Blaschke accompanied Hitler to the Führerbunker but was ordered to leave the city as the Red Army approached. After the war he was detained and interrogated by the Allies, and classified as a 'fellow traveller'. He was imprisoned from 1945 to 1947, and transferred to Nuremberg-Langwasser in 1947. Here he was first sentenced to three years in a labour camp as part of one of numerous denazification proceedings.

But by September 1948 he was classified as a 'lesser offender'. After his lawyer's objection, he was even downgraded to a mere 'follower' and released on parole in December 1948. After his release he continued to practice dentistry in Nuremberg until his death in 1959.

In 1991, after the fall of the Soviet Union and during the process of re-examining Stalin-era crimes, Käthe Heusermann was officially rehabilitated by the Russian Republic. This act, often described in Russian sources as 'rehabilitation', meant the government formally overturned her 1940s –1950s conviction, acknowledged the injustice of her arrest and imprisonment, and restored her civil rights.

This post-Soviet rehabilitation paralleled many similar cases, as Russian authorities exonerated individuals wrongfully imprisoned under Stalin and his successors, especially those who were arrested on fabricated charges or as innocent witnesses.

While continuing to deny that Hitler was dead, the Russians, through 'Operation Myth', continued to delve into Hitler's death. This involved the Bunker inspection in the spring of 1946, when the scene of the burial was re-examined, as well as Hitler's study. The medical examiners analysed the bloodstains in the study and on the stairs leading out to the garden.

They concluded that:

On the basis of the great number of streams and spots of blood on the sofa it must be concluded that the wound was accompanied by a profuse shedding of blood, which was as good as life threatening. At the moment of the wounding the person in question was sitting in the right-hand corner of the sofa, next to the arm . . . Such a quantity of blood spots and rivulets, as well as the characteristic appearance, indicate that the wound was confined to the head, and not the chest or stomach . . . The damage to the head resulted from a gunshot wound and not from a blow to the head with a heavy instrument.

Proof of this is to be found in the fact there are no bloodstains on the back of the sofa, the sofa itself or on the back frame. After the head wound the wounded man lost consciousness and remained motionless for a while, sitting with his head inclined towards the right arm of the sofa.

Up above in the garden two fragments of a male skull, from the left and right parietal bones were found . . . The left-side one betrayed an injury that, according to the coroner Semenovsky, suggested the exit hole of a bullet. He further affirmed that 'the shot was directed from the bottom upwards and from right to left, and from the back'.

Therefore, 'Operation Myth' concluded, Hitler had shot himself, as the witnesses Linge and Günsche had stated.

At the same time the NKVD planned a new autopsy on the body SMERSH had found, to test conclusively the theory that there had been a simultaneous intake of cyanide. The NKVD's bureaucratic rivals, SMERSH, refused to allow it. Despite making strenuous efforts, the 'Myth' special commission did not manage to persuade military counter-intelligence to give up the already dissected bodies of Hitler and Eva Braun. This made the NKVD officers reluctant to commit themselves, so they renounced the opportunity to inform Stalin of the results of their investigation. This allowed further speculation about Hitler's death to arise, ranging from 'exclusively suicide by poison' to a *coup de grâce* (administered by either Linge or Günsche).

The 'missing' parts of skull are still held by the Russians, who adamantly assert they belong to Hitler. But this contention has now been severely tested. In 2009, University of Connecticut archaeologist Nick Bellantoni was allowed to physically and anthropologically examine the skull fragment in the Russian State Archives. He noted that the bone was 'very thin' compared to a male skull, and the sutures suggested an individual under 40 years old (Hitler was 56 at death). Therefore its true provenance remains unknown

Bellantoni and molecular biologist Linda Strausbaugh took a small sample from the skull fragment and also from bloodstains on the sofa where Hitler reportedly shot himself. The DNA analysis of the skull fragment found only female DNA – unequivocally ruling out Adolf Hitler, a male, as the bone's source. The blood from the sofa matched a male profile, but this could not be directly tied to Hitler without living relative comparison. These findings were corroborated by image and stain analysis, matching the blood stains on the sofa to wartime photographs, thus confirming that at least the bloodstain's provenance fits the historical record.

Anthropological features (bone thickness, suture maturity) did not match an older male. Forensic odontological comparisons that confirmed Hitler's death relied on entirely separate remains: specifically, the jawbone and dental work identified by his dentist and compared to Hitler's dental records and X-rays. Therefore, the only scientifically confirmed remains of Hitler are the jawbone and teeth, identified by dental records and other forensics.

Russian officials have disputed the DNA findings, insisting on the fragment's authenticity, but have not provided contradictory DNA or allowed open international comparison to direct Hitler relatives. The Russian reaction to the claim that the skull fragment long believed to be Adolf Hitler's was actually from a woman was one of immediate rejection and official denial. The Russian State Archives and FSB

(Federal Security Service), the successor to the Soviet KGB, publicly disputed the findings from the University of Connecticut team, which had used DNA analysis to show that the fragment belonged to a woman under 40, not Hitler, a 56-year-old man at death.

FSB officials asserted that the American researchers did not work in full cooperation with Russian authorities, and that there was no credible basis for comparison, asking 'with what could they have compared the DNA?' because no living relatives of Hitler had been sampled.

Russian authorities maintained that their archives contained the genuine mortal remains of Hitler, stating, 'Moscow is the only place with the mortal remains of Hitler' and insisting the artifacts on display were authentic.

Russian archivists and historians continue to display the skull fragment in exhibitions, dismissing the American findings, and arguing that the chain of Soviet custody was secure, although independent Russian scientists have at times quietly admitted doubts about the fragment's provenance.

Chapter 20

OPERATION 'ARCHIVE'

Only one last question remained. What eventually happened to the bodies? After more than two hours in front of the camera this was the inevitable question.

Elena Rzhevskaya took a deep breath. 'Well, she said, 'after the bodies were buried and dug up again then re-buried, in and around Berlin, they eventually found their way to Magdeburg, and there they were buried until 1970, when they were finally disposed of.' And that was all she knew, and it took several more years before the story finally came out.

The documents relating to the disposal were finally released, and now we know what happened – codenamed 'Operation Archive'. It turns out the actual location of the bodies was a military camp near Magdeburg, not far from the (then) West German border, which the Soviets decided to abandon and return to East German civilian control. Worried that the site could become a shrine for neo-Nazis if its existence was discovered, the KGB leadership decided on complete destruction.

On 4 April 1970, the KGB exhumed the graves on the Magdeburg site, and the remains of Hitler, Eva Braun, the Goebbels family, and others were removed. These remains were taken to the outskirts of the town of Schönebeck, 11km from Magdeburg. There, the bodies were thoroughly burned on a bonfire in an open field. After cremation, the remains were ground into ashes, collected, and thrown into the Biederitz River, a tributary of the Elbe.

This procedure was documented in two KGB protocols: one for the opening of the graves and another detailing the physical destruction of the remains.

March-April, 1970
Report of Y.V. Andropov to CPSU Of Special Importance
Top secret Series 'K'
copy No.2
13 March, 1970 CPSU CC

In February, 1946, in Magdeburg (GDR) in the grounds of a military base which is now occupied by KGB Special Department of the 3rd Army of the GSFG, the corpses of Hitler, Eva Braun, Goebbels, his wife and children were buried (10 corpses altogether).

At present, the above-mentioned military base, being surplus to our requirements, is being turned over to the (East) German authorities by the Army Command.

Taking into consideration the possibility of construction or other excavations on the site, which could result in the discovery of the burial place, I would consider it advisable to conduct the exhumation of the remains and cause their complete destruction by burning.

This would be undertaken in strict secrecy by the operative group of the KGB Special Department of 3rd Army of the Group of Soviet Forces in Germany and documented in due form.

Chairman of the State Security
Committee
Andropov

On the document there is a note: 'Agreement of CPSU CC received'.

Reported from the 1 Section of the General Department of the CPSU CC comrade SOLOVIEV N.A.

Strictly personal. Do not open in the office A copy
Top secret copy No.2 Serial 'K'

The letter of 3rd Department of KGB attached at the USSR CM to SS of KGB attached at the USSR CM m/p p/b 92626 26 March, 1970

TO THE CHIEF OF THE SPECIAL SECTION OF THE KGB attached at the USSR CM military unit army post 92626 to Colonel Comr. Kovalenko N.G.

Attached herewith an execution copy of the order approved by the Command of the KGB attached at the USSR CM.
Enclosed: 2nd copy of the plan in 2 pages, our No. 3/C/ 143

CHIEF OF 3KGB DEPARTMENT Lieutenant General Fedorchuk

Top Secret
Copy No.
Series 'K'
'APPROVED'
CHAIRMAN OF THE COMMITTEE OF STATE SECURITY
ATTACHED AT THE USSR COUNCIL OF MINISTERS Y. V.
ANDROPOV.
26 March, 1970
PLAN FOR CARRYING OUT OPERATION 'ARCHIVE

The aim of the operation: To exhume and physically annihilate the remains of the war criminals buried in Magdeburg on 21 February 1946 in the military base in the Westendestrasse, near building no 36 (now Klausenerstrasse).

Participants in the realisation of the said operation to include: Chief of Special Section of KGB m/u 92626 Colonel KOVALENKO N.G., operatives of the Section

To carry out the operation:

1. Two to three days before the start of the work, a tent is to be erected over the place of burial by a platoon of guards of Sp. Sec., its size to be sufficient to conceal the work taking place under it, as required by the plan.
2. The approaches to the tent to be guarded by soldiers, and during the works by operatives assigned to Operation 'Archive'.
3. To set up a secret counter-observation post overlooking the nearest house, inhabited by local civilians, to discover whether the site is open to possible observation, In case of such observation, to take the appropriate measures to stop it as the situation requires.
4. The excavation to be performed at night, the discovered remains to put in specially-prepared boxes and taken to the vicinity of the training fields of engineer and tank regiments of the GSEG near the Faulsee (Magdeburg district, GDR) where they are to be burned, and then thrown into the lake.
5. Execution of these actions according to the prepared plan of action is to be confirmed by compiling the appropriate Reports:
   a) the Report on uncovering the burial site (the Report is to indicate the condition of the boxes and their contents, and their being put into the specially prepared boxes);
   b) Report on the burning of the remains.

The Reports to be signed by all officers of Spec. Sec. m/u 92626 named here.

6. After exhumation of the remains, the place of burial is to be put back in order. The tent is to be taken down 2-3 days after the main work has been completed.

7. The cover story: because the operation is to be undertaken on a military base, approach to which is forbidden for the local population, the necessity to explain the cause and nature of the work performed would arise only in respect to the Army officers, members of their families and non-commissioned officers living on the base. The essence of the cover story: the works (erection of the tent, the excavations) are being performed in order to check the evidence of a criminal arrested in the USSR, according to whom important archive documents might be buried in this place.

8. In case the first excavation turns out to be futile due to inaccurate information as to the place of the 'Archive', a trip to the site is to be arranged by Major General com. Gorbushin V.N., retired, living in Leningrad, and with his help to perform the actions for execution under this Plan.

CHIEF OF 3 KGB DEPARTMENT Lieutenant-General Fedorchuk
20 March, 1970 inc. no 1758 10.4.70
Top Secret
The only copy Series 'K'
the city of Magdeburg m/u p/b 92626
4 April, 1970

THE REPORT
(OF EXCAVATION OF THE REMAINS OF THE WAR CRIMINALS)

According to the 'Archive' plan of operation, approved by the Chairman of the KSS (KGB translator) attached to the USSR Council of Ministers on 26 March, 1970, an operative group, consisting of Chief of Special Section of KGB m/u 92626 Colonel Kovalenko N.G. and operatives of the Section, performed the excavation of the remains of the war criminals on a military base in the Westendestrasse, near building no 36 (now Klausenerstrasse).

The excavation discovered that the alleged remains of the war criminals were buried in five wooden boxes, placed one over the other in a form of a cross, three of them from north to south, the two others from east to west. The boxes had decomposed and turned into rotten wood, the remains mixing with the soil.

Having been dug up, the soil was thoroughly examined and the remains (skulls, shinbones, ribs, vertebrae and so on) were placed in a box.

The remains were in an advanced state of decay, especially those of the children, which prevented the exact count of how many had been discovered. According to an examination of the shinbones and skulls, the remains could belong to between 10 and 11 bodies.

After the excavation, the place was put back in proper order. The excavation was performed during the night and morning of 4 April, 1970.

Observation of the nearest house, where local German civilians live, did not detect any suspicious actions on their part.

The Soviet citizens living on the base showed no direct interest in the works or the tent erected over the place of work.

The box containing the remains of the war criminals was under guard by the operatives until the morning of 5 April, when physical annihilation was performed.

Chef of Special Section of KGB m/u p/b 92626 Colonel KOVALENKO N.G.

Operatives of the Special Section KGB m/u p/b 92626 (signatures) inc. no 1758

10.4.70
Top Secret
The only copy
Series 'K'
the city of Magdeburg m/u p/b 92626
4 April, 1970

THE REPORT
(OF PHYSICAL ANNIHILATION OF THE REMAINS OF THE WAR CRIMINALS)

According to the 'Archive' plan of operation' the operative group consisting of Chief of Special Section of KGB m/u p/b 92626 Colonel Kovalenko N.G. and operatives of the Section . . . performed the burning of the remains of the war criminals exhumed from the burial site on the military base in the Westendestrasse near building no 36 (now Klausenerstrasse).

Annihilation of the remains was performed by burning on the waste ground in the vicinity of the city of Schänebeck, 11km from Magdeburg.

The remains, burned with charcoal, were crushed to dust, collected and thrown into the river at Bideritz, as confirmed by this Report.

Chief of Special Section of KGB m/u p/b 92626 Colonel Kovalenko N.G.
Operatives of the Special Section KGB m/u p/b 92626 (signatures)
5 April, 1970

Chapter 21

INCONSISTENCIES

When the Russian search teams entered the bunker searching for Hitler and the other leaders of the Third Reich, their only priority was finding them. Those captured inside were interrogated about Hitler's whereabouts which continued until his body was finally discovered.

But the various interrogations, which occurred over a long period of time, and in different places, did not conclusively determine whether Hitler poisoned himself or shot himself at the same time, which would have been possible because the cyanide which he had taken was not instantaneous.

According to Elena Rzhevskaya, this was not important to them. She said the original search teams did not care about the manner of death, only that they had achieved their task. But these interrogations did reveal some inconsistencies which have led to questions about the manner of Hitler's death. And after more than 80 years, it is still not possible to tell whether Hitler took poison and shot himself or whether someone executed a coup de grâce.

It is generally accepted, however, that there was a gunshot. Hitler did in fact own a gun, a Walther 7.65mm. According to one witness, his bodyguard Hans Rattenhuber, it had a special finish which made it easily recognisable.

A Walther 7.65mm pistol is extremely loud, especially when fired inside a building. It typically produces a sound pressure level of about 153–157 decibels, louder than a jet engine at take-off, and can cause permanent damage to unprotected hearing. At the accepted time of Hitler's suicide, his secretary, Traudl Junge, says she heard a shot 'that was loud and echoed throughout the rooms'. Goebbel's son Helmuth, who was with her, exclaimed 'that was a direct hit', believing it was an artillery shell which had hit the building.

Others, such as Heinz Linge, does not say in any of his testimonies whether he heard a shot, and neither do Erik Kempka, his chauffeur, or Otto Günsche, who said he didn't hear a shot. However, there is strong evidence from the same witness, and others, that even if there was a shot Hitler would have had trouble because of his physical condition. Several people gave evidence that both his hands were shaking badly, which may have prevented him from carrying it out. Several key witnesses say they went into Hitler's room and discovered his corpse with a gunshot wound to the right temple. Linge, in particular, gave a quite detailed description.

He said there was a wound in the right temple 'the size of a pfenning', and two streams of blood ran down his cheek. The wall and the sofa were bespattered with blood. The Walther pistol lay by the floor next to his right foot, and Eva Braun's 6.35mm lay next to it. Linge was quite certain that Hitler had shot himself, and he repeated this over many years to various interrogators, and in his autobiography.

The problem arises because Rattenhuber tells a slightly different story. On 20 May 1945, in his interrogation in Moscow, he said that after returning from carrying out his duties elsewhere, he returned to Hitler's reception room where he was struck by the powerful smell of bitter almonds, and was told that Hitler was dead

He said that although he had expected it he was shocked, and slumped into an armchair in despair. At that moment Linge came in and said he had had to carry out the hardest order the Führer had ever given him. He looked at Linge in surprise. 'He explained to me that before his death, Hitler ordered him to leave the room for 10 minutes, then to return, wait 10 minutes more and then "carry out the order". Having said that, Linge quickly went to Hitler's room and returned with a Walther pistol which he placed on the table before me. By its special external finish, I recognised it as the Führer's personal pistol.'

He said Artur Axmann, who was present, took the gun from him and said he would hide it for 'Better times'. Now it was clear to me what Hitler's order had been. Obviously Hitler, doubting the effectiveness of the poison after all the injections he had been given for such a long time, ordered Linge to shoot him after he had taken the poison. Linge had shot Hitler. In his testimony, however, Axmann made no mention of this, or taking the gun and hiding it.

Erik Kempka said he and Günsche went into the room and both saw the pistols on the floor. They held them in in their hands but said they did not check to see if they had been fired. But he did not say who he gave the guns to. The question is, how did other witnesses see the gun on the floor if Linge took it out with him and gave it to Axmann? Is Rattenhuber telling the truth or Linge?

Elena Rzhevskaya was convinced that Linge had shot Hitler post mortem, and intimated that it was also the opinion of her colleagues at the time. But it is almost impossible, now, to determine the truth. The original post mortem verdict, of death by cyanide poison, now seems conclusive.

The post-war fate of the pistol is unclear. While it was seen at the scene and presumably collected by Soviet officers who took control of the bunker, there is no credible public record confirming that Hitler's suicide weapon was preserved, catalogued, or displayed by Soviet or later Russian authorities.

No major Western or Russian archive has ever produced what is incontrovertibly documented as the 'Hitler suicide pistol'. Although several Walther pistols with Hitler associations have surfaced in private collections or auctions, none can be definitively proven to be the exact gun used in the bunker.

EPILOGUE

Even though she was a member of Marshal Zhukov's staff, and was an important cog in the transmission of information between Zhukov and Stalin in May, 1945, she never actually met him during the war.

So, as she says, she was very surprised when, one day in November, 1965, she received a telephone call:

'Yelena Moiseyevna? This is Zhukov.'

He wanted to meet her, and asked her to come to his dacha. According to Rzhevskaya, this was unusual, as she had been warned earlier that Zhukov, who was awarded the title Hero of the Soviet Union four times, the Soviet Union's highest distinction for heroic feats in service to the state and society, and a member of the Order of Lenin, was under constant watch by the KGB, and was traumatised by it.

She said that during the war nothing could tarnish the heroic image of Marshal Zhukov, although even then, and particularly after the war ended, she heard a lot about his rudeness, his cruelty, and outbursts of often unjustified rage.

> I heard he was callous about the cost in lives. I was not entirely without prejudice towards him myself. Mark Gallai, a Hero of the Soviet Union and the first pilot to shoot down a German aircraft over Moscow, told me, 'If it had not been for Rokossovsky, we would never have known a different style of command was possible, but this does not mean Zhukov was anything other than a really big commander, and we owe more to him than to anyone else.'

Zhukov told her he was doing research for his own autobiography and wanted to check some facts with her. He had read her book *Berlin, May 1945* and discovered her role for the first time. But the tone of the meeting, says Rzhevskaya, was tense.

He said that although he knew Hitler was dead, as he had reported to Stalin, he did not know that his body had been found.

I did not know Hitler had been found, but now I have read about it in your book and believe it, even though there are no references to archives, which would be customary. I have faith in you, though, and in your conscience as a writer. I am writing my memoirs and have just now got as far as Berlin. Now I have to decide how I am to write about this.

If I now write that I did not know, it will be taken to mean that Hitler was not found, and politically that would be the wrong thing to do. That would play into the hands of the Nazis.

Rzhevskaya said it was a question she had not seen coming, but knew that strict secrecy had surrounded everything connected with the discovery of Hitler, and that it was reported by order of Stalin directly to him, bypassing the army command; bypassing, as she now learned, even Marshal Zhukov.

She told Zhukov: 'Why that was so, is something only Stalin could explain.'

Zhukov immediately rejected that. 'Under any circumstances, I should have been informed of this. I was, after all, Stalin's deputy. How is it possible that I did not know that?'

Zhukov told Rzhveskaya that there was a dilemma.

'I wanted to ask you', Zhukov said, 'to help me out with a few things here. Since what I write in my book will decide the fate of yours . . . If I write that I know nothing about this, you will not be believed.'

Rzhevskaya said she had no clear and convincing answer to that. Having come into possession of such an important historical fact, and perhaps not yet sure what use to make of it, Stalin had instinctively turned it into a secret. 'Perhaps his decisions were affected, as I wrote, by the difficulty and volatility of the relationship between these two men. It shows us Zhukov as someone whose directness was innate, something Stalin valued, but for just as long as the war continued.'

In the event, Zhukov made only one mention in his book about Hitler's body. He recounted the negotiations for the surrender of Berlin with General Krebs. 'I reported to [Stalin] about Hitler's suicide and the letter from Goebbels proposing armistice. Stalin answered: "Now he's done it, the bastard. Too bad he could not have been taken alive. Where is Hitler's body?" According to General Krebs Hitler's body was burned.'

Rzhevskaya said Zhukov described Stalin's personality very trenchantly and boldly (which, even 21 years later, made the censor very, very cross), but without prejudice. He had nothing but contempt for Khrushchev's caricature of Stalin as conducting military operations around the globe. Zhukov said that at the beginning of the war Stalin really did not know anything. His only military experience was of the Civil War. 'But he got the right idea after Stalingrad.'

Rzhevskaya asked Zhukov if Stalin had any personal charm. He said, 'No', and shook his head emphatically.

> Quite the reverse. He was intimidating. Do you know the kind of eyes, what kind of expression he had? Scornful. He could sometimes be in a good mood, but that was unusual. If he had scored some success in international affairs, or military, then he might even sing, sometimes. He was not without a sense of humour, but rarely showed it. People went to him as if they were going to something dreadful. Yes, when he summoned people, they went as if in dread.
>
> But without him, it would have been difficult in the war . . . He was strong-willed. The situation really was desperate. You yourself have no idea how desperate. We had absolutely nothing, 'no steel, no powder'. And yet, it came from somewhere. It was taken from virtually anywhere. It was like a miracle.

Elena Rzhevskaya's struggle to bring the truth to light eventually bore fruit in Russia, and in later life she became something of a celebrity. Russian television even made a documentary about her.

Russian journalist Olaf Koens featured her in *The Moscow Times* in 2020, saying 'all young people who meet 91-year-old Yelena Rzhevskaya want to ask her about is the day she held Hitler's jaw. But she'd be happier if they just said "hello".'

Every May, says Koens, come the dozens of journalists who are trying to get hold of the translator who carried a jaw in a box, and later became a well-known writer. '"All those young people are interested in is that story about the jaw", she sighs. "I've told it so many times, yet people still wonder about it. I don't leave the house much more any longer, but when I do, it would be nice if people said 'hello' once in a while".' And not just in May.

Her achievements were also formally recognised. In 1996 she was awarded the Andrei Sakharov Prize for Writer's Civic Courage. The prize was created in October 1990 by the 'Writers in Support of Perestroika' association in the Soviet Union. This literary prize was established to honour writers who demonstrated exceptional civic courage, often by standing up for historical truth, human rights, and resisting censorship or political repression. The award cited how she risked her personal safety and career to serve historical truth and confront the abuse of state power.

We concluded the interview late in the day of June and the camera crew began packing up. Elena Rzhevskaya studied a small toy Koala I had brought from Australia, and she asked me about the country.

Her role in the bunker was known to many people but for many years she politely, but resolutely refused to be interviewed. The (West) German magazine *Der Spiegel* had made repeated requests, as had several others. I asked her why she had agreed to give me this exclusive audience. She smiled, 'Because you came from such a long way away.'

I had one last question: 'Who do *you* think shot Hitler?' There was no hesitation. 'Linge. It was Linge who shot the corpse.'

As we bade each other goodbye she said 'Now I have to go and change, I have a very important engagement this evening'.

I asked her what that could be. 'Don't you know the date?' she said. 'Yes, I replied, it's June 21st.'

'Quite so', she replied. 'Tonight it will be the 50th Anniversary of Germany's attack on Russia, and I'm off to the Kremlin to commemorate the occasion, and meet any of those comrades who are still with us.'

APPENDIX

Hitler's Will & Marriage Document
On the night of 29 April 1945 the Führer dictated his will to his secretaries Gerda Christian and Traudl Junge. The will was typed in three or four copies. The following morning three men were chosen to get the documents out of the bunker.

SS-Standartenführer Wilhelm Zander, a close aide of Martin Bormann, adjutant Willy Johannmeyer and journalist Heinz Lorenz made it out of the bunker and successfully escaped Berlin, made their way across Germany as the Nazi regime collapsed, and eventually entered the territory held by Western Allies

Willy Johannmeyer was tasked with delivering his document set to Field Marshal Ferdinand Schörner, who was the commander of Army Group Centre in Bohemia. Zander was to deliver his documents to Admiral Karl Dönitz, whom Hitler had designated as his successor and new Reich President, and Lorenz was instructed to take his set of documents to Munich for preservation and eventual publication. The goal was to ensure these documents survived and could reach senior Nazi officials or other intended recipients.

After the war, the British captured Lorenz and his testimony, plus the documents he carried, which were used to authenticate events surrounding Hitler's death. Johannmeyer successfully hid the documents by burying them in his family's garden. He disclosed the hiding place after being captured by the Americans, who also captured Zander who had gone into using the alias 'Wilhelm Paustin'. He admitted his identity and the crucial documents were recovered from his hiding place.

Adolf Hitler's will, along with his political testament and marriage certificate, is preserved at the National Archives and Records Administration in Maryland, USA.

The original documents were subsequently transferred to the custody of the US government. They have been displayed at various times, including exhibits at the National Archives in Washington, D.C., and have undergone authentication by the FBI and US Army intelligence.

The following documents contain a letter from Secretary of War Robert P. Patterson to President Harry Truman, the certificate of marriage between Adolf Hitler and Eva Braun, the private will of Adolf Hitler, a letter from Martin Bormann, and the political testament of Adolf Hitler.

The private will concerns the distribution of the property of Adolf Hitler. The letter from Martin Bormann, private secretary of Adolf Hitler, is to Admiral Dönitz, and it transfers the political testament of Adolf Hitler to his custody.

The political testament discusses Hitler's political motivations and stresses his reluctance to create war. The political testament also provides for his political succession. Also included are English translations of the marriage certificate, the private will, and the political testament.

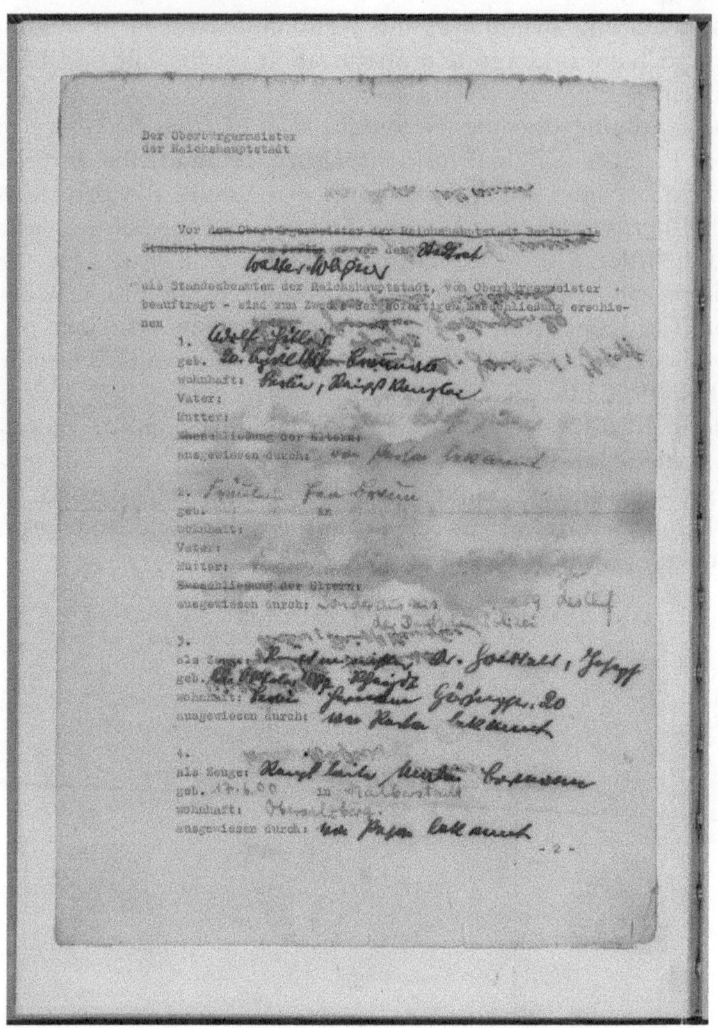

The front of Hitler's and Eva Braun's marriage certificate.

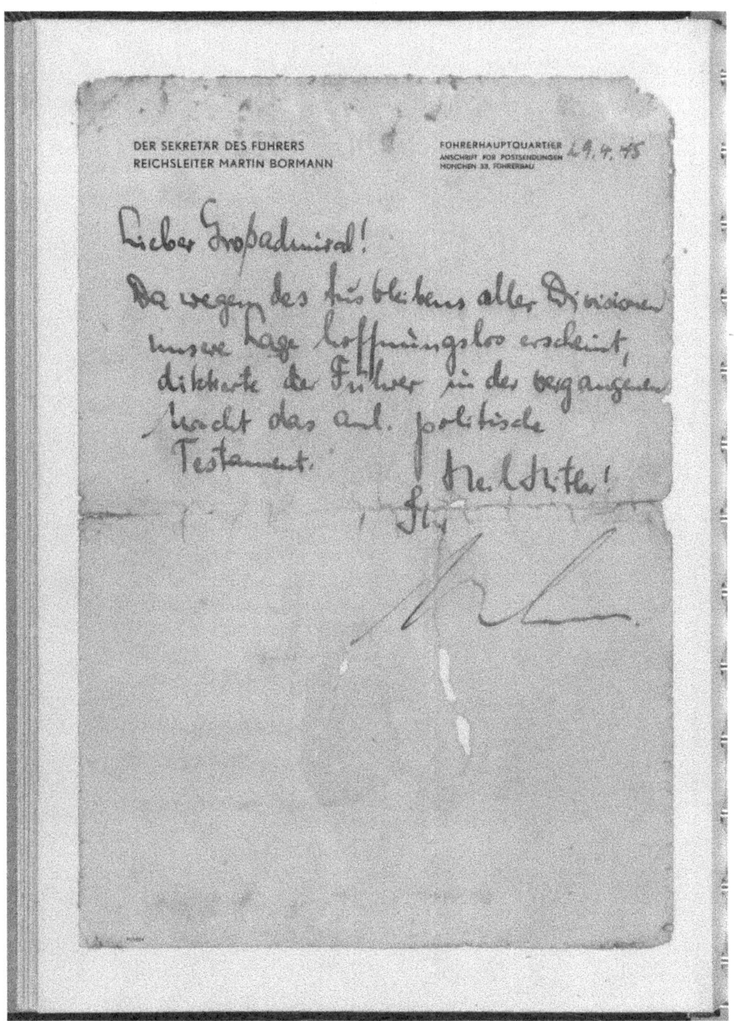

The letter that Bormann wrote to Grossadmiral Karl Dönitz, and which transfers the political testament of Adolf Hitler to the custody of the latter. Along with a copy of Hitler's will, it was handed to Hauptschriftführer Heinz Lorenz, who was instructed to leave Berlin at once in civilian clothes and take the documents to Dönitz.

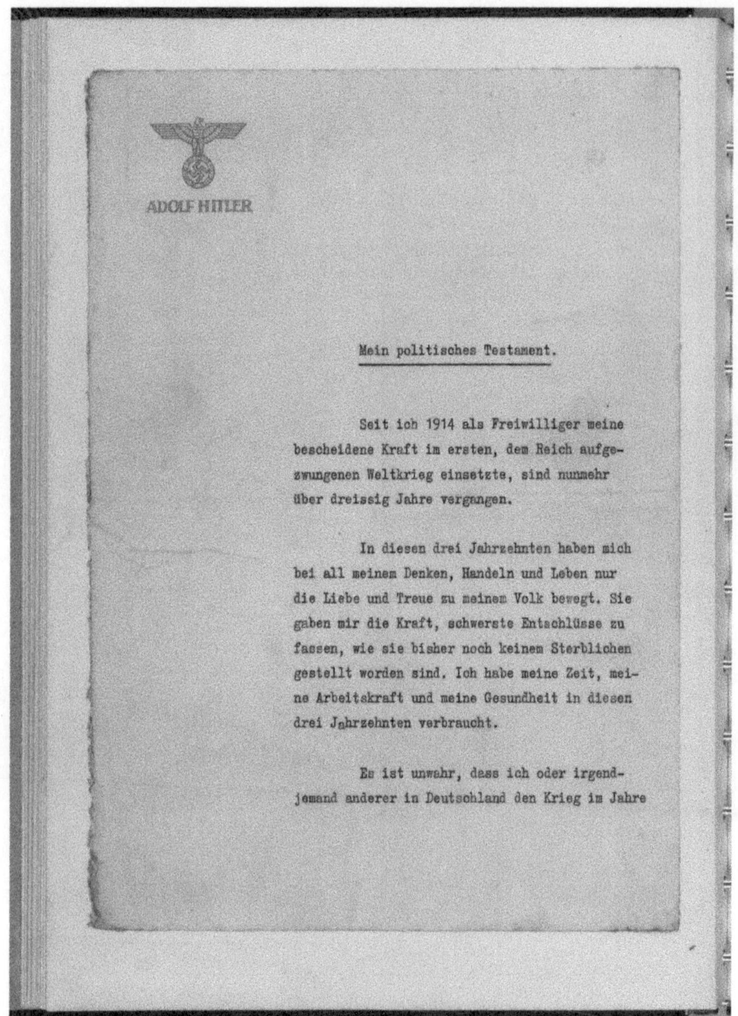

The first page of Hitler's political testament.

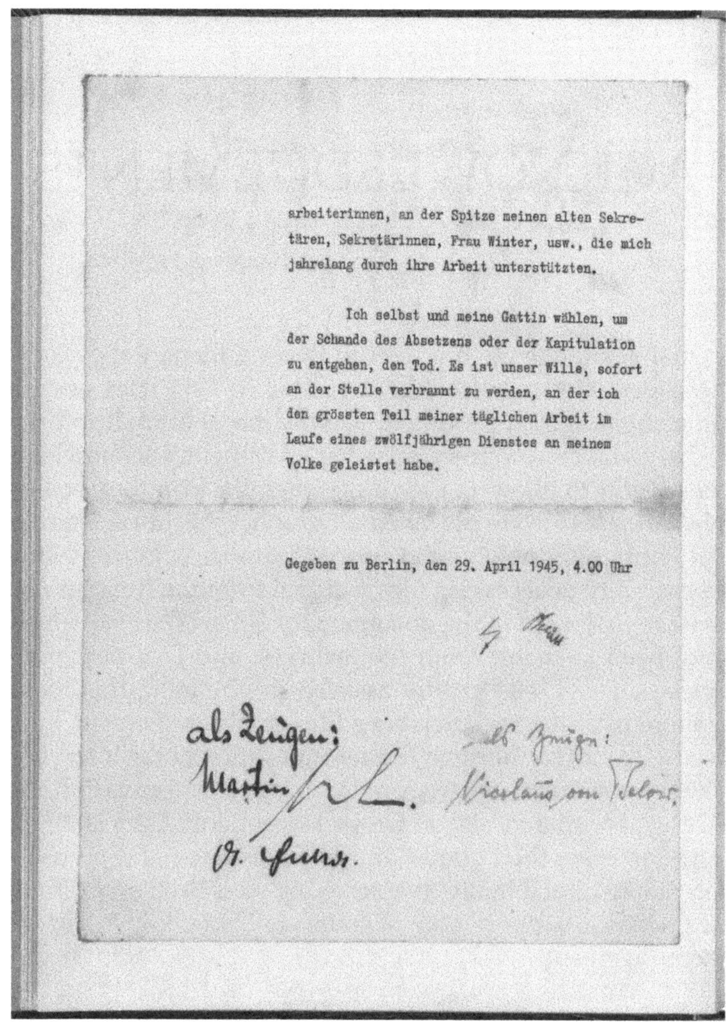

arbeiterinnen, an der Spitze meinen alten Sekre-
tären, Sekretärinnen, Frau Winter, usw., die mich
jahrelang durch ihre Arbeit unterstützten.

Ich selbst und meine Gattin wählen, um
der Schande des Absetzens oder der Kapitulation
zu entgehen, den Tod. Es ist unser Wille, sofort
an der Stelle verbrannt zu werden, an der ich
den grössten Teil meiner täglichen Arbeit im
Laufe eines zwölfjährigen Dienstes an meinem
Volke geleistet habe.

Gegeben zu Berlin, den 29. April 1945, 4.00 Uhr

The last page of Hitler's political testament, one of the documents carried by Heinz Lorenz. Below Hitler's signature are those of the witnesses, all four of whom died shortly after endorsing the document. Goebbels and his wife committed suicide, whilst Burgdorf and Krebs committed suicide together in the bunker on the night of 1/2 May. Bormann's exact time and place of death remain uncertain; his remains were discovered north of the bunker in 1972 and identified by DNA analysis in 1998. Therefore, he was most likely killed the same night trying to escape from the Führerbunker.

Courtesy U.S. National Archives and Records Administration.

ACKNOWLEDGEMENTS

I must first acknowledge my debt to the late Elena Rzhevskaya who told her story on camera for the first time in 1991. Her warmth and encouragement was appreciated, as was the good-natured way she allowed my film crew to re-arrange her apartment. I acknowledge also her permission to allow me to quote liberally from her book, *Berlin, May 1945*. Thanks also to my cinematographer, Nicholas Sherman, the Russian immigrant, newly arrived in Australia, who first alerted me to the possibility of accessing film material from the Russian Archives. This footage first aired in the documentary *Hitler. The Final Chapter* has not since been available from the archives, and I suspect may have been reclassified. I was greatly assisted in obtaining this footage by Igor Voitenko, of the St. Petersburg film company Lennauchfilm. My thanks also to Tanya Sherman for her translation of the interview with Elena Rzhevskaya, and my interpreters in Moscow, Tanya Fidinova and Luba Descy. My thanks also to Gwyn Harper and Associate Professor Dr. Tony Sasse, for their good-natured persistence, and perusal of the finished manuscript. Finally, thanks to my sons Brett and Timothy for their enthusiastic support, and, of course my wife, Robyn, for her love and encouragement.

Melbourne 2025

BIBLIOGRAPHY

Bezymenski, L. (1968), *The Death of Adolf Hitler. Unknown Documents from Soviet Archives*. London: Michael Joseph, London.

Bruck Family. (Continuous). Retrieved from BruckFamilyBlock.com: https://bruckfamilyblog.com/category/fedor-bruck/

Central Archive of the Federal Security Service of the Russian Federation. (n.d.).

Chaney, O. P. (1972), *Zhukov*. Devon, UK: David & Charles Ltd.

Linge, H. (2009), *With Hitler To the End*. London: Frontline Books.

Lucas, J. (1986), *Last Days of the Reich*. Minneapolis, Minnesota USA: Arms & Armour Press Ltd.

Parshina, J.-C. B. (2018), *The Death of Hitler*. London: Hodder & Stoughton.

Payne, R. (1973), *The Life & Death of Adolf Hitler*. London UK: Transworld Publishers Ltd.

Ryan, C. (1980), *The Last Battle*. London: William Collins & Co (New English Library).

Rzhevskaya, E. (1991, 21 June) (C. Jones, Interviewer).

Rzhevskaya, E. (1988), *Berlin, May 1945*. Moscow, Russian Federation: Moscow Publishing Gioyuse 'Pravda'.

Rzhevskaya, E. (2018), *Memoirs of a Wartime Translator (English Translation of Berlin, May 1945)*. Barnsley, UK: Pen & Sword Books Ltd.

Shtemenko, G. S. (1978), *The Last Six Months*. London: William Kimber & Co Ltd, London.

Trevor-Roper, H. (1955), *The Last Days of Hitler*. London, United Kingdom: Macmillan & Co Ltd (Great Pan).

Vinogradov, V. (2005), *Hitler's Death. Russia's Last Great Secret*. London: Chaucer Press.

Werth, A. (1964), *Russia At War 1941-1945*. London: Pan Books Ltd, London.

Zhukov, G. G. (2013), *Marshal of Victory (Autobiography)*. Barnsley, UK: Pen & Sword Military (Pen & Sword Books Ltd).

INDEX

Places

Organisations / Terms